Women Memoirists

volume one

Women Memoirists

volume one

Edited and with an Introduction by

Harold Bloom

CHELSEA HOUSE PUBLISHERS

Philadelphia

ON THE COVER: Kay Sage, American, 1898–1963. *I Saw Three Cities*, 1944. Oil on canvas, 91.5 x 71.0 cm. The Art Museum, Princeton University. Gift of the Estate of Kay Sage Tanguy. Photo by Clem Fiori.

CHELSEA HOUSE PUBLISHERS

EDITOR-IN-CHIEF   Stephen Reginald
MANAGING EDITOR   James D. Gallagher
PRODUCTION MANAGER   Pamela Loos
PICTURE EDITOR   Judy Hasday
ART DIRECTOR   Sara Davis
SENIOR PRODUCTION EDITOR   Lisa Chippendale

WOMEN WRITERS OF ENGLISH AND THEIR WORKS:
   Women Memoirists: Volume One

SERIES EDITOR   Jane Shumate
CONTRIBUTING EDITOR   Tenley Williams
SENIOR EDITOR   Therese De Angelis
INTERIOR AND COVER DESIGNER   Alison Burnside
EDITORIAL ASSISTANT   Anne Hill

First Printing
1 3 5 7 9 8 6 4 2

Library of Congress Cataloging-in-Publication Data

Women memoirists / edited and with an introduction by Harold Bloom.
    p.   cm. — (Women writers of English and their works)
   Includes bibliographical references.
   ISBN 0-7910-4485-8 (v. 1 : hc). — ISBN 0-7910-4501-3 (v. 1 : pbk.)
   1. American prose literature—Women authors—History and criticism. 2. English prose literature—Women authors—History and criticism. 3. Women authors, American—Biography—History and criticism. 4. Women authors, English—Biography—History and criticism. 5. Autobiography—Women authors. I. Bloom, Harold. II. Series.
PS366.A88W64   1998   97-35879
810.9'9287—dc21   CIP

CONTENTS

R0127181674

HAROLD BLOOM

I APPROACH THIS SERIES with a certain wariness, since so much of classical feminist literary criticism has founded itself upon arguments with that phase of my own work that began with *The Anxiety of Influence* (first published in January 1973). Someone who has been raised to that bad eminence—*The Patriarchal Critic*—is well advised that he trespasses upon sacred ground when he ventures to inquire whether indeed there are indisputable differences, imaginative and cognitive, between the literary works of women and those of men. If these differences are so substantial as pragmatically to make an authentic difference, does that in turn make necessary different aesthetic standards for judging the achievements of men and of women writers? Is Emily Dickinson to be read as though she has more in common with Elizabeth Barrett Browning than with Ralph Waldo Emerson?

Is Elizabeth Bishop a great poet because she triumphantly meets the same aesthetic criteria satisfied by Wallace Stevens, or should we evaluate her by criteria she shares with Marianne Moore, but not with Stevens? Are there crucial gender-based differences in the representations of Esther Summerson by Charles Dickens in *Bleak House*, and of Dorothea Brooke by George Eliot in *Middlemarch*? Does Samuel Richardson's Clarissa Harlowe convince us that her author was a male when we contrast her with Jane Austen's Elizabeth Bennet? Do women poets have a less agonistic relationship to female precursors than male poets have to their forerunners? Two eminent pioneers of feminist criticism, Sandra Gilbert and Susan Gubar, have suggested that women writers suffer more from an anxiety of authorship than they do from influence anxieties, while another important feminist critic, Elaine Showalter, has suggested that women writers, early and late, work together in a kind of quiltmaking, each doing her share while avoiding any contamination of creative envy in regard to other writers, provided that they be women. Can it be true that, in the aesthetic sphere, women do not beware women and do not suffer from the competitiveness and jealousy that alas do exist in the professional and sexual domains? Is there something in the area of literature, when practiced by women, that changes and purifies mere human nature?

I cannot answer any of these questions, yet I do think it is vital and clarifying to raise them. There is a current fashion, in many of our institutions of higher education, to insist that English Romantic poetry cannot be studied in the old way, with an exclusive emphasis upon the works of William Blake, William Wordsworth, Samuel Taylor Coleridge, Lord Byron, Percy Bysshe Shelley, John Keats, and John Clare. Instead, the Romantic poets are taken to include Felicia Hemans, Laetitia Landon, Charlotte Smith, and Mary Tighe, among others. It would be heartening if we could believe that these are unjustly neglected poets, but their current revival will be brief. Similarly, anthologies of 17th-century English literature now tend to include the Duchess of Newcastle as well as Aphra Behn, Lady Mary Chudleigh, Anne Killigrew, Anne Finch, Countess of Winchilsea, and others. Some of these—Anne Finch in particular—wrote well, but a situation in which they are more read and studied than John Milton is not one that is likely to endure forever. The consequences of making gender a criterion for aesthetic choice must finally destroy all serious study of imaginative literature as such.

In their *Norton Anthology of Literature by Women*, Sandra Gilbert and Susan Gubar conclude their introduction to Elizabeth Barrett Browning by saying that "she constantly tested herself against the highest standards of male-defined poetic genres," a true if ambiguous observation. They then print her famous "The Cry of the Children," an admirably passionate ode that protests the cruel employment of little children in British Victorian mines and factories. Unfortunately, this well-meant prophetic affirmation ends with this, doubtless its finest stanza:

XIII

They look up with their pale and sunken faces,
    And their look is dread to see,
For they mind you of their angels in high places,
    With eyes turned on Deity.
"How long," they say, "how long, O cruel nation,
    Will you stand, to move the world, on a child's heart,—
Stifle down with a mailèd heel its palpitation,
    And tread onward to your throne amid the mart?
Our blood splashes upward, O goldheaper,
    And your purple shows your path!
But the child's sob in the silence curses deeper
    Than the strong man in his wrath."

If you read this aloud, then you may find yourself uncomfortable, on a strictly aesthetic basis, which would not vary if you were told that this had been composed by a male Victorian poet. In their selections from Elizabeth Bishop, Gilbert and Gubar courageously reprint Bishop's superb statement explaining her refusal to permit her poems to be included in anthologies of women's writing:

> Undoubtedly gender does play an important part in the making of any art, but art is art and to separate writings, paintings, musical compositions, etc., into sexes is to emphasize values in them that are *not* art.

That credo of Elizabeth Bishop's is to me the Alpha and Omega of critical wisdom in regard to all feminist literary criticism. Gender studies are precisely that: they study gender, and not aesthetic value. If your priorities are historical, social, political, and ideological, then gender studies clearly are more than justified. Perhaps they are a way to justice, or at least to more justice than women have received throughout thousands of years of male domination and aggression. Yet that is a very different matter from the now vexed issue of aesthetic value. Biographical criticism, like the different modes of historicist and psychological criticism, always has relied upon a kind of implicit gender studies and doubtless will benefit, as other modes will, by a making explicit of such considerations, particularly in regard to women writers.

Each volume in this series contains copious refutations of, and replies to, the traditionally aesthetic stance that I have advocated here. These introductory remarks aspire only to a questioning, and not a challenging, of feminist literary criticism. There are no longer any Patriarchal Critics; they are all dinosaurs, fabulous beasts fit for revival only in horror films. Sometimes I sadly think of myself as Bloom Brontosaurus, amiably left behind by the fire and the flood. But more often I go on reading the great women writers, searching for the aesthetic difference that yet may prove to be there, but which has not yet been found.

OF THE DOZEN or so talented writers surveyed in this volume, one could not choose Alice James as the most eminent. Fanny Burney's *Evelina* and Zora Neale Hurston's *Their Eyes Were Watching God* are memorable novels, and several of the other authors have composed lasting works. But I focus upon the *Diary* of Alice James partly because of its intrinsic values of thought and consciousness, but partly because of its author's famous predicament. She was the youngest child and only daughter of Henry James Sr. and Mary James, and so she numbered among her four older brothers William James, psychologist and philosopher, and Henry James Jr., novelist and person-of-letters. A lifelong depressive, Alice James composed her diary only during her final years, from 1889 to 1892. It manifests her remarkable qualities: fierce wit, ironic detachment, courage, endurance, pride, and grand strength of will. Unfortunately, the *Diary*'s style is mixed and its tone radically uneven. Yet it shares in the James family's project of self-reliance and self-apotheosis, ultimately at one with Emerson's kind of American religion. In its religious recognitions, the *Diary* is very much part of Emersonian tradition, as we should expect from the daughter of Emerson's disciple Henry James Sr.

There are many felicities in Alice James's *Diary*, but the reader needs to cultivate the patience to wait for them. I treasure in particular one passage about the novelist Henry James Jr., to which R. W. B. Lewis first called my attention, in his admirable *The Jameses: A Family Narrative* (1991). The greatest of our novelists generally kept himself at a defensive remove from the sufferings of others, but Alice James, writing in March 1890, gives us a unique portrait of the creator of Isabel Archer and Milly Theale:

> Henry the patient, I should call him. Five years ago in November, I crossed the water and suspended myself like an old woman of the sea round his neck where to all appearances I shall remain for all time. I have given him endless care and anxiety but notwithstanding this and the fantastic nature of my troubles I have never seen an impatient look upon his face or heard an unsympathetic or misunderstanding sound cross his lips. He comes at my slightest sign and hangs on to whatever organ may be in eruption and gives me calm and solace by assuring me that my nerves are his nerves and my stomach his stomach—this last a pitch of brotherly devotion never before approached by the race. He has never remotely hinted that he expected me to be well at any given moment, that burden which fond friend and relative so inevitably impose upon the cherished invalid. But he has always been the same since I can remember and has almost as strongly as Father that personal susceptibility—what can one call it, it seems as if

it were a matter of the scarfskin, as if they perceived thro' that your mood and were saved thereby from rubbing you raw with their theory of it, or blindness to it.

This would be an extraordinary vision of anyone but is particularly poignant of a Henry James whose gentleness and empathy were more often evoked by literature than by life. As critics frequently have surmised, the novelist's love for his tragic sister informed the sequence of beautiful representations of women that are at the center of his work. In a letter to a friend, Henry James expressed a sorrowful tribute to his departed sister:

> [E]ven with everything that made life an unspeakable weariness to her, she contributed constantly, infinitely to the interest, the consolation, as it were, in disappointment and depression, of my own existence . . . Her talk, her company, her association and admirable acute mind and large spirit were so much the best thing I have, of late years, known here.

Some recent feminist critics have suggested that Alice James was martyred to her father's and brothers' supposedly patriarchal wills. But Alice James made herself into an invalid, and her long lesbian relationship with Katherine Peabody Loring was acceptable to her family and to her friends. The Swedenborgian mystic Henry James Sr. was anything but a domestic tyrant, and the two great brothers, William and Henry, are among the double handful of enlightened consciousnesses that our country has brought forth. Alice James subdued her own gifts, as she did her life, and was nobody's victim, unless she was her own.

MAYA ANGELOU
b. 1928

MAYA ANGELOU was born Marguerite Johnson in St. Louis, Missouri, on April 4, 1928. Her life has been varied and often tragic: as a young child she was left by her parents in the care of her grandmother; later, reclaimed by her mother, she was raped by her mother's boyfriend. Growing up during the Depression, she attended public schools in Arkansas and California, although she also studied music privately and studied dance with Martha Graham. She held a variety of odd jobs, including streetcar conductor, Creole cook, nightclub waitress, prostitute, and madam. She bore a son, Guy, when she was 16 and has been married twice: in her early twenties she married Tosh Angelos, a white man whose name she adapted for herself when she became a dancer; she was later married to Paul Du Feu from 1973 to 1981.

Angelou was a member of the cast of *Porgy and Bess* in 1954/55 and acted in several off-Broadway plays, including *Cabaret for Freedom* (1960), a musical she wrote with Godfrey Cambridge. At about this time she moved to Brooklyn, where she met John Oliver Killens, James Baldwin, and other authors who encouraged her to write. As she developed her craft, however, she became involved in the civil rights movement: she met Martin Luther King Jr., was appointed the northern coordinator of the Southern Christian Leadership Conference, and organized demonstrations at the United Nations. She fell in love with the South African freedom fighter Vusumzi Make, the relationship precipitating several years of intense activity in Egypt and later in Ghana.

Angelou's first published book was *I Know Why the Caged Bird Sings* (1969), an account of the first 16 years of her life; a tremendous critical and popular success, it was nominated for a National Book Award and was later adapted for television. Two more autobiographical volumes followed: *Gather Together in My Name* (1974) and *Singin' and Swingin' and Gettin' Merry Like Christmas* (1976), along with three volumes of poetry, several dramas and television plays, and two screenplays. She also continued to pursue her acting career and was nominated for a Tony Award in 1973 for her Broadway debut in *Look Away*.

In the 1980s Angelou solidified her reputation with two more autobiographies, *The Heart of a Woman* (1981) and *All God's Children Need Traveling Shoes* (1986), along with several more volumes of poetry.

l

Although she has won greater acclaim for her memoiristic works than for her poetry and drama, the peak of her fame may have come in 1993, when she composed the poem "On the Pulse of Morning" for President Bill Clinton's inauguration.

Maya Angelou, who has received honorary degrees from Smith College, Mills College, and Lawrence University, currently lives in Sonoma, California.

CRITICAL EXTRACTS

SIDONIE ANN SMITH

Maya Angelou's autobiography ⟨*I Know Why the Caged Bird Sings*⟩, like ⟨Richard⟩ Wright's, opens with a primal childhood scene that brings into focus the nature of the imprisoning environment from which the self will seek escape. The black girl child is trapped within the cage of her own diminished self-image around which interlock the bars of natural and social forces. The oppression of natural forces, of physical appearance and processes, foists a self-consciousness on all young girls who must grow from children into women. Hair is too thin or stringy or mousy or nappy. Legs are too fat, too thin, too bony, the knees too bowed. Hips are too wide or not wide enough. Breasts grow too fast or not at all. The self-critical process is incessant, a driving demon. But in the black girl child's experience these natural bars are reinforced with the rusted iron social bars of racial subordination and impotence. Being born black is itself a liability in a world ruled by white standards of beauty which imprison the child *a priori* in a cage of ugliness: "What you looking at me for?" This really isn't me. I'm white with long blond hair and blue eyes, with pretty pink skin and straight hair, with a delicate mouth. I'll try again. The black and blue bruises of the soul multiply and compound as the caged bird flings herself against these bars:

> The Black female is assaulted in her tender years by all those common forces of nature at the same time that she is caught in the tripartite crossfire of masculine prejudice, white illogical hate and Black lack of power.

Within this imprisoning environment there is no place for this black girl child. She becomes a displaced person whose pain is intensified by her consciousness of that displacement:

> If growing up is painful for the Southern Black girl, being aware of
> her displacement is the rust on the razor that threatens the throat.
> It is an unnecessary insult.

If the black man is denied his potency and his masculinity, if his autobiography narrates the quest of the black male after a "place" of full manhood, the black woman is denied her beauty and her quest is one after self-accepted black womanhood. Thus the discovered pattern of significant moments Maya Angelou superimposes on the experience of her life is a pattern of moments that trace the quest of the black female after a "place," a place where a child no longer need ask self-consciously, "What you looking at me for?" but where a woman can declare confidently, "I am a beautiful, Black woman."
—Sidonie Ann Smith, "The Song of a Caged Bird: Maya Angelou's Quest After Self-Acceptance," *Southern Humanities Review* 7, no. 4 (Fall 1973): 368

FRANK LAMONT PHILLIPS

Maya Angelou begins the second book of her autobiography, *Gather Together in My Name*, with a brief history of Black American thought and culture after the second World War; it is not a precise history, certainly not history as viewed coolly and through statistics. It is not even "accurate," but viewed from the vantage of almost 30 years, as one might hear it on the streets: biased, authoritative, hip, almost wildly funny, like certain urban myths. It seems right, and if this is not history as it was, it is history as it should have been. ⟨. . .⟩

Maya Angelou is not the stylist that ⟨Chester⟩ Himes is, nor a Richard Wright. She manages, however, a witty poetic flow (intensely more successful than in her book of poems, *Just Give Me a Cool Drink of Water 'Fore I Diiie*) that is sometimes cute, sometimes lax, often apt. The events of her life make interesting if somewhat lurid reading: an unwed mother, she is unlucky in love; she becomes a prostitute, enduring every nadir of fortune, her motherly instincts intact, her ability to adapt to adversity functioning.

Miss Angelou has the right instincts, that mythomania which one who is given to prattling about his life seems to possess. She applies it cannily, preserving the fiction that one can recall and, from a distance, whole conversations and surrounding trivia—as if she were a reel of recording tape, consuming for later regurgitation a problematic life. Further, she is schooled in situation ethics, licensing them retroactively to cover her having been a prostitute, making it seem almost enviable that she pulled it off so well.

It can also be said that Miss Angelou possesses an ear for folkways; they spawn abundantly in the warm stream of narration, adding enough mother wit and humor to give the events a "rightness." To some extent she is coy, never allowing us a really good, voyeur's glimpse into the conjugal bed that several male characters enjoy with her; rather, she teases. And though the author is never mawkishly sentimental, she shows herself to have been, like most of us, silly, only more so than many of us will admit. Yet she is proud. She stumbles, falls, but like the phoenix, rises renewed and wholly myth.

—Frank Lamont Phillips, [Review of *Gather Together in My Name*], *Black World* 24, no. 9 (July 1975): 52, 61

STEPHANIE A. DEMETRAKOPOULOS

Increasingly puzzling and unsettling, the more one tries to work with it, is Maya Angelou's *I Know Why the Caged Bird Sings*. Writing during her thirties, Angelou ⟨. . .⟩ never comes to terms with the matriarchal face that her biological mother embodies. She paints it over with a daughterly love that the mother does not deserve and that is singularly unconvincing.

The most positive and convincing face of the matriarchate and the one that provides the foundation of Angelou's personality is her father's mother, the grandmother to whom she is strangely and without explanation sent at age three just because the parents are divorced. She calls her Momma, and the first part of the book is a hymn to her. ⟨. . .⟩

⟨. . .⟩ Everyone in Stamps admired "the worth and majesty of my grandmother." Momma is proud of being black, disapproving even of Shakespeare since he was white. Her matriarchal realm includes her son Willy, crippled from birth, whom she continues to protect and shelter as if he were a child. She rules with deep love and an iron hand, often from principles she does not bother to explain to Angelou and her brother Bailey: "Her world was bordered on all sides with work, duty, religion and 'her place.' I don't think she ever knew that a deep-brooding love hung over everything she touched." She stands strong and silent even before the obscenely vicious baiting of the local white children; Angelou seems in the rest of her narrative to emulate this strength during such horrors as the rape by Mr. Freeman and the knifing by her father's mistress.

It is not until the appearance of her father that Angelou questions the worth of being female, but the father's obvious preference for Bailey makes her wish to have been a boy. Then she meets her frivolous and beautiful mother who could pass for white and finds that even as a female, she is inferior to the prevailing cultural standards. The oppressiveness and lack of maternal love in her mother's Venus-like role are reflected in the gradual destruction of Bailey as he attempts to internalize his mother's image, to come to terms with her sending them away twice to Momma. The mother's cold yet heated sexuality is apparent throughout. In the matriarchate of her mother, Mr. Freeman (the mother's live-in lover) seems to have all life force suspended, sitting inanimate until the mother appears. He seems to be useful only for sexual purposes, and he uses Angelou as an extension of her mother. Then, in the most shocking callousness one could adopt toward a child, the mother returns her daughter to Momma because Maya is depressed after the rape.

In her own behavior at the end of her book, Angelou splits the feminine archetype of her mother's cold Venus and her grandmother's primal warm sheltering Demeter aspects. She offers herself to a neighborhood boy for her first voluntary sexual experience. This partakes of the anonymity of the temple whore and Venus' use of the male as sexual cohort only. This act also reflects Angelou's inability to feel that a man could find her desirable, even though her mother's third husband, who appears on the scene in Angelou's early teens, has been kind to her. In a psychologically bizarre ending, Angelou finds her adulthood through her acceptance and love of her baby son. Her mother brings him to her bed, and when she awakens, she finds that she has instinctively slept so as not to hurt him. This acting out of her grandmother's qualities of sheltering, warm, fortress-like physicality reflects her comfort with the Demeter archetype, not with the adult woman's Venus or Hera (the wife archetype) couplings with the male. It seems a celebration of womanhood through becoming the Primal Great Good Mother, but skipping all the steps in between of establishing authentic contact with the male world and/or making one's own matriarchal realm. She says she feels close to her own mother at the end, but that too is difficult to believe. Her mother has thoroughly betrayed her, but never does Angelou show us that she or her mother has consciously confronted this rejection. In a way, having the baby can be seen as Angelou's counter-betrayal. At any rate, the emergence of the baby from the womb of this girl-child who has not even been truly sexually awakened in any concrete way seems a tragic way to end the book and begin life as an adult. Birth as self-actualization or gender realization would appear a very limited step toward consciousness; at any rate, I always feel tricked at the book's conclusion. However, perhaps it is psychologically apt and even life-affirming in that Angelou does not lose but consolidates her sense of the strength of her grandmother and all she symbolizes.

—Stephanie A. Demetrakopoulos, "The Metaphysics of Matrilinearism in Women's Autobiography," *Women's Autobiography* (1980), excerpted in *Twentieth-Century American Literature*, ed. Harold Bloom (New York: Chelsea House Publishers, 1985), 203–4

SONDRA O'NEALE

Unlike her poetry, which is a continuation of traditional oral expression in Afro-American literature, Angelou's prose follows classic technique in nonpoetic Western forms. The material in each book while chronologically marking her life is nonetheless arranged in loosely structured plot sequences which are skillfully controlled. In *Caged Bird* the tenuous psyche of a gangly, sensitive, withdrawn child is traumatically jarred by rape, a treacherous act from which neither the reader nor the protagonist has recovered by the book's end. All else is cathartic: her uncles' justified revenge upon the rapist, her years of readjustment in a closed world of speechlessness despite the warm nurturing of her grandmother, her grand-uncle, her beloved brother Bailey, and the Stamps community; a second reunion with her vivacious mother; even her absurdly unlucky pregnancy at the end does not assuage the reader's anticipatory wonder: isn't the act of rape by a trusted adult so assaultive upon an eight-year-old's life that it leaves a wound which can never be healed? Such reader interest in a character's future is the craft from which quality fiction is made. Few autobiographers however have the verve to seize the drama of such a moment, using one specific incident to control the book but with an underlining implication that the incident will not control a life.

The denouement in *Gather Together in My Name* is again sexual: the older, crafty, experienced man lasciviously preying upon the young, vulnerable, and, for all her exposure by that time, naïve woman. While foreshadowing apprehension guided the reader to the central action in the first work, Maya presses the evolvement in *Gather Together* through a limited first-person narrator who seems to know less of the villain's intention than is obvious to the reader. Thrice removed from the action, the reader sees that L. D. Tolbrook is nothing but a slick pimp, that his seductive sexual refusals can only lead to a calamitous end; that his please-turn-these-few-tricks-for-me-baby-so-I-can-get-out-of-an-urgent-jam line is an ancient inducement for susceptible females, but Maya the actor in the tragedy cannot. She is too much in love. Maya, the author, through whose eyes we see a younger, foolish "self," so painstakingly details the girl's descent into the brothel that Black women, all women, have enough vicarious example to avoid the trap. Again, through using the "self" as role model, not only is Maya able to instruct and inspire the reader but the sacrifice of personal disclosure authenticates the autobiography's integral depth.

—Sondra O'Neale, "Reconstruction of the Complete Self: New Images of Black Women in Maya Angelou's Continuing Autobiography," *Black Women Writers (1950–1980): A Critical Evaluation*, ed. Mari Evans (New York: Anchor Books/Doubleday, 1984), 32–33

CHRISTINE FROULA

Mr. Freeman's abuse of Maya ⟨in *I Know Why the Caged Bird Sings*⟩ occurs in two episodes. In the first, her mother rescues her from a nightmare by taking her into her own bed, and Maya then awakes to find her mother gone to work and Mr. Freeman grasping her tightly. The child feels, first, bewilderment and terror: "His right hand was moving so fast and his heart was beating so hard that I was afraid that he would die." When Mr. Freeman subsides, however, so does Maya's fright: "Finally he was quiet, and then came the nice part. He held me so softly that I wished he wouldn't ever let me go. . . . This was probably my real father and we had found each other at last." After the abuse comes the silencing: Mr. Freeman enlists the child's complicity by an act of metaphysical violence, informing her that he will kill her beloved brother Bailey if she tells anyone what "they" have done. For the child, this prohibition prevents not so much telling as asking, for, confused as she is by her conflicting feelings, she has no idea what has happened. One day, however, Mr. Freeman stops her as she is setting out for the library, and it is then that he commits the actual rape on the terrified child, "a breaking and entering when even the senses are torn apart." Again threatened with violence if she tells, Maya retreats to her bed in a silent delirium, but the story emerges when her mother discovers her stained drawers, and Mr. Freeman is duly arrested and brought to trial. ⟨. . .⟩

Maya breaks her silence when a woman befriends her by taking her home and reading aloud to her, then sending her off with a book of poems, one of which she is to recite on her next visit. We are not told which poem it was, but later we find that the pinnacle of her literary achievement at age twelve was to have learned by heart the whole of Shakespeare's *Rape of Lucrece*—nearly two thousand lines. Maya, it appears, emerges from her literal silence into a literary one. Fitting her voice to Shakespeare's words, she writes safe limits around the exclamations of her wounded tongue and in this way is able to reenter the cultural text that her words had formerly disrupted. But if Shakespeare's poem redeems Maya from her hysterical silence, it is also a lover that she embraces at her peril. In Angelou's text, Shakespeare's Lucrece represents that violation of the spirit which Shakespeare's and all stories of sleeping beauties commit upon the female reader. Maya's feat of memory signals a double seduction: by the white culture that her grandmother wished her black child not to love and by the male culture which imposes upon the rape victim, epitomized in Lucrece, the double silence of a beauty that serves male fantasy and a death that serves male honor. The black child's identification with an exquisite rape fantasy of white male culture violates her reality. Wouldn't everyone be surprised, she muses, "when one day I woke out of my black ugly dream, and my real hair, which was long and blond, would take the place of the kinky mass that Momma wouldn't let me straighten? My light-blue eyes were going to hypnotize them. . . . Because I was really white and because a cruel fairy stepmother, who was understandably jealous of my beauty, had turned me into a too-big Negro girl, with nappy black hair, broad feet, and a

space between her teeth that would hold a number two pencil." Maya's fantasy bespeaks her cultural seduction, but Angelou's powerful memoir, recovering the history that frames it, rescues the child's voice from this seduction by telling the prohibited story.
—Christine Froula, "The Daughter's Seduction: Sexual Violence and Literary History," *Signs* 11, no. 4 (Summer 1986): 634–37

SELWYN R. CUDJOE

The violation that began in *Caged Bird* takes on a much sharper focus in *Gather Together*. To be sure, Angelou is still concerned with the questions of what it means to be black and female in America and exactly where she fits into the scheme of things. But her development is reflective of a particular type of black woman, located at a particular moment of history and subjected to certain social forces that assault the black woman with unusual ferocity. Thus, when Angelou arrives in Los Angeles she complains bitterly that her mother "hadn't the slightest idea that not only was I not a woman, but what passed for my mind was animal instinct. Like a tree or a river, I merely responded to the winds and the tides" (GT 23). In responding to her mother's indifference to her immaturity, she complains that "they were not equipped to understand that an eighteen-year-old mother is also an eighteen-year-old girl" (GT 27). It is from this angle of vision, that of a "tree in the wind" possessing mostly "animal instinct" to an "unequipped" eighteen-year-old young woman, that we must respond to the story that she tells.

Neither politically nor linguistically innocent, *Gather Together* reflects the imposition of values of a later period of the author's life. Undoubtedly, in organizing the incidents of the text and having recourse to memorization, the selection of incidents, the fictive principle, and so on come into full play. For example, it is difficult to believe that Angelou set out to organize the prostitution of Jonnie Mae and Beatrice because she wanted to revenge those "inconsiderate, stupid bitches" (GT 45). Nor can we accept the fact that she "turned tricks" for L. D. because she believes that "there was nothing wrong with sex. I had no need for shame. Society dictated that sex was only licensed by marriage documents. Well, I didn't agree with that. Society is a conglomerate of human beings, and that's just what I was. A human being" (GT 142).

It rings hollow as a justification. Society is not a mere conglomerate of human beings. Society is a conglomeration of *social beings* whose acts make them *human* or *nonhuman*. To the degree that those acts affirm or negate our humanity they can be considered correct or incorrect. Such reasoning only keeps the argument within the context in which it is raised. The point is that one cannot justify the prostitution of one's body or that of others simply by asserting: "I didn't agree with that."

The importance of the text (its social significance, if you may) lies in its capacity to signify to and from a larger social context than that from which it originates. In spite of the imperial tone she sometimes adopts, Angelou is an extremely lonely young woman drifting through this phase of her life. She is more isolated in the bustle of California than she was in the rural quietude of Stamps. The kidnapping of her child, her most significant achievement so far, and her escape from a life of drugs (because of the generosity of Troubadour Martin) give her a new understanding of life, a rebirth into a higher level of dialectical understanding.

Yet, in a curious way, the book fails. Its lack of moral weight and absence of an ethical center deny it an organizing principle and rigor capable of keeping the work together. It is almost as though the incidents in the text were simply gathered together under the name of Maya Angelou but not so organized to achieve that complex level of signification that one expects in such a work. The absence of these qualities makes *Gather Together* conspicuously weak. The language of the text, more controlled, begins to loosen up—this is its saving grace. Where there were patches of beautiful writing in *Caged Bird*, here there is a much more consistent and sustained flow of eloquent and honey-dipped prose, while the simplicity of the speech patterns remains. The writing flows and shimmers with beauty, but the rigorous, coherent, and meaningful organization of experiences is missing.

—Selwyn R. Cudjoe, "Maya Angelou: The Autobiographical Statement Updated," in *Reading Black, Reading Feminist: A Critical Anthology*, ed. Henry Louis Gates Jr. (New York: Meridian, 1990), 292–94

DOLLY A. MCPHERSON

Through the genre of autobiography, Angelou has celebrated the richness and vitality of Southern Black life and the sense of community that persists in the face of poverty and racial prejudice, initially revealing this celebration through a portrait of life as experienced by a Black child in the Arkansas of the 1930s (*I Know Why the Caged Bird Sings*, 1970). The second delineates a young woman struggling to create an existence that provides security and love in post–World War II America (*Gather Together in My Name*, 1974). The third presents a young, married adult in the 1950s seeking a career in show business and experiencing her first amiable contacts with Whites (*Singin' and Swingin' and Gettin' Merry Like Christmas*, 1976). The fourth volume (*The Heart of a Woman*, 1981) shows a wiser, more mature woman in the 1960s, examining the roles of being a woman and a mother. In her most recent volume, Angelou demonstrates that *All God's Children Need Traveling Shoes* (1986) to take them beyond familiar borders and to enable them to see and understand the world from another's vantage point.

While the burden of this serial autobiography is essentially a recapturing of her own subjective experiences, Angelou's effort throughout her work is to describe the influences—personal as well as cultural, historical and social—that have shaped her life. Dominant in Angelou's autobiography is the exploration of the self—the self in relationship with intimate others: the family, the community, the world. Angelou does not recount these experiences simply because they occurred, but because they represent stages of her spiritual growth and awareness—what one writer calls "stages of self." ⟨. . .⟩

A study of Maya Angelou's autobiography is significant not only because the autobiography offers insights into personal and group experience in America, but because it creates a unique place within Black autobiographical tradition, not because it is better than its formidable autobiographical predecessors, but because Angelou, throughout her autobiographical writing, adopts a special stance in relation to the self, the community and the world. Angelou's concerns with family and community, as well as with work and her conceptions of herself as a human being, are echoed throughout her autobiography. The ways in which she faces these concerns offer instruction into the range of survival strategies available to women in America and reveal, as well, important insights into Black traditions and culture.

—Dolly A. McPherson, *Order out of Chaos: The Autobiographical Works of Maya Angelou* (New York: Peter Lang, 1990), 5–6

MARION KRAFT

This last volume of autobiographical works by Maya Angelou ⟨*All God's Children Need Traveling Shoes*⟩ is a powerful example for the African continuum in the African diaspora and for various transcultural influences in contemporary Black women's writings. ⟨. . .⟩ Angelou demystifies Africa but celebrates it as her ancestral home, the spirit of which has survived in the New World, and she transforms her different experiences into a new cross-cultural identity, the African American heritage. Thus, Angelou concludes her-story:

> Many years earlier I, or rather someone very like me and certainly related to me, had been taken from Africa by force. This second leave-taking would not be so onerous, for now I knew my people had never completely left Africa. We had sung it in our blues, shouted it in our gospel and danced the continent in our breakdowns. As we carried it to Philadelphia, Boston and Birmingham we had changed its color, modified its rhythms, yet it was Africa which rode in the

bulges of our high calves, shook in our protruding behinds and crackled in our wide open laughter (208).

Maya Angelou's prose works are not merely autobiography. They are selected
episodes of her personal life that tell a collective story. She writes from within
the tradition of storytelling, the slave narratives and early African American
autobiographical writings, all of which have also always served a political and
educational purpose. Yet, in the European tradition, she centers herself as the
picaresque heroine, who moves through various stages of imaginative and real
selves. She is the trickster *Brer Rabbit*, a bold wanderer, but above all, the Black
woman artist—creating herself. This self-creation has been supported by
female bonding, her African worldview, the spirit that governs it, and her
Christian belief. In an interview Angelou confirms that it is this transcultural
spirituality that is the underlying core of her survival, her life and her works,
that renders power to her voice and that is the connecting link between the
various aspects of different identities in herself:

> When I think of spirit, I think of the energy of life. African religions
> encourage the supplicant to respect the spirit in the tree, in the water,
> in the flower, in the air, in a child. I, too, am aware of the presence of
> spirit in everything. And because I am a religious woman, I cannot—
> don't know how to and don't wish to—separate spirit from the spirit
> of God. So spirit to me is God. [. . .]
>
> My grandmother, who was one of the greatest human beings I've ever
> known, used to say, "I am a child of God and I'm nobody's creature."
> That to me defined the Black woman, through the centuries.

Maya Angelou's different lives and her processes of self-consciousness, her
political commitment and her spirituality are reflected in her autobiographical
works, in which her different ways of self-portraiture are connected to the
story of her people, whose grace and persistence, as she asserts herself, form
the basis of her personal power and strength.

—Marion Kraft, *The African Continuum and Contemporary African American Women Writers: Their
Literary Presence and Ancestral Past* (Frankfurt am Main: Peter Lang, 1995), 107–8

B I B L I O G R A P H Y

Cabaret for Freedom (with Godfrey Cambridge). 1960.
I Know Why the Caged Bird Sings. 1969.

Just Give Me a Cool Drink of Water 'fore I Diiie: The Poetry of Maya Angelou.
    1971, 1988.
Gather Together in My Name. 1974, 1985.
Oh Pray My Wings Are Gonna Fit Me Well. 1975.
Singin' and Swingin' and Gettin' Merry Like Christmas. 1976.
And Still I Rise. 1978.
The Heart of a Woman. 1981.
Shaker, Why Don't You Sing? 1983.
All God's Children Need Traveling Shoes. 1986.
Mrs. Flowers: A Moment of Friendship. 1986.
Poems: Maya Angelou. 1986.
Now Sheba Sings the Songs. 1987.
Conversations with Maya Angelou. Ed. Jeffrey M. Elliot. 1989.
Selected from I Know Why the Caged Bird Sings and The Heart of a Woman. 1989.
I Shall Not Be Moved. 1990.
Maya Angelou Omnibus. 1991.
On the Pulse of Morning. 1993.
Soul Looks Back in Wonder. 1993.
Lessons in Living. 1993.
Life Doesn't Frighten Me. 1993.
Wouldn't Take Nothing for My Journey Now. 1993.
I Love the Look of Words. 1993.
And My Best Friend Is Chicken. 1994.

VERA BRITTAIN
1893–1970

VERA MARY BRITTAIN was born on December 29, 1893, in Newcastle-under-Lyme, England, the elder of two children of Thomas Arthur Brittain, a successful paper manufacturer, and Edith Mary Bervon Brittain, an accomplished amateur singer and the daughter of a church organist and composer. In 1911, a teacher introduced Vera to Olive Schreiner's *Woman and Labour*, and she began to embrace feminist perspectives and possibilities. Vera wanted to become a writer but could not withstand class and gender assumptions of the day; she returned home to make her debut and assume her expected social duties.

By 1914, however, Brittain was committed to a different path, and she entered Somerville College, at Oxford, that fall. She was an excellent student, but World War I changed Oxford: the college became a military hospital, and staff and students participated in relief efforts. Brittain abandoned her studies to become a nurse in the Voluntary Aid Detachment (VAD), serving in London, Malta, and France, from 1915 to 1919. During this period she became engaged to Roland Leighton, a friend of her brother. Both young men would be killed in the war.

Brittain did not abandon her ambitions as a writer during her service but recorded her observations in diaries, letters, and poems. The 1918 publication of *Verses of a VAD* launched her career as a professional writer. The following year Brittain returned to Oxford, where she met fellow aspiring writer Winifred Holtby; the women formed a lasting friendship and working partnership. In 1925, having received her bachelor's and master's degrees, Brittain married political scientist and philosopher G. E. G. Catlin, with whom she would have two children.

During the 1920s, Brittain published her first two novels, *The Dark Tide* (1923) and *Not Without Honour* (1924), and pursued a career as a journalist and author of works on feminism and international issues. *Women's Work in Modern England* (1928) encouraged women to seek autonomy and to resist stereotypical definitions; in it she argued that "mothercraft is a science which has to be taught" but that professional advice need not destroy "the application of female values in a world where all values that have been thought to matter have hitherto been male." In *Halcyon; or, The Future of Monogamy* (1929) Brittain argued that monogamy, freely chosen, is the most egalitarian arrangement.

13

By the late 1920s, "Great War" literature had become popular. Brittain began her own account of the war, *Testament of Youth*, in 1929; it was published in 1933. This romanticized narrative about young people who had supported the war is also an antiwar statement about the deaths of her brother and fiancé. A traditional narrative form marketed as a best-seller, *Testament of Youth* breaks new ground, as her biographer, Deborah Gorham, notes, because it is "a reasoned analysis of why the war happened and how to prevent a future war"—a type of analysis traditionally offered only by male writers. The book also made Brittain a sought-after spokesperson for peace during the 1930s.

Honourable Estate (1936), a political and feminist novel that was not enthusiastically received, is Brittain's most ambitious and best-realized work. An autobiographical travel book, *Thrice a Stranger*, appeared in 1938; it was followed by *Testament of Friendship* (1940), a biographical tribute to Winifred Holtby, who died in 1935, a year that also marked the suicide of Brittain's father and the defeat of her husband's bid for a seat in Parliament. Hereafter Brittain devoted her energies mainly to historical writing projects and to the cause of pacifism, on which she spoke and published widely.

Vera Brittain suffered a fall in 1966 while hurrying to give a lecture in London. She never fully recovered from her injuries and died on March 29, 1970.

CRITICAL   EXTRACTS

VERA BRITTAIN

Until a very few months ago, no eyes but mine had seen the diary which is here reproduced, and even my own had not seen it for several years. These intimate, undisciplined outpourings were forced from my immaturity by the urgent need of self-expression. I have decided to publish them now because I have come to believe that our need of understanding, one of another, is at least equally urgent.

I belong to the few who believe in all sincerity that their own lives provide the answers to some of the many problems which puzzle humanity. I should like to help the experienced, who think they understand youth, to realise how easy it is to mistake illusion for conviction, bewilderment for weakness, enthusiasm for indiscretion or self-will. It is in the hope that these records of my own ardours, absurdities, weaknesses, and failures will enlighten the old who are puzzled about the young, and console the young who are confused about themselves, that I venture to expose them to the searchlight of public criticism.

—Vera Brittain, "Foreword" to A Chronicle of Youth (about 1922), in Vera Brittain: War Diary, 1913–1917: Chronicle of Youth, ed. Alan Bishop (London: Victor Gollancz Ltd, 1981), 13

CLARE LEIGHTON

It is over half a century since Roland ⟨Leighton⟩ was killed. Time is supposed to hold the power of softening the effect of grief, but as I read this diary of Vera Brittain's with its vivid account of life in the First World War, I found myself as emotionally destroyed as though my brother's death had happened but a short while before.

When Dr Alan Bishop asked me to write this Preface I hesitated before saying I would do so. Why, I felt, must I re-live that terrible time of wholesale destruction? But, as I wavered, my decision was forced upon me. A friend reproached me. "It is your duty to write this and it is also your contribution to history," she insisted. "Don't forget that you are, today, the sole living person who closely experienced the tragedy of your brother's death. You would never forgive yourself if you were a coward and shrank from this. The world needs to be reminded of the wanton horror of that war, with its destruction of the flower of a generation of young men."

Perhaps, too, it is of importance to chronicle a war as seen and experienced through the eyes and emotions of the young. It is strange how vividly a visual memory can be stamped into the soft wax of the very young. The impression is deep and hardens over the years, never to be softened and erased by time. So it is that to this day the sound of a bugle or even the sight of a soldier in uniform can frighten me.

As I write this I find myself back in childhood. It is a cold morning in January and I am in the garden of our cottage in Sussex. My father is with me. I carry two heavy kettles. They are filled with boiling water, for we are about to bury the tunic—blood-stained and bullet-riddled—in which Roland has been killed. . . . Father watches the windows of the house, for my mother must not see this tunic that Father has hidden from the packages of Roland's effects returned from France. I am to thaw the frozen earth so that it may be buried out of sight.

Over here, in America, where I am now living, children have not been so directly exposed to the fears and horrors of war. War is something you see on television or read about in history books. It does not impinge upon one's daily

life. But my generation in England chanced to grow up with the repeated associations of war. Behind the brave, happy trivia of daily life loomed this hideous
spectre. 〈. . .〉

All that was so long ago. But it has left me with a deep terror of war and
a pleading with the world to see that we are not beguiled into it. The wages
of war continue long after the young men are forgotten, and we who lived
through it have a deep responsibility.

Thus it is that I feel the importance of this book. Vera Brittain knew and
suffered, and we are fortunate to be able to read and learn the lesson of the
waste and horror of war.

—Clare Leighton, "Preface" to *Vera Brittain: War Diary, 1913–1917: Chronicle of Youth*, ed.
Alan Bishop (London: Victor Gollancz Ltd, 1981), 11–12

ALAN BISHOP

This is not a depressing diary. Movingly, memorably, it records the decimation
of Vera Brittain's generation; but it also records courage, endurance, loyalty,
generosity, happiness, love. As a woman's detailed account of the First World
War, it is almost unique; and it must stand high among all accounts of the first
part of that War. But it is much more than a "war diary".

If the young Vera Brittain is representative of the "war generation", she is
equally representative of a generation of young women who rebelled against
a society that insisted they were inferior to men. Her diary shows clearly some
of the forces and feelings that cemented her early feminism into a lifelong
commitment. In other respects, too, one's understanding of recent social
developments is extended: through the diary's description of a leisured provincial society, for instance, and of the subsequent disruption and destruction of
many of its values. From the beginning of the War, Vera Brittain paid very
close attention to national and international as well as local affairs, her keenly
analytical mind giving her a sensitive awareness of the shifting times she was
living through.

This diary is also of great interest and value as a psychological document,
adding to one's knowledge and understanding, not only of one of the great
women of our time, but of the intricacies of human behaviour under stress.
The girl who took up her pen to begin a daily "Reflective Record" was complex in personality and exceptional in her abilities. To her idealistic and ambitious spirit, the Buxton of 1913 was a prison; so she set out determinedly to
find freedom and fulfilment. The process of maturation that led her out of
rebellious frustration to academic endeavour at Somerville College, Oxford,
then on to the dedicated drudgery of wartime nursing, is vividly unfolded. The
narrative of her relationship with Roland Leighton—its deep and confused

feelings, its discussions and misunderstandings, quarrels and joys—is a moving revelation of the complicated contradictions we gloss as "love". Perhaps even more moving is the halting record of her near-despair, and of the agonisingly slow stages of her recovery, after Roland's death. The sifting of moral, religious and philosophical questions throughout this diary may remind some readers of the great spiritual autobiographies of English nonconformism, such as John Bunyan's *Grace Abounding*.

The diary is also notable for its emphatic literary qualities. As a schoolgirl, Vera Brittain had written poetry and fiction, and her firm ambition by 1913 was to become a novelist. Her natural ability as a writer makes this diary a joy to read: its maturing style is fluent, lucid and direct, but ornate description and the occasional purple patch contribute variety. As is indicated by the frequent occurrence of quotations, Vera Brittain was extremely receptive to literary influence; the novels of George Eliot, the poems of Wordsworth, and Rupert Brooke's *1914* sonnets affected her with particular force. One recognises, too, a writer's tendency to shape experience towards literary models; as when she enacts Lyndall, the heroine of Olive Schreiner's *Story of an African Farm*—a novel which, from May 1914, was a dominant influence. The diary's literary qualities are attractive and distinctive, authenticating rather than diminishing its documentary authority.

One should also note, perhaps, that the events recorded in the diary have fortuitously patterned it as a tripartite structure of great aesthetic force. The first section, running to the summer of 1914, acts as a prologue, introducing characters and establishing themes and background. Then the long central section develops the relationship of Vera Brittain and Roland Leighton in the spreading shadow of the war. His experiences on the Western Front, described in the excerpts from his fine letters, are counterpointed with hers as a student at Oxford and as a V.A.D. nurse; there are several brilliantly detailed episodes and character-sketches; and Roland's death is an almost unbearably wrenching climax. The final section, composed of the 1916 and 1917 entries, can be read as an epilogue, its ending muted, ironic, open. Does any other diary project so powerfully, so fully, qualities suggestive of a great novel?

But it will be read primarily because it possesses, in abundance, qualities characteristic of a great diary. Vera Brittain's wide range of interests and experiences, her sharp observation, and her patent determination to record with total honesty, make this a trustworthy and very informative account of lives being lived. Moreover her personality is vigorously transmitted—a personality immediately and continuously fascinating. With characteristic integrity and strength of mind, Vera Brittain in later life was the first to acknowledge youthful failings such as her tendency to make acerbic personal comments; but the open expression of these failings helps to guarantee her sincerity—and

they are balanced by a parallel harshness of self-criticism and by generous enthusiasms.
—Alan Bishop, "Introduction" to *Vera Brittain: War Diary, 1913–1917: Chronicle of Youth*, ed. Alan Bishop (London: Victor Gollancz Ltd, 1981), 16–18

SANDRA M. GILBERT

Even the most conventionally angelic of women's wartime ministrations, must have suggested to many members of both sexes that, while men were now invalid and maybe in-valid, their sisters were triumphant survivors and destined inheritors. Certainly both the rhetoric and the iconography of nursing would seem to imply some such points. To be sure, the nurse presents herself as a servant of her patient. "Every task," writes Vera Brittain of her days as a VAD, "had for us . . . a sacred glamour" ⟨*Testament of Youth*, 1979, 210⟩. Yet in works by both male and female novelists the figure of the nurse ultimately takes on a majesty which hints that she is mistress rather than slave, goddess rather than supplicant. After all, when men are immobilized and dehumanized, it is only these women who possess the old (matriarchal) formulas for survival. Thus, even while memoirists like Brittain express "gratitude" for the "sacred glamour" of nursing, they seem to be pledging allegiance to a *secret* glamour— the glamour of an expertise which they will win from their patients. "Towards the men," recalls Brittain, "I came to feel an almost adoring gratitude . . . for the knowledge of masculine functioning which the care of them gave me" ⟨165–66⟩. ⟨. . .⟩

⟨. . .⟩ A number of texts by men and women alike suggest that the revolutionary socioeconomic transformations wrought by the war's "topsy turvy" role reversals did bring about a release of female libidinal energies, as well as a liberation of female anger, which men usually found anxiety-inducing and women often found exhilarating.

On the subject of erotic release, a severely political writer like Vera Brittain is notably restrained. Yet even she implies, at least subtextually, that she experienced some such phenomenon, for while she expresses her "gratitude" to the men from whom she learned about "masculine functioning," she goes on to thank the war that delivered their naked bodies into her hands for her own "early release from . . . sex-inhibitions" ⟨165–66⟩. Significantly, too, as if to confirm the possibility that Brittain did receive a wartime sex education, Eric Leed records the belief of some observers that "women in particular 'reacted to the war experience with a powerful increase in libido.'" Was the war a festival of female misrule in which the collapse of a traditional social structure "permitted," as Leed also puts it, "a range of personal contacts that had been impossible in [former lives] where hierarchies of status ruled?" ⟨. . .⟩

Perhaps more important than the female eroticism that the war energized, however, was the more diffusely emotional sense of sisterhood its "Amazonian countries" inspired in nurses and VADs, land girls and tram conductors. As if to show the positive aspect of the bacchanalian bonding ⟨D. H.⟩ Lawrence deplores in his "Tickets, Please," women like Vera Brittain, May Sinclair, and Violetta Thurstan remembered how their liberation into the public realm from the isolation of the private house allowed them to experience a female (re)union in which they felt "the joys of companionship to the full . . . in a way that would be impossible to conceive in an ordinary world" ⟨*Field Hospital and Flying Column*, 1915, 174⟩. For Radclyffe Hall, too, the battalion of sisters "formed in those terrible years" consisted of "great-hearted women . . . glad . . . to help one another to shoulder burdens" ⟨*Well of Loneliness*, 1928, 336⟩. In a variation on this theme, Winifred Holtby told in *The Crowded Street* how her alienated heroine, Muriel Hammond, finally achieved a purposeful life through the friendship of Delia Vaughan, a feminist activist (modeled in part on Vera Brittain, as Muriel is on Holtby herself) whose fiancé was killed in the war.

—Sandra M. Gilbert, "Soldier's Heart: Literary Men, Literary Women, and the Great War," *Signs* 8, no. 3 (Spring 1983): 433–37, 442

MURIEL MELLOWN

On her death in 1970 Vera Brittain left behind, in addition to innumerable newspaper and journal articles, 29 books, including five novels, two volumes of poetry, two autobiographies, biographies, travel books, and a variety of social studies. This diverse material is marked by a remarkable intellectual consistency. Whatever the form of her work, Brittain wrote—even in her fiction—to express her views on life and in particular her views on women. During the early years in Oxford and London she formulated distinct theories about woman's position and autonomy and the rights of woman to think, to act, and to be heard. At Oxford she had received an historian's training, and her historical sense allowed her to see the long tradition of female oppression which she was combating. As she espoused the feminist cause, she brought to bear the keen intelligence which had enabled her—without tutoring, guidance or instruction—to win a Somerville Exhibition. Her theories are consistent, precisely thought out, and clearly articulated into a coherent system.

Vera Brittain's ideas reflect the new direction of the feminist movement in the 1920s. Women now had won the right to an education and the power of the vote. In the second stage of the women's movement the need was to utilise these gains in order to effect extensive legal and social reforms and Vera Brittain devoted much of her life to this end. The basis of her efforts was a set

of six distinct, specific goals: sweeping changes in human attitudes, a new con-
cept of marriage, the advancement of women to professional and economic
equality, the improvement of social services for women, radical developments
in sexual morality, and a new understanding of women's psychology and
capacities. These six goals constitute the main planks of her feminist theory,
which was aimed at ending sexual inequality. ⟨. . .⟩

Vera Brittain ⟨sought⟩ to bring about through her writings a fresh understanding of women's psychology and abilities. In her view female psychology
is distinguished from male by a capacity for friendship and loyalty and by a
deep-seated instinct for peace. Her understanding of the importance of friendship among women is most completely revealed in *Testament of Friendship* (1940).
Though primarily a biography of Winifred Holtby, this work was also
designed to explore the subject of women's friendship, just as *Testament of Youth*
was written to attest to the role of women in war. In the prologue Brittain
explains: 'From the days of Homer the friendships of men have enjoyed glory
and acclamation, but the friendships of women, in spite of Ruth and Naomi,
have usually been not merely unsung, but mocked, belittled and falsely interpreted' (p 2). Thus the work is not only a glowing tribute to Holtby but also
a powerful and detailed analysis of their friendship and the gamut of emotions
it involved. Its main theme is that 'loyalty and affection between women is a
noble relationship' (p 2). Years later Brittain must have had herself and
Winifred Holtby in mind when she wrote in *Radclyffe Hall* of the 'intensity of
love which can exist between woman and woman'. That she was not speaking
only of an erotic relationship is made clear by her comment: 'Such love can
exist between mother and daughter, sister and sister, or friend and friend; its
distinction lies in its intensity, and its freedom from selfishness or the desire to
possess' (p 45).

Yet the biography is more than an account of the relationship of Vera
Brittain and Winifred Holtby. Holtby's warm, sympathetic, outgoing nature
brought her many friends, and the book describes the full range of her connections—with Stella Benson, Dot McCalman, Jean McWilliam, Phyllis
Bentley, Storm Jameson, and many others. In fact, the work becomes a celebration not merely of individual relationships but also of women's friendships
in general. In short, it records the commitment to women which has always
been a part of the women's movement.

—Muriel Mellown, "Vera Brittain: Feminist in a New Age (1896–1970)," in *Feminist Theorists:
Three Centuries of Key Women Thinkers*, ed. Dale Spender (New York: Pantheon Books, 1983),
317, 326–27

MARVIN RINTALA

In 1960, Vera Brittain was invited to lecture to the Royal Society of Literature and chose as her topic "Literary Testaments." Nowhere in this lecture did she mention her own books, and nothing else she ever wrote was so impersonally detached in tone, but nothing else she ever wrote was so self-revealing. Her arguments that modern autobiographies entitled *Testament* are common and that autobiographies of the powerful are no longer popular with readers fall flat, since she is, as always, talking about herself. Some of her other arguments in this lecture present problems of conceptual clarity, but even those problems may help us better understand the human being who was making those arguments.

Brittain began her lecture by citing two different dictionary definitions of testament: a solemn covenant, and an act determining posthumous distribution of personal property. She seems not to have realized the possible mutual exclusiveness of these definitions. She clearly assumed that her *Testaments* met both definitions. Even taking these two definitions separately, the difficulties presented by her political consciousness and her writing are substantial. Indeed, since she was always "a severely political writer," it is impossible to separate her political consciousness and her writing. Writing was for her an intensely political act, her characteristic way of participating in the political process. She hoped "to write and utter words which reached at least a few whose benevolence had power to change the state of the world." She recognized also, however, that the act of writing both intensified and clarified her political consciousness.

The first definition of testament, as a covenant, presupposes, of course, two or more parties to an agreement. Brittain spoke of a covenant between author and reader, and she took seriously the responsibility of writing. She may have lived well from her writing, but she lived, to use Max Weber's distinction, for as well as off her work. She was a professional writer with a message about which she cared deeply, but any reader's receptivity to her message was discouraged both by the endless recitation of personal trivia and by the breathless intensity of it all.

Brittain failed to acknowledge, and perhaps to understand, the religious origins of covenants. God had made at most two, and the Scottish Presbyterians not many more—at least until their most devoted heir wrote that Covenant of the League of Nations in which Brittain believed so strongly until she renounced it so completely. She, however, offered three major *Testaments* and endless minor ones. In ignoring the religious origins of covenants, she was symbolizing the most important reason why her personal commitment to pacifism and, to a lesser extent, her personal commitment to social justice were of such small political impact. Peace and social justice are values which in a profoundly conservative modern British political culture have been advanced chiefly by the nonconformist Protestant conscience. This conscience has found expression in parties, first the Liberal and later the Labor, and numerous pressure groups. Other than her contacts with Quakers, Brittain had surprisingly few "chapel" contacts in her political activity ⟨. . . .⟩

The second kind of testament, bequeathing personal property, can be revised often, but only the last word is valid. Its contents are, or are meant to be, secret until the death of its writer. Only then is it published. Brittain, however, published her first major *Testament* when she was forty, the second at forty-seven, and the third when she was sixty-four. Her first *Testament* lacks the immediacy of youth, and the last lacks reflectiveness of age. The story of the third ends seven years before its first publication. She apparently chose to be silent about the last two decades of her life, even though she seems once to have contemplated a fourth, and presumably final, *Testament*. Her life before 1950 may have been a series of open books, but all of them were written by her.

More seriously, the second meaning of testament assumes that the property which is being distributed in fact belongs to the person writing the testament. Brittain claimed to speak for an entire generation, at least of women. She thought she had left "the permanent record of a generation." Surely millions of European women grieved to the ends of their lives over the deaths in 1914–1918 of those whom they loved. Whether all, or even most, of them drew the same political lessons as Brittain did is, however, at best uncertain. Brittain made no effort to ascertain the answer to the crucial question. Furthermore, those of her personal experiences which came while she was a war nurse in the First World War were relatively atypical. Most European women did not watch soldiers die. Most European men did so watch. Ten million of them did not have the opportunity to watch. They were being watched. With the exception of a few who had literary precociousness, or wealthy families to publish their last letters or poems, these ten million died intestate. Vera Brittain chose to write her own story, not theirs. That was apt, for she was one of life's survivors.

   —Marvin Rintala, "Chronicler of a Generation: Vera Brittain's Testament," *Journal of Political and Military Sociology* 12, no. 1 (Spring 1984): 31–33

JEAN KENNARD

Both Brittain's and ⟨Winifred⟩ Holtby's work shows the need to struggle with certain concepts or problems—companionate marriage, for example, is a central topic in Brittain's fiction—a fact which suggests that writing was their way of dealing with life. Brittain wrote of one of her later novels, *Born 1925*, "in this novel I have sought to work out some of my own problems vicariously." Events, people they knew, and particularly each other and each other's work thus became texts to be read and interpreted in print. For their readers, then, their written work can become an opportunity, among other things, to understand their psychological development and their relationship with each other. ⟨. . .⟩

For Brittain and Holtby, dealing with life through literature involved two major activities: writing as a form of catharsis and writing as a means of self-definition. In *On Being an Author* Brittain devotes several pages to quoting other writers on the subject of writing as catharsis. She describes her own coming to terms with the personal tragedies of World War I through writing *Testament of Youth*. The author, she claims, "is one of the few men and women who can set himself free from fear and sorrow. He can, if he chooses, write these scourges of the spirit out of his system." Similarly, Holtby describes writing her first novel, *Anderby Wold*, as a way of curing the heartbreak she felt when her father sold the family farm.

While in a general sense it is obviously true that all writers express their own personalities in their work, the particular process of self-definition that both Brittain and Holtby underwent through their writing seems to have been a peculiarly female one. ⟨. . .⟩ Talking of the way in which women writers use their texts as part of a self-defining process, Judith Gardiner suggests that "the author often defines herself through the text while creating her female hero in a process analogous with learning to be a mother, that is, learning to experience oneself simultaneously as a well-nurtured child and as one's own nurturing parent, and, at the same time, learning that one's creation is separate from oneself."

—Jean Kennard, *Vera Brittain & Winifred Holtby: A Working Partnership* (Hanover, New Hampshire: University Press of New England, 1989), 12–13

MAROULA JOANNOU

Testament of Youth, for all its anti-war sentiments and its emphasis on the authority of a woman's perspective, ultimately belongs within the realm of 'dominant memory' as opposed to 'popular memory'. ⟨. . .⟩ The autobiography constructs a picture of autobiographical self in relation to society which, if it does not strictly mirror the thinking of the social and political establishment of the time, is still a picture that the establishment did not find uncongenial. *Testament of Youth* offers a view of war 'from above' which does not question the idea of nation or the ideology of Englishness under which the war is conducted, rather than a view which properly reflects the discontents and ambivalent feelings about the war of those 'below'.

An example of a 'popular memory' text written by a woman is Maya Angelou's autobiography, *I Know Why the Caged Bird Sings*. To judge from her autobiography, Angelou's *bios* (experience) and her *aute* (sense of identity) are clearly no less the product of her specific class and racial position than are Brittain's. *I Know Why the Caged Bird Sings* tells the story of a young, poor, black woman who was raped at the age of eight. It tells, movingly and searingly, the story of how Angelou later became pregnant as the result of a single, loveless sexual encounter at the age of sixteen. No matter how seriously Angelou takes herself, she remains poor, black, and a woman with multiple disadvantages. She cannot assume significance within the dominant order of white middle-class America except, somewhat ironically, as the author of a successful auto-biographical text which vividly dramatises a black woman's experience of poverty, and racial and sexual prejudice. In the process of writing a past the author must inevitably write from the vantage point of a survivor. In this sense what holds true for Brittain also holds true for Angelou. But if the jettisoning of some, or all, of the conditions which motivated the writer to write does not itself necessarily invalidate her representations, we should perhaps ask what does? The answer, I think, is related to the text's reception; to its repudiation by readers who see themselves as subject to (and their own role as attempting to change) the myriad of oppressive ideologies which constrict the lives of women and from which success almost inevitably abstracts the autobiographer. This is the point at which the question 'when is a feminist text not a feminist text?' must be put.

What ironically confirms Vera Brittain's membership of the dominant order is her perception of the world as hostile. This is most acutely felt after her return to Somerville College, Oxford, after the war. Yet the rebel whose text projects a hostile world against which she struggles to define her own identity is only able to take herself seriously because her right to a place within the dominant order is *already assured*. It is only in the certainty of membership that the certainty of rebellion can be asserted. Objectively, there were few external barriers to prevent Vera Brittain becoming a success after leaving Oxford University. Maya Angelou's sense of the world as hostile is real not illusory. That reality is clearly not the projection of her subjective personal angst. It is the result of the deeply entrenched racist attitudes that her autobiography painfully evokes. Such racism is amply confirmed in countless oral and written testimonies which make up the 'popular memory' of black people in the southern states of America. ⟨. . .⟩

One of the typical features of the autobiographical mode is that the relationship between the authorial subject—the 'I' central to the narrative (and to a particular social group such as the working class)—and the narrative movement is peculiarly complex. As Julia Swindells notes, a class-conscious autobiographer 'invests in furthering not only the individual, the autobiographical-self, moving through the narrative and through society'. This type of autobiography 'carries the freight of a narrative direction which subsumes the autobiographical "I", with its conventional association with individualism, in the interests of a particular social group' ⟨*Victorian Writing and Working Women*, 1985, 139⟩. In *Testament of Youth* the central figure claims a direct relationship to not one but two groups. The formulation 'my generation of obscure young women' harnesses 'my generation' and 'obscure young women' in an uneasy and somewhat incongruent union.

Let us examine the formulation carefully. In what, if any, sense might the privileged, middle class, Vera Brittain, a promising Oxford undergraduate in 1914 (and a published novelist and successful journalist when *Testament of Youth* was published in 1933) be said to speak for 'obscure young women'? What it seems we are faced with is a double tension. There is a stress in these words on uniqueness, on subjectivity implicit in the dramatisation of self, and there is also a stress on representativeness, implicit in the obligation of the professional writer and social historian to produce an account of events which is ramifying and extends beyond its individual context. This double imperative, the impulse to merge the self with the group (and to mingle the unique and the representative) is perhaps the surest indicator of Brittain's dilemma in attempting to establish the discursive authority to interpret herself as a woman, and of her burning desire to write as a feminist ⟨. . . .⟩

—Maroula Joannou, *'Ladies, Please Don't Smash These Windows': Women's Writing, Feminist Consciousness and Social Change 1918–38* (Oxford: Berg Publishers, 1995), 33–36

LINDA ANDERSON

What is so interesting about Brittain's writing ⟨. . .⟩ are the contradictions, the difficulties she reveals in achieving a consistent subject position. Brittain as autobiographer must seek a place within discourses already marked by sexual difference; the positions she adopts are pragmatic or rhetorical moves within a historical field whose meaning can never be completely known to her. Hence in Brittain's writing a claim to feminine selflessness also reveals and shields an assertion of autonomy whilst the very framing of this binary opposition—the contradictory pairing of autonomy and selflessness—is not a 'natural' or 'timeless' one but itself constructed through and by history. What I want to advance here is an argument about history, about where it is and about how texts or language can provide access to it. It may be that we must begin to see history not in the same terms that Brittain did—as a moment, a crisis, a set of circumstances to be entered upon—but rather as already there within the subject. This is an idea that Naomi Schor suggests in her essay about 'the

status of difference' in Georges Sand's writing when she writes: 'history inhabits sexual difference'. According to Schor, trying to understand the meaning of
sexual difference, 'peering obsessively into the abyss of sexual difference and
its vicissitudes', may mean we miss the crucial way that 'history is already at
work in that difference'. While we focus exclusively on the meaning of sexual
difference what we may lose sight of, following Schor's argument, are the historical conditions which shaped that particular representation of it; what we
may overlook is the problematic way history is neither inside or outside discourse and identity but *both*. The female subject constructed as belonging to
the private rather than the political 'masculine' realm and thus seen as occu-
pying a place outside history could *by that very fact* be just as much the subject
of a set of historical and political discourses. In many ways, of course, the
importance of Brittain to this book is that her autobiographical writing does
seem to enter the public world in a different way, to adopt a genre and to
assume a much simpler and more confident form of public address than does
Alice James's or Virginia Woolf's. War sanctioned a narrative, it seems, that
joined Brittain both literally and symbolically to the cataclysmic events of her
era, events which decimated and irrevocably transformed her generation. Yet
war, so much assumed to belong to the category of the external, the outside,
must also be thought about in terms of gender and a particular conception of
the subject. Brittain, writing 'for her generation', authorising herself as speaking *for* a momentous historical moment, is also spoken *by* it, by a history which
is not where it seems to be, which she is not yet, nor can ever be, wholly in
possession of.
    —Linda Anderson, *Women and Autobiography in the Twentieth Century: Remembered Futures* (London:
    Prentice Hall/Harvester Wheatsheaf, 1997), 87–88

B I B L I O G R A P H Y

Verses of a VAD. 1918.
The Dark Tide. 1923.
Good Citizenship and the League. 1924.
Not Without Honour. 1924.
Women's Work in Modern England. 1928.
Halcyon; or, The Future of Monogamy. 1929.
Testament of Youth. 1933.
Poems of the War and After. 1934.
Honourable Estate. 1936.

Thrice a Stranger: New Chapters of an Autobiography. 1938.
Testament of Friendship: The Story of Winifred Holtby. 1940.
War-Time Letters to Peace Lovers. 1940.
England's Hour. 1941.
Humiliation with Honour. 1942.
One of These Little Ones . . . A Plea to Parents and Others for Europe's Children. 1942.
Law Versus War. 1944.
Seed of Chaos: What Mass Bombing Really Means. 1944.
Account Rendered. 1945.
Conscription or Cooperation? 1946.
On Becoming a Writer. 1947. Reprinted as *On Being an Author.* 1948.
Born 1925. 1948
In the Steps of John Bunyan. 1950.
Search after Sunrise. 1951.
The Story of St. Martin's: An Epic of London. 1951.
Lady into Woman: A History of Women from Victoria to Elizabeth II. 1953.
Testament of Experience. 1957, 1980.
Long Shadows (with G. E. W. Sizer). 1958.
Selected Letters of Winifred Holtby and Vera Brittain (1920–1935). 1960.
The Women at Oxford: A Fragment of History. 1960.
The Pictorial History of St. Martin-in-the-Fields. 1962.
Pethick-Lawrence: A Portrait. 1963.
The Rebel Passion: A Short History of Some Pioneer Peace-Makers. 1964.
Envoy Extraordinary: A Study of Vijaya Lakshmi Pandit and Her Contribution to Modern India. 1965.
Radclyffe Hall: A Case of Obscenity? 1968.
Chronicle of Youth: Vera Brittain's War Diary, 1913–1917. 1981.
Vera Brittain, Diary of the Thirties, 1932–1939: Chronicle of Friendship. 1986.
Vera Brittain, Diary 1939–1945: Wartime Chronicle. 1989.

FRANCES (FANNY) BURNEY
1752–1840

FRANCES (FANNY) BURNEY was born on June 13, 1752, in King's Lynn, Norfolk, England, the second of six children of Esther Sleepe and Charles Burney, a musician, composer, and author of *History of Music 1776–1789*. Esther died, probably of cancer, when Fanny was 10, and her father married widow Elizabeth Allen, who had several children of her own. The household was a large and uproarious one that was often visited by Charles Burney's friends, such as David Garrick, Joshua Reynolds, Samuel Johnson, Edmund Burke, Richard Sheridan, the Bluestocking Circle, and many members of London's aristocratic and literary society. Fanny, who was largely self-educated, would absorb the atmosphere of this company. Her early writings— published posthumously as *Early Diary* in 1889—were influenced by her father's friend Samuel Crisp. To him she addressed her first journal letters, describing musical evenings at the Burney's London home during which famous European performers entertained. Fanny was considered the least gifted of the Burney children and so was able to move unnoticed among the estimable guests, sharing her observations with Crisp.

In 1778, at age 26, Burney anonymously published her first novel, *Evelina; or, The History of a Young Lady's Entrance into the World*. This novel of manners, a landmark of the genre, is remarkable for its social satire and its representation of the nuances of London dialect; it pointed the way for the work of Jane Austen, an admirer of Burney's. The novel was wildly successful, and, when the identity of its shy author was discovered, Fanny Burney debuted in London literary society under the guidance of the fashionable Mrs. Thrale. During frequent visits at the Thrales' between 1779 and 1783, Burney developed a friendship with Dr. Johnson. Her journals from this period reflect her secret delight in her fame and are notable for her impressions of contemporary scenes and celebrities.

Burney's next novel, *Cecilia; or, Memoirs of an Heiress*, was published in five volumes in 1782. With a more complex plot but lacking the freshness and spontaneity of *Evelina*, it was nonetheless equally successful. Burney's success, however, was overshadowed by the deaths of Henry Thrale in 1781, of Crisp in 1783, and of Dr. Johnson in 1784. Burney also suffered a disappointment in her love for a young clergyman.

After being presented to Queen Charlotte and King George III in 1785, Burney was invited to court as second keeper of the robes, a position she retained for five unhappy years. Although her health began to suffer, her novels reflect her busy family and social life. Her accounts of this time—published posthumously as *Diary and Letters of Madame d'Arblay* between 1842 and 1846—loyally omit gossip of King George's madness but describe public events like the trial of Warren Hastings. Burney was allowed to resign in 1791.

At the age of 41, Burney married Alexandre d'Arblay, a former adjutant general to Lafayette. Together they had one son. With the proceeds from her 1796 potboiler, *Camilla; or, a Picture of Youth*, the family built a house in Surrey, where they moved in 1797. In 1802 the d'Arblays visited France, and, caught in the renewed Napoleonic Wars, they were forced to remain there for 10 years. During this period Burney underwent a mastectomy (without anesthesia), an experience she recounts in rivetingly detailed letters to her husband and friends. Her description of this event has been described by Julia Epstein as "one of the most astonishing, and bravest, medical passages in literature."

After the failure of her 1814 novel *The Wanderer; or, Female Difficulties* and the 1815 Battle of Waterloo, the d'Arblays returned to England and settled in Bath, where Alexandre died in 1818. Burney and her son then moved to London, where she edited and published her father's memoirs as *The Memoirs of Dr. Burney* in 1832.

Fanny Burney died on January 6, 1840, in London.

C R I T I C A L   E X T R A C T S

FANNY BURNEY

This year was ushered in by a grand and most important event! At the latter end of January, the literary world was favored with the first publication of the ingenious, learned, and most profound Fanny Burney! I doubt not but this memorable affair will, in future times, mark the period whence chronologers will date the zenith of the polite arts in this island!

This admirable authoress has named her most elaborate performance, *Evelina; or, a Young Lady's Entrance into the World.*

Perhaps this may seem a rather bold attempt and title for a female whose knowledge of the world is very confined, and whose inclinations, as well as situation, incline her to a private and domestic life. All I can urge is, that I have only presumed to trace the accidents and adventures to which a "young woman" is liable; I have not pretended to show the world what it actually *is*, but what it *appears* to a girl of seventeen: and so far as that, surely any girl who is past seventeen may safely do? The motto of my excuse shall be taken from Pope's *Temple of Fame*:

> In every work, regard the writer's end;
> None e'er can compass more than they intend.

A thousand little odd incidents happened about this time, but I am not in a humor to recollect them; however, they were none of them productive of a discovery either to my father or mother. My aunt Anne and Miss Humphries being settled at this time at Brompton, I was going thither with Susan to tea, when Charlotte acquainted me that they were then employed in reading *Evelina* to the invalid, my cousin Richard. This intelligence gave me the utmost uneasiness—I foresaw a thousand dangers of a discovery—I dreaded the indiscreet warmth of all my confidants. In truth, I was quite sick with apprehension, and was too uncomfortable to go to Brompton, and Susan carried my excuses. Upon her return, I was somewhat tranquillized, for she assured me that there was not the smallest suspicion of the author, and that they had concluded it to be the work of a *man!*

—Fanny Burney, *Diary* (1778, 1779), excerpted in *The New Moulton's Library of Literary Criticism: Early Victorian*, ed. Harold Bloom (New York: Chelsea House Publishers, 1989), 4044

WILLIAM HAZLITT

Women, in general, have a quicker perception of any oddity or singularity of character than men, and are more alive to every absurdity which arises from a violation of the rules of society, or a deviation from established custom. This partly arises from the restraints on their own behaviour, which turn their attention constantly on the subject, and partly from other causes. The surface of their minds, like that of their bodies, seems of a finer texture than ours; more soft, and susceptible of immediate impulses. They have less muscular strength; less power of continued voluntary attention—of reason, passion, and imagination: but they are more easily impressed with whatever appeals to their senses or habitual prejudices. The intuitive perception of their minds is less disturbed by any abstruse reasonings on causes or consequences. They learn the idiom of character and manners, as they acquire that of language, by rote, without troubling themselves about the principles. Their observation is not

the less accurate on that account, as far as it goes; for it has been well said, that
'there is nothing so true as habit.'

There is little other power in Miss Burney's novels, than that of immediate
observation: her characters, whether of refinement or vulgarity, are equally
superficial and confined. The whole is a question of form, whether that form
is adhered to or infringed upon. It is this circumstance which takes away dignity and interest from her story and sentiments, and makes the one so teazing
and tedious, and the other so insipid. The difficulties in which she involves her
heroines are too much 'Female Difficulties'; they are difficulties created out of
nothing. The author appears to have no other idea of refinement than that it
is the reverse of vulgarity; but the reverse of vulgarity is fastidiousness and
affectation. There is a true and a false delicacy.

—William Hazlitt, *Lectures on the English Comic Writers* (1818), excerpted in *The New Moulton's
Library of Literary Criticism: Early Victorian*, ed. Harold Bloom (New York: Chelsea House
Publishers, 1989), 4040

JOHN WILSON CROKER

At first sight the *Diary* seems a minute record of all that ⟨Burney⟩ saw, did, or
heard, and we find the pages crowded with names and teeming with matters
of the greatest apparent interest—with details of the social habits and familiar
conversation of the most fashionable, most intellectual, and, in every sense,
most illustrious personages of the last age. No book that we ever opened, not
even Boswell's *Johnson*, promised at the first glance more of all that species of
entertainment and information which memoir-writing can convey, and the
position and respectability of the author, with her supposed power of delin-
eating character, all tended to heighten our expectation; but never, we regret
to say, has there been a more vexatious disappointment. We have indeed
brought before us not merely the minor notabilities of the day, but a great
many persons whose station and talents assure them an historic celebrity—
King George III, Queen Charlotte, and their family—Johnson, Burke, Sir
Joshua, and their society—Mrs. Montague, Mrs. Thrale, Mrs. Delany, and
their circles—in short, the whole court and literary world; and all in their eas-
iest and most familiar moods:—their words—their looks—their manners—
and even their movements about the room—pencilled, as it would seem, with
the most minute and scrupulous accuracy:—but when we come a little closer,
and see and hear what all these eminent and illustrious personages are saying
and doing, we are not a little surprised and vexed to find them a wearisome
congregation of monotonous and featureless prosers, brought together for one
single object, in which they, one and all, seem occupied, as if it were the main
business of human life—namely, the *glorification of Miss Fanny Burney*—her tal-

ents—her taste—her sagacity—her wit—her manners—her temper—her delicacy—even her beauty—and, above all, her *modesty!*

We really have never met anything more curious, nor, if it were not
repeated *ad nauseam*, more comical, than the elaborate ingenuity with which—
as the ancients used to say that *all roads led to Rome*—every topic, from whatso-
ever quarter it may start, is ultimately brought home to Miss Burney. There can
be, of course, no autobiography without egotism; and though the best works
of this class are those in which *self* is the most successfully disguised, it must
always be the main ingredient. We therefore expected, and, indeed, were very
willing, that Miss Burney should tell us a great deal about herself; but what we
did not expect, and what wearies, and, we must candidly add, disgusts us, is to
find that she sees nothing beyond the tips of her own fingers, and considers
all the rest of man and womankind as mere satellites of that great luminary of
the age, the *author of Evelina.* 〈. . .〉

In truth nothing can be so vapid as that mode of reporting conversation
must inevitably be, *even in the cleverest hands.* Boswell, the best and most graphic
of narrators, never attempts so hopeless a task for above two or three consec-
utive paragraphs, but more commonly contents himself with preserving the
general spirit of the discourse—catching here and there the most striking
expressions, and now and then venturing to mark an emphasis or an attitude.
A clever artist may *sketch* a very lively likeness of a countenance which he has
only seen *en passant*, but if he were to attempt—in the absence of the object—
to fill up the outline with all the little details of form and colour, he would find
that his efforts only diminished the spirit and impaired the resemblance. So it
is of reporting public *speeches*—and so still more of reporting *conversations.* But
even if Miss Burney had had more of Boswell's happy knack, it would not have
much mended the matter, for her sole and exclusive object was—not to relate
what Burke, or Johnson, or anybody else should say on general subjects, but
what flattering things they said about *Fanny Burney.* The result is, that we have
little amusement and less faith in the details of those elaborate dialogues,
which occupy, we believe, more than half her volumes—their very minuteness
and elaboration sufficiently prove that they cannot be authentic; and they are,
moreover, trivial and wearisome beyond all patience. How—we will not say,
the author of *Evelina* and *Cecilia*, but—how any person of the most ordinary
degree of taste and talents could have wasted time and paper in making such
a *much ado about nothing* we cannot conceive; nor did we—till we had read this
book—imagine that *real life and proper names* could by any *maladresse* of a narrator
be made so insufferably flat, stale, and unprofitable.

    —John Wilson Croker, "Madame D'Arblay's *Diary and Letters,*" *Quarterly Review* (June 1842),
    excerpted in *The New Moulton's Library of Literary Criticism: Early Victorian*, ed. Harold Bloom
    (New York: Chelsea House Publishers, 1989), 4047–48

ANNIE RAINE ELLIS

This is believed to be the only published, perhaps the only existing, record of the life of an English girl, written by herself, in a century before that which is now in its wane. Such a portrayal of a young Englishwoman, and her times, would be interesting even if the girl had not been (as was this one) a born author, who lived among men and women more or less distinguished, herself became famous, and was admired by the admired, as well as praised by the common voice; whose brilliant reputation as a novelist was revived, some fifty years ago, by her fresh and still greater renown as a chronicler of English social and court-life, during many and marked years of the long reign of George the Third.

The novelist and the chronicler are shown in these still earlier diaries which are now for the first time published, as developing from year to year. Sketches revealing the future "character-monger" alternate here with innocent, tender, and generous thoughts, and feelings of affection to kinsfolk and friends, more than commonly lasting, as well as warm; with traits of a disposition very mobile, but singularly steady; very lively, but very sweet; discreet, and considerate almost to moral precocity. The character of Frances Burney shows itself on every leaf of these journals, even as the story of her first youth tells itself as we turn them. They were the offspring of that real pleasure in writing, even in the mechanical part of it, which Richardson attributes to his heroine, Clarissa, which he had felt himself; for it is not to be divined, but known. These journals gave Frances in old age, the delight which she had looked forward to receiving from them in her youth. No stronger proof of a clear conscience and a healthy mind could well be shown. In them there are erasures, there are long passages removed and destroyed, but the context shows that the feelings of others, not her own, were to be considered and spared.

—Annie Raine Ellis, "Preface" to *The Early Diary of Frances Burney* (1889), excerpted in *The New Moulton's Library of Literary Criticism: Early Victorian*, ed. Harold Bloom (New York: Chelsea House Publishers, 1989), 4048–49

HENRY CRAIK

Frances Burney was the first in her kind. She handed on the tradition of her art to Jane Austen, in whose hands the portraiture became more delicate, the shades of discrimination more subtle, the current of the story ran in a more secure and well-cut channel, and its interest was developed with greater art. But Frances Burney made Jane Austen possible; and if her touch was less delicate, it was perhaps more bold, and the colours were laid on with a stronger brush.

The story of *Evelina* is told by a series of letters, and this is one reason why the style is better than in the later novels. The authoress was then in all the freshness of her genius. She wrote by herself and for herself, troubled herself little about models, and was hampered by no advice. She looked upon authorship as something at which she might make a girlish attempt, but which she could never seriously profess. But the simplicity of style is helped also by the epistolary form. Most of the letters are written by a girl of seventeen, and the author never forgets how such a heroine would write. Of the rest the chief are written by the girl's guardian, and in their kind they are perfect, as expressions of tender and delicate affection. Four years later, when *Cecilia* was written, the epistolary style was abandoned. The narrative style came in its place, and fashion in that day almost forced narrative to adopt a solemn and inflated style. Frances Burney had in the interval become a literary character. She was never left to herself, and was surrounded day after day by the most finished talkers of the time, whose talk was above all things literary in form.

—Henry Craik, "Madame D'Arblay," in *English Prose*, vol. 4, ed. Henry Craik (1895), excerpted in *The New Moulton's Library of Literary Criticism: Early Victorian*, ed. Harold Bloom (New York: Chelsea House Publishers, 1989), 4043

PATRICIA MEYER SPACKS

If the collection of Fanny Burney's journals and letters creates the effect of autobiography, a coherent narrative implying an imaginative grasp of experience, her four novels also have aspects of psychic autobiography. One can readily perceive in them versions of the journals' central theme: the discipline and the liberation of a woman's fears of disapproval and of being found wanting—fear, in fact, of the other people who comprise society. But novels, with their capacity to express wish and fantasy as well as reality, allow Fanny Burney to enlarge her communication of her own nature. Her fiction illustrates complex feminine identities of indirection.

Ian Watt, noting that women wrote most novels in the eighteenth century, hints also—in terms more tactful than mine—that most of those novels were bad. In Jane Austen, he suggests, we first encounter an unmistakable example of the fact "that the feminine sensibility was in some ways better equipped to reveal the intricacies of personal relationships and was therefore at a real advantage in the realm of the novel" ⟨*The Rise of the Novel*, 1957, 310⟩. He does not explain why earlier female writers had proved unable to exploit this advantage. Indeed, the fact—like many facts about literary quality—is profoundly inexplicable. One can describe the aspects of Fanny Burney's novels that make them more moving and more meaningful than Jane Barker's, and it is possible to demonstrate how Jane Austen excels Fanny Burney. *Why* is another matter; *why* reduces one to vaguenesses like *talent* and *genius*.

To define the strengths and weaknesses of Fanny Burney's fictional achievement, however, may lead at least to speculation about the reasons for her superiority to her female contemporaries. Her strengths are more far-reaching than has been generally recognized. *Evelina* has been praised as though it consisted only of a collection of skillful character sketches. Joyce Hemlow has demonstrated its affinities to the "courtesy book," as an effort to outline a scheme of acceptable womanly conduct ⟨*The History of Fanny Burney*, 1958, 91–95⟩. It has been admired ever since its own time for the accuracy of its social detail and conversation. But it also manifests a high level of psychological insight closely related to the self-knowledge that emerges from even the youthful diaries. Fanny Burney may write better fiction than other women of her era partly because she has come to terms more fully than they with the realities of the female condition. She is therefore "equipped to reveal the intricacies of personal relationships" as they actually exist in the world and is not blinded by wishful fantasy or by anger, although both manifest themselves in her work.

Self-discovery of a woman in hiding constitutes the subject of the novels, as of the journals. Fanny Burney's heroines hide specifically because they are women, driven to concealments in order to maintain their goodness. They do not, except in brief moments, openly resent their fates. Yet the tension suggested by a formulation that asserts the simultaneity of discovery and hiding pervades Miss Burney's fiction. She constructs elaborate happenings to articulate conflict, locate happiness, and apportion blame. Her transformations of life in fiction, while insisting on the essential order of experience, also hint their author's awareness of the psychic costs of such affirmation. Anxiety dominates the Burney novels, despite their happy endings. However minute its pretexts—and often they seem trivial indeed—its weight is real, deeply experienced by the central characters and, to a surprising extent, shared even by readers who can readily dismiss its nominal causes. In fact, the causes lie deep; the heroines suffer profound conflicts. ⟨. . .⟩

No one now reads Fanny Burney's novels, except for *Evelina*, where comedy and youthful exuberance qualify the pervasive anxiety and one can even smile at the anxiety, for its causes are, by and large, so trivial. Yet the later novels, creaky of plot and increasingly impenetrable in rhetoric, seriously explore the possibilities for women to assert individual identities. More clearly than Fanny Burney's letters and diaries, the novels betray her anger at the female condition, although she also acknowledges the possibility of happiness within that condition. Imagining female defiance, she imagines also its futility in those heroines dominated, like herself, by fears of doing wrong. The atmosphere of anxiety she vividly evokes suggests what conflicts attend a woman's search for identity. The Burney female characters face endless struggle between what they want to have (independence, specific husbands, friends, pleasure, work) and what they want to be (angelically perfect): between the impulses to action and to avoidance. However important or negligible the specific images of this conflict, it stands behind the action and the characterization of all the novels.

The record of the journals, extending chronologically far beyond the writer's marriage, makes it clear that her commitment to D'Arblay, fulfilling as it was, did not mark the happy ending to her experience as it did for all her fictional heroines. Marriage resolved or simplified conflicts, granting Fanny Burney permission to act (through writing) while yet remaining conspicuously good; it thus provided energy. It also generated new dramas: classic Oedipal struggles, symbolic dilemmas about where and how to live, and conflicts of interest between Fanny's old family and her new—dramas that the journals expose more freely than they had revealed the problems of the author's youth, although in fact the problems remain in many respects essentially the same. The plot of the diaries thus necessarily differs from that of the novels, which never explore post-marital experience.

Yet the fictional inventions uncover the inner realities of the writer's mature as well as her youthful life. Indeed, comparison of Fanny Burney's personal record with her novels suggests the possibility that fiction may more vividly than autobiography delineate the shape of an author's private drama. The external events of Miss Burney's life, as reported in her diaries, supply small excitements, minor clashes, and tiny resolutions. The events of her novels increasingly emphasize important happenings—in *The Wanderer*, political as well as personal happening. Her heroines must cope with grotesque misunderstandings, malicious enemies, and bitter strokes of fate. They suffer more than they can comprehend—more perhaps even than their author comprehends. They express both their creator's wishes and her conviction that such wishes must be punished: the real essence of the inner drama that is more palely reflected in the relatively trivial events she chooses to record in diary and letters.

—Patricia Meyer Spacks, "Dynamics of Fear: Fanny Burney," *Imagining a Self* (1976), excerpted in *The Critical Perspective: Early Victorian*, ed. Harold Bloom (New York: Chelsea House Publishers, 1988), 3860–61, 3865

KRISTINA STRAUB

Occupations for middle-class women ⟨of the 18th century⟩, from the relatively harmless vocation of the needle to a morally and socially dangerous addiction to "diversions," are tainted with suggestions that women are dim-witted or corrupt or, at best, in the process of becoming one or the other through constant exposure to tedium or triviality. But while women are encouraged, at least to an extent, to cultivate an intellectual and spiritual refinement that might place them above the dangers of female pastimes, they are seldom encouraged to break with traditional definitions of womanly work or play. The middle-class girl was taught the rightness of her work role at the same time that she also seems to have been implicitly tutored in a quiet contempt for it. Fanny Burney writes in her diary of July, 1768, "I make a kind of rule, never to indulge myself in my two *most* favorite pursuits, reading and writing, in the morning—no, like a very good girl I give that up wholly, accidental occasions and preventions excepted, to needle work, by which means my reading and writing in the afternoon is a pleasure I cannot be blamed for by my mother, as it does not take up the time I ought to spend otherwise" (*The Early Diary*, 1:15). This passage suggests more than a young woman's self-submission to social convention (although it certainly suggests that): it expresses, of course, Burney's fear of blame for venturing outside the traditional work role, but it also implies her desire to place herself and her energies outside that role. Like the modern bumper stickers that announce "I'd rather be running," or "I'd rather be reading Jane Austen"—attempts to deny the uninspiring anonymity of the expressway or city intersection at rush hour—Burney's statement says what she would really rather be doing, and, by implication, being. But her fear of blame is too great to allow her to disclose this desire directly, and she presents her self-identification as one who would rather read and write than sew in the moral context of her duty to the traditional work role. In other words, Burney is ambivalent toward the occupations that define her, on one hand, as a "very good girl" and, on the other hand, as a rather boring, trivial person. She cannot be comfortable without the conventional role, but she is left unsatisfied, incomplete if she invests herself entirely in it. Burney's attempt to define herself in this passage from *The Early Diary* is not hypocritical, therefore, so much as it is duplicitous by necessity—a double-dealing forced by her own irreconcilable desires—the need to take herself seriously as a thinking (and writing) human being opposed to the need to see herself as conventionally feminine in her employments. ⟨. . .⟩

In sum, young women like Burney were encouraged to engage in daily occupations that were, in turn, held in such low esteem as to make ego-investment in them foolish or perverse. This cultural ambivalence towards women's employments situates femininity awkwardly in occupational roles that women, themselves, are not supposed to care about or take seriously. Women are seen as curiously both "in" and "out" of what they do, performers with little investment in their performance. This potentially debilitating or, at least, demoralizing psychological positioning of the female subject in relation to its employments is transformed by Burney ⟨. . .⟩ into a social and psychological strategy for retaining both her femininity and her self-respect. Her fiction and her journals establish the female subject within the conventional territory of feminine employments and pastimes while disassociating the subject's worth from that territory. The result is a duplicity that has more to do with social adjustment than with dishonesty: Burney and her heroines are always in the contradictory position of conforming to conventional modes of female employment while remaining somehow separate from the stereotypical roles those modes imply.

—Kristina Straub, *Divided Fictions: Fanny Burney and Feminine Strategy* (Lexington: University of Kentucky Press, 1987), 82–83, 89

MARGARET ANNE DOODY

Each of Burney's heroines makes an "entrance into the world," and the world she enters becomes increasingly more problematic with each novel. Juliet endeavors to enter society not in order to make a debut but to earn her own living. The society she enters is arid and apathetic, given to division and rejection, and apparently possessing no power to heal itself. The strange inner world presented through the characters of *Camilla* is now the world of the novel itself—fantastic, shifting, with abrupt transitions and dreamlike images, especially the image of Stonehenge. *The Wanderer* is a tragicomedy about disjunction and disintegration, looking at history in the light of human suffering, the pain that no novelist can bring to a closure. If all the novels show young ladies making entrances into the world, and the world as hazardous, in *The Wanderer* it is no longer certain that any entry can be truly achieved, that a place in the world can be found. England can be entered (even desperately), but still it remains closed. English society is not accessible to a woman who craves "self-dependence." Beyond that truth is another even starker truth. The world is forever alien. We all—men and women—must remain partly strangers in it and to it. The individual identity cannot be recognized by the world, cannot fit into the world; neither can the dark outer world swallow up and incorporate the troubling identity. There remains self alone, woman alone: Elle is / Ellis. Burney had given us a wonderful gallery of comic characters from Mr. Smith and Madame Duval to Sir Jaspar Herrington and Mrs. Ireton. Yet all these gain their significance from their place in the story of a heroine who is trying to comprehend the world of which these comic characters are expressions. They represent the hard edges of the intractable world, as well as illustrating in themselves the struggle for identity and control.

Undoubtedly, some readers will be shocked at having the nice little comic writer taken away. Some will feel horrified at what they will regard as a changeling-substitution of a mad Gothic feminist for the cheerful little Augustan chatterbox. It is, of course, my contention that the comic, the grotesque, and the macabre elements in Burney's writings are all united, and that the themes and insights of *The Wanderer* are already adumbrated in the violence of *Evelina*, where old women are thrown into a ditch or forced to run a footrace. Hazlitt said *The Wanderer* exhibited not a decay of Burney's talent but "the perversion" of it. It is neither a decay nor a perversion; *The Wanderer* is a culmination, saying clearly what readers could have found in the earlier works.

In her various works Burney was trying to develop not only her own themes but also—inseparable from these—her own language. The language of all her works after *Evelina* is often charged with clumsiness and false expression, but it should be realized that it represents her attempt to mold language and obtain the meaning she wants. Recent research on the new edition of the *OED* has shown to what an extent Burney contributed to English language and usage. She is not only an early recorder of words in modern usages, but also a word-coiner. One of the pleasures of reading the letters is the light play of nonce-words, "un-Julyish"; "that unsniggered him." In her fiction Burney takes the liberty of trying to form a language suited to her purposes. ⟨. . .⟩

It is, of course, hard for women writers to hear that they must strictly obey the rules of a masculine definitive language. The man who varies from the beaten path may be termed a strong stylist, but a woman who does so is merely mistaken and ignorant. Yet to defer utterly to the superior language is to render oneself incapable of writing—the iron pen will indeed make no mark. The masculine-defined ordered language may truly not say or do everything that a woman wishes it to do. Burney presumably used inverted structures a great deal (to instance one mannerism that critics found a detestable "gallicism") because she thought many things were back-to-front. Burney's use of language reminds me both of Charlotte Brontë and Emily Dickinson—very different stylists, who were both experimenters in language, and who were both cited by critics for insufficient command of what everyone knows is the proper way of writing. Like Brontë and Dickinson, Burney can sometimes be abstract, rhetorical, distant, tangential, or crowded; like them, she can use to full effect the force of strong or complex words. Burney is to be classified among those writers who experiment with style. If she sometimes failed, she sometimes succeeded, and succeeded on her own terms—but to succeed in one's own terms is to show an audacity that tempts the Guardians of the canon to put the female "mannerist" in her place.

Embarrassed as she was, Burney was in her own way heroic. She was encumbered and constrained (as we all are) by her circumstances, including her era and its mores, her family history, and her personal emotional needs. Those constraints shape every individual. But Burney had courage and intelligence. Had she written timid, blushing, pleasing novels, she might have met with even more contemporary approval, but she might not have attained even that peculiar position she has occupied hitherto: if never quite in the canon, always on the border of it. She remains to delight and disturb us. She is not a writer who induces cultural contentment.

—Margaret Anne Doody, *Frances Burney: The Life in the Works* (New Brunswick: Rutgers University Press, 1988), 387–89

JULIA EPSTEIN

On 30 September 1811, in Paris, Burney underwent a simple mastectomy of the right breast to remove a growth her surgeons believed to be a cancerous tumor. A wine cordial, possibly containing laudanum, served as the sole anesthetic agent. During the months that followed, Burney slowly and painfully composed a detailed narrative of her illness and operation for her family and friends in England. This narrative appears at first reading to represent an oddly paraliterary document: its nonprofessional descriptive history encapsulates the psychological and anatomical consequences of cancer in a text that is part medico-surgical treatise and part sentimental fiction. While its wealth of detail makes it a significant document in the history of surgical technique, its intimate confessions and elaborately fictive staging, persona-building, and framing make it likewise a powerful and courageous work of literature in which the imagination confronts and translates the body. The formal, stylized operation and intimately encoded response retold in Burney's letter constitute two approaches to the same timeless human need: the need to avoid pain and suffering.

Burney's letter is preoccupied with that need, and is preoccupied as well with the narrative possibilities for representing violence. Can this story be told? Burney's letter asks. By questioning the narratability of her medical experience and bodily violation, Burney's mastectomy document also questions the very nature of narrative representation, in the private story of painful experience as well as in the highly codified genre of the medical case history. Writing, like the act of surgery, is an invasion of privacy that can be simultaneously wounding and therapeutic. Burney insists on narrating the violence and pain she found to be pervasive in the late eighteenth-century European social world. Her extraordinary letter, the circumstances of its composition and later revision, and the literary, medical, and cultural context of her experience serve as paradigms for Burney's inscription of herself into this world. The letter presents a fictive iconography of the body in narrative representation. The way Burney presents the embattled female body in this familiar letter maps the iconography as well of her embattled fictional heroines. That

mapping itself—the careful inscription of a trapped female (body) in the world—empowers the female voice in all Burney's writings.
—Julia Epstein, *The Iron Pen: Frances Burney and the Politics of Women's Writing* (Madison: University of Wisconsin Press, 1989), 54–55

BIBLIOGRAPHY

Evelina; or, The History of a Young Lady's Entrance into the World. 1778.
Cecilia; or, Memoirs of an Heiress. 1782.
Brief Reflections Relative to the Emigrant French Clergy. 1793.
Edwy and Elgiva. 1795.
Camilla; or, a Picture of Youth. 1796.
The Wanderer; or, Female Difficulties. 1814.
The Memoirs of Dr. Burney. 1832.
Diary and Letters of Madame d'Arblay. 1842–46.
The Early Diary of Frances Burney. 1889.
Selected Letters and Journals. 1987.

ANNIE DILLARD
b. 1945

ANNIE DILLARD was born Meta Anne Doak on April 30, 1945, in Pittsburgh, Pennsylvania, the eldest of three daughters of an affluent family. Her parents, Frank and Pam Lambert Doak, were intellectual nonconformists who encouraged independent thought and social responsibility in their children. Attracted to the natural sciences from an early age, Annie reread *The Field Book of Ponds and Streams* every year. By 14, she had begun to write poetry and to collect favorite poems from Edna St. Vincent Millay, Rupert Brooke, Wilfred Owen, T. S. Eliot, Rimbaud, and Verlaine. She developed firm religious convictions, attending (though her parents did not) the local Presbyterian church and a fundamentalist church camp. The many Bible verses Dillard memorized surface in her poetry of the period. In *An American Childhood* (1987) she recounts how she prayed each night for a grateful heart—but she had become a rebellious teenager ready to abandon the church for what she perceived as its hypocrisy. Taking refuge in her poetry, she became increasingly interested in the transcendental views of Ralph Waldo Emerson.

In 1963 Annie entered Hollis College in Roanoke, Virginia. She enrolled in the creative writing program, studied theology, became a member of Phi Beta Kappa in her junior year, and received a bachelor's degree in English in 1967. At the end of her sophomore year, she married her creative writing teacher, Richard Henry Wilde Dillard. He would have a major influence on her work, and she appears in much of his, although they would divorce in 1975. Dillard received a master's degree in 1968, with a thesis entitled "Walden Pond and Thoreau." Her poems were published in magazines and journals, including *Southern Poetry Review* and *Atlantic*.

The writing of *Pilgrim at Tinker Creek* (1974) began after Dillard's near-fatal pneumonia in 1971. She spent her recovery camping alone near the creek, and the book is drawn from 20 volumes of the journal in which she described her observations and speculations. *Tickets for a Prayer Wheel*, a collection of poems, was published the same year. With *Pilgrim at Tinker Creek* Annie Dillard became a literary celebrity. It was a Book-of-the-Month Club selection, drew largely enthusiastic reviews, and in 1975 received the Pulitzer Prize for general nonfiction.

The attention held no charm for Dillard, however; she saw fame as a corrupting influence. She moved to Puget Sound, Washington, in order to devote herself to writing, and accepted a position as scholar-in-residence at Western Washington University. Living in an isolated log cabin, Dillard completed and published *Holy the Firm* in 1978. It too received favorable reviews, but it was more philosophically complex than *Tinker Creek* and less popular among general readers. It is Dillard's favorite. After they lived together for several years, Dillard married novelist and professor of anthropology Gary Clevidence in 1980; they divorced in 1987.

In 1982 Dillard's selected essays were published in *Teaching a Stone to Talk*, which received excellent reviews, and a book of literary theory appeared, *Living by Fiction*, which was more modestly acclaimed. The same year Dillard was a member of a State Department delegation of scholars, publishers, and writers sent to China; the experience resulted in *Encounters with Chinese Writers*, published in 1985. Dillard's daughter was born in summer 1984, and soon afterward, with the help of a Guggenheim foundation grant, she began writing a book about her own childhood and the nature of consciousness: *An American Childhood* (1987). *The Writing Life*, in which Dillard describes her love-hate relationship with her craft, was published in 1989.

Dillard has received honorary degrees from Boston College, Connecticut College, and the University of Hartford, and she is a member of International P.E.N., Century Association, Poetry Society of America, Western Writers of America, and Phi Beta Kappa. In 1987 she married Robert D. Richardson, biographer of Henry David Thoreau; they live in Middletown, Connecticut. Annie Dillard is writer-in-residence at Wesleyan.

C R I T I C A L   E X T R A C T S

JOHN B. BRESLIN

Once again the Greeks were there ahead of us with their insistence that the love of wisdom begins with wonder. The author of ⟨*Pilgrim at Tinker Creek* and *Tickets for a Prayer Wheel*⟩ would wholeheartedly agree, and add, it should end in praise. The two, wonder and praise, serve as warp and woof for the elaborate tapestry Annie Dillard has woven out of her days at Tinker Creek. Like a good craftswoman, she understands that the horizontal and vertical threads must be carefully intertwined to establish the pattern she wants, and so we pass easily ⟨. . .⟩ from observation to reflection, from creative to creature, from wonder to praise.

And yet, if we stop to think of it for a moment, that transposition itself is cause enough for wonder. Not everyone who has looked closely at the ways of nature has been led, ineluctably, to praise nature's God. Indeed, it is not hard to imagine someone watching a female praying mantis devouring her mate in the course of copulation who might register a decidedly negative vote on the question of a benevolent Creator. Or take the water bug that serves as a recurring symbol for Miss Dillard of nature's depredations on itself. At one moment she is observing a small frog in the creek; suddenly it begins to collapse before her eyes "like a deflating football." It is the giant water bug at work, dissolving the frog's innards to a fine juice which it then drinks up as a midday snack.

In a fascinating chapter called "Fecundity," the author pursues the question further. "Nature," she has discovered, "is as careless as it is bountiful, and . . . with [its] extravagance goes a crushing waste that will one day include our own cheap lives." One might well paraphrase Aristotle and say it is death that makes the world go round, so necessary are mass exterminations of life to the process of evolution. Getting exercised over this cycle doesn't make much sense, but it does indicate the line that separates us from the natural world. "We value the individual supremely, and nature values him not a whit." And what of the God who presides over both?

Here the author's background reveals itself. Besides an innocent and enquiring eye and a disposition toward enormous patience, Miss Dillard brought to Tinker Creek a lot of books and a good deal of theology. The pattern she finds amid the ambiguities of nature is not in nature itself. How decide whether the ecstatic vision she experiences of the cedar tree alive with lights, or the giant water bug drinking down the frog, is more expressive of the way things really are? Only the human spirit can settle such a question and opt for a vision in which "the dying pray at the last not 'please,' but 'thank you,' as a guest thanks his host at the door."

Miss Dillard would subscribe, I think, to Rudolph Otto's description of God as *mysterium tremendum et fascinans*, a mystery that fills us with a sense of dread while it draws us inescapably to itself. Her attitude toward His creation is much the same. In her journal and in her poems she reverses the biblical curse, for, having eyes, she *does* see and having ears, she *does* hear. None of nature's mysteries is too small for her attention or her respect. She is curious, but not nosy. Only the contemplative gaze will serve to reach the heart of the mystery; a microscope helps at times, but its usefulness is limited to enlarging the possibilities of the human eye. That alone can see.

—John B. Breslin, [Reviews of *Pilgrim at Tinker Creek* and *Tickets for a Prayer Wheel*], *America* (20 April 1974): 312–14

BOBBIE BURCH LEMONTT

Although set on an island in Puget Sound, Annie Dillard's *Holy The Firm* has an
inward rather than outward focus. By studying "hard things—rock mountain
and sea salt . . . to temper [her] spirit on their edges" (p. 19), Ms. Dillard
intensely explores enigmatic questions about the mythic, mystical and mysterious nature of existence. Her explanation of the means by which the artist can
answer such questions transforms a western paradise into a philosophical pur-
gatory.

Ms. Dillard structures *Holy The Firm* as a world of symbols in three parts.
"Newborn and Salted" (Part I) illustrates an awakening into an environment
where "days are gods." This pantheistic paradise is pierced with "God's Tooth"
(Part II) when a plane falls into the firs and pain is felt by the uninitiated. A
child named Julie becomes the victim of senseless suffering and a vehicle for
poignant sacrifice. Thus, "Holy The Firm" (Part III) attempts to bridge the gap
between a desire for meaning and the knowledge of meaninglessness by turning creative service into metaphor. Consequently, *Holy The Firm* becomes an
act of spiritual flagellation.

The narrator seems frustrated by feelings about the inability of language
to capture fully her subjective reality. Using overly thoughtful and tough language, she attempts to verbalize reactions to an apparently unlimited but yet
deterministically circumscribed world. To state directly that "nothing will happen in this book . . . there is only a little violence in the language" (p. 24) is
extreme literary self-consciousness. The use of allusions and the exploitation
of semantic possibilities in language approaches heavy-handedness. The
extravagant enthusiasm of a voice which sees the world as an "illuminated
manuscript" sounds pretentious and loquacious. And the underlying sense of
lost innocence appears too pervasive, vocal, and hysterical. However, the
haunting beauty of a moth suspended in candle flame, the grotesque violence
of a 7-year-old child's burnt face, and the magical simplicity of a cat carrying
an homunculus in its wren-drenched mouth are images which burn into the
eidetic memory without being strained or self indulgent. When such images
are seen paradigmatically, the actual and the imaginary combine to intensify a
sense of wonder, guilt and urgency. Thus, there is a brutal honesty in the idea
that "if days are gods, then gods are dead, and artists [are] pyrotechnic fools."

By raising questions concerning reality, faith, and art, Ms. Dillard's per-
sonalized and intricate study is a protean reflection of her role as an artist.
Ultimately, *Holy The Firm* sits atop the philosopher's stone on the island of
Samos. In this situation the view is always the same and the author remains
cloistered by her own efforts.

—Bobbie Burch Lemontt, [Review of *Holy the Firm*], *Western American Literature* 13, no. 3 (Fall
1978): 274

DAVID L. LAVERY

The impressionist Claude Monet wanted to paint each of his subjects without knowing what it was: he hoped evidently that his ignorance would de-gloss things, subverting the tendency of the eye—in conjunction with human memory—to stereotype the visible world and rob it of its uniqueness. Although a writer, a creator of verbal imagery alone, Annie Dillard nonetheless shares with Monet the hope of seeing the world raw.

It is her project as a writer, in *Pilgrim at Tinker Creek*, *Tickets for a Prayer Wheel*, and *Holy the Firm* (hereafter designated as *PTC*, *TPW*, and *HF*, respectively), to attain the secret of vision—the "pearl of great price" (*PTC*, 34)—and thereby to be able "to look spring in the eye" (*PTC*, 124). It is through vision that she hopes to enact the most difficult of tasks: learning the neighborhood (*PTC*, 130). All that she has been and all that she does—from her experiences as a big city child to her own wide reading—it is all in order to enable her "to look at the creek" beside which she lives (*PTC*, 104). Twice, in both *Pilgrim at Tinker Creek* and *Tickets for a Prayer Wheel*, she quotes the unfathomable question, first proposed by Thoreau, to which she hopes to find the answer: "With all your science can you tell how it is and whence it is, that light comes into the soul?" The search for an answer to this question constitutes nothing less than the intrinsic movement of her books.

She senses in advance that attainment of such a secret will grant to her special powers: when the scales drop from her eyes, in fact, she hopes to "see trees like men walking" (*PTC*, 32). Yet the "uncertainty of vision" (*PTC*, 3) troubles her deeply. The "pearl of great price" is no simple acquisition. Above all, she knows, it is not to be secured through the Faustian pursuits which usually characterize the intellectual quests of western man.

Nor can it be discovered in the ecstasy of a Dionysian frenzy. As May Sarton sagaciously observes in *Mrs. Stevens Hears the Mermaids Singing*, there can be no such thing as a Dionysian woman, a female Dylan Thomas, for such a woman would be mad. As a woman writer, Dillard likewise senses that her art must be in keeping with natural process and earthly rhythms. The woman writer, Anais Nin once observed in her *Diaries*, must never forget

> that everything that is born of her is planted in her . . . she was born
> to represent union, communion, communication, she was born to
> give birth to life, and not to insanity. . . . The art of woman must be
> born in *the womb-cells of the mind*. She must be the link between the syn-
> thetic products of man's mind and the elements. (My italics)

Because Annie Dillard knows this, she understands that "although the pearl may be found, it may not be sought" (*PTC*, 34). It will be discovered, she intuits, only by not trying to secure it.

—David L. Lavery, "Noticer: The Visionary Art of Annie Dillard," *The Massachusetts Review* 21, no. 2 (Summer 1980): 255–57

BRUCE A. RONDA

Whereas ⟨*Pilgrim at Tinker Creek*⟩ pursues questions of self-definition and meaning through natural observation and reflection, Dillard's second book, *Holy the Firm*, centers our attention on the human community and on the author's involvement with the sufferings of others. The image of flame as pain and illumination dominates this brief book. Dillard recalls a camping experience when a large moth flew into her candle, caught its wing in the melting wax and burned. Its shell, propped upright, formed a second wick: "She burned for two hours without changing, without bending or leaning—only glowing within . . . like a hollow saint." The moth's immolation gave her more light for reading. This union of flame and sight is picked up several pages later when Dillard imagines that the cat has dragged in a small, slightly scorched god who perches on her shoulder and, singing in her ear, points out new islands in the sound. But did the moth or the god suffer? Or did Dillard suffer because of their burning? These questions prepare us for the book's central moment, the crash of the plane and the burning of Julie Norwich.

The plane, we are told, fell like a moth, and only Julie was injured, singled out for a kind of brutal rite of passage into adulthood. As in *Pilgrim*, Dillard's desire for intense experience, her very openness to moths or scorched gods, has made her vulnerable to Julie's anguish and to all human suffering:

> And you can get caught holding one end of a love, when your father
> drops, and your mother; when a land is lost, or a time, and your
> friend blotted out, gone, your brother's body spoiled and cold, your
> infant dead, and you dying; you reel out love's long line alone,
> stripped like a live wire loosing its sparks to a cloud, like a live wire
> loosed in space to longing and grief everlasting [pp. 42–43].

Ultimately, Dillard concludes, the only response to such brutal reminders of our creatureliness is worship. She buys a bottle of communion wine and sets out for the parish church. On the road, she has a remarkable visionary experience.

> The world is changing. . . . It is starting to utter its infinite particulars, each overlapping and lone, like a hundred hills of hounds all giving tongue. . . . Above me the mountains are raw nerves, sensible and exultant; the trees, the grass, the asphalt below me are living petals of mind, each sharp and invisible, held in a greeting or glance full perfectly formed. . . . Walking faster and faster, weightless, I feel the wine. . . . It sheds light in slats through my rib cage, and fills the buttressed vaults of my ribs with light pooled and buoyant. I am moth; I am light. I am prayer and I can hardly see [p. 68].

In sketching out some of the major themes of Dillard's prose, three points emerge that need to be made explicit and placed in a larger context. First, Dillard is a mystical, or preferably a contemplative, writer who deserves more careful study than she has yet received. Second, Dillard experiences her contemplative life very much as a late 20th century person, heir to the demythologizing that characterizes our time and culture. Third, Dillard's reflections are marked, indeed dominated, by the experience of suffering. ⟨. . .⟩

⟨. . .⟩ In Dillard's writing, one feels the awful inner tension between wanting to control and wanting to let go; one sees the amoral careen of nature that separates it from our sympathy. While there are moments of genuine celebration and ecstasy in her books, the more characteristic sequence is vulnerability, insight and pain. This connection between knowing deeply and suffering deeply makes her a mystic for our time.

—Bruce A. Ronda, "Annie Dillard and the Fire of God," *The Christian Century* 100, no. 16 (18 May 1983): 484–86

WILLIAM J. SCHEICK

For Dillard ⟨. . . .⟩ great art is "juncture itself, the socketing of eternity into time and energy into form" ⟨*Living by Fiction*, 164⟩. Great art conveys "the rim of knowledge" (*LF*, 170), where beauty and terror intersect. In her own art Dillard tries to depict this frayed intersection of matter and spirit, of the temporal and the eternal, of opaque surfaces and translucent depths, of terror and beauty. In her art Dillard relies on a narrative fringe, a liminal edge where the reader glimpses the rim or hemline between time and eternity.

Holy the Firm is an excellent example of this narrative technique. Like *Pilgrim at Tinker Creek*, *Holy the Firm* cues the reader to its author's technique whenever it specifically refers to the "serrate margin of time," to "the fringey edge where elements meet and realms mingle, where time and eternity spatter each other with foam" (*HF*, 20, 21). *Holy the Firm* also emphasizes the figure of the artist as someone who encounters the "lunatic fringe" (*TC*, 144), someone who *sees* the intersection of matter and spirit in the world as well as in himself or herself. In Dillard's opinion, the artist spans "all the long gap with the length of his love, in flawed imitation of Christ on the cross stretched both ways unbroken and thorned. So must the work be also, in touch with, in touch with, in touch with; spanning the gap, from here to eternity" (HF, 72). In *Holy the Firm* Dillard achieves a narrative fringe suggesting this terrible and beautiful Christlike intersection of time and eternity.

Ostensibly *Holy the Firm* consists of a journal record of three days, 18-20 November, recording Dillard's thoughts about a seven-year-old girl named Julie Norwich, who on the 19th had her face severely burned and disfigured by an exploding airplane. At first the reader of *Holy the Firm* might anticipate a narrative governed by a linear, sequential sense of time. The narrative, however, consists of various fragments without evident transitions, a narrative collage, depriving the reader of a comfortable sense of continuity at the level of narrative surface. At one point Dillard suddenly and without transition warns the reader, who has already been having trouble detecting a temporal narrative progression in the book, that "nothing is going to happen in this book. There is only a little violence here and there in the language, at the corner where eternity clips time" (HF, 24). Referring here to a correspondence between her narrative technique (her narrative fringe) and the liminal edges (the intersections of eternity and time) glimpsed in nature, Dillard suggests that for a sense of continuity in her book one must look not at the surface of temporal details; but into the depths of their eternal significance.

—William J. Scheick, "Annie Dillard: Narrative Fringe," in *Contemporary American Women Writers: Narrative Strategies*, ed. Catherine Rainwater and William J. Scheick (Lexington: University Press of Kentucky, 1985), 54–55

GARY MCILROY

The appearance of other people in ⟨Thoreau's⟩ *Walden* and ⟨Dillard's⟩ *Pilgrim at Tinker Creek* is ⟨a⟩ measure of the writers' attitudes toward society. While Thoreau's friends and acquaintances make up a large part of his narrative, Dillard's do not, despite the fact that she mentions many of their names, e.g., the Whites, the Garretts, Maren and Sandy, Thomas McGonigle, Rosanne Coggeshall, Matt Spireng, and "Sally Moore, the young daughter of friends." These are merely references, however. The social interchange is usually off-stage. Her description of playing baseball tells us more:

> My mind wanders. Second base is a Broadway, a Hollywood and
> Vine; but oh, if I'm out in right field they can kiss me goodbye. . . . I
> have no idea how many outs there are; I luck through the left-
> handers, staring at rainbows. The field looks to me as it must look to
> Wes Hillman up in the biplane: everyone is running, and I can't hear
> a sound. The players look so thin on the green, and the shadows so
> long, and the ball a mystic thing, pale to invisibility (TC, 107–108).

Her playing parallels the movement of her book. She moves so far away from society that she sees it only as a world of shadows and symbols. She is a displaced romantic, out of touch with the fashion of the time:

> I have often noticed that these things, which obsess me, neither bother nor impress other people even slightly. I am horribly apt to approach some innocent at a gathering and, like the ancient mariner, fix him with a wild, glitt'ring eye and say, "Do you know that in the head of the caterpillar of the ordinary goat moth there are two hundred twenty-eight separate muscles?" The poor wretch flees. I am not making chatter; I mean to change his life (TC, 132).

We are reminded of Thoreau:

> Sometimes when, in a conversation or a lecture, I have been grasping at, or even standing and reclining upon, the serene and everlasting truths that underlie and support our vacillating life, I have seen my auditors standing on their *terra firma*, the quaking earth, . . . watching my motions as if they were the antics of a ropedancer or mountebank pretending to walk on air. . . . ⟨*The Journal of Henry D. Thoreau*, 1906, 237–38⟩

Dillard knows the danger, we may assume, of a too-close association with the legends surrounding Thoreau. She does not want to be perceived as a hermit, so she speaks of people in passing, assuring us she is part of the community. But by naming her goldfish Ellery Channing, a teasing reference to "the most intimate and most lasting friendship of Thoreau's life," she announces firmly that her personal life will remain private. At the same time she commits herself to a metaphorical rendering of her life in society through her relationships and encounters with the animal world. Although the goldfish only cost her twenty-five cents at a local pet store, she realizes that this simple transaction—"I handed the man a quarter, and he handed me a knotted plastic bag bouncing with water in which a green plant floated and the goldfish swam"—involves the intricate mystery of a living thing. "This Ellery" has "a coiled gut, a spine radiating fine bone, and a brain." He also has a heart. Dillard recalls how years ago she looked through a powerful microscope and saw the individual red blood cells of a goldfish pulsating through a section of its transparent tail:

> I've never forgotten the sight of those cells; . . . I think of it lying in bed at night, imagining that if I concentrate enough I might be able to feel in my fingers' capillaries the small knockings and flow of those circular dots, like a string of beads drawn through my hand (TC, 125).

This rosary of cells, a symbol of the sanctity of life, is a common bond between Dillard and the fish, between animal life and human life in general, and between Dillard and other people. The symbolic richness of the goldfish is expanded by Dillard's later discussion of the spiritual significance of the fish in Tinker Creek, and especially by the affinity between fish and the early Christian church.

Ellery Channing is Dillard's most powerful cultural symbol, representing her detachment from society as well as her acknowledgement of the common bond of all living things. It is the detachment, however, which carries the greatest weight. Her relationship to the social world in *Tinker Creek*, and what may be read as her underlying attitude toward it, is ambiguous and largely indifferent. She does not succeed in encompassing within her vision any but the most fragmentary consequences for society at large. The Pilgrims' errand into the wilderness was a community's joint venture; the Transcendentalists' return to nature was a limited fellowship of the spirit; Dillard's exploration of the Virginia woodlands is the solitary search of the soul.

—Gary McIlroy, "*Pilgrim at Tinker Creek* and the Social Legacy of *Walden*," *The South Atlantic Quarterly* 85, no. 2 (Spring 1986): 114–16

CATHERINE PETROSKI

Autobiography by definition would seem to require a singular subject. In *An American Childhood*, we get both more and less: Those people who figure large in ⟨Dillard's⟩ early life assume almost mythic proportions, but the author wisely spares her reader the undifferentiated, and what could be trivial, aspects of her childhood. Somehow, we experience the sensation of a summer's droning tedium without being bored for a second.

Dillard follows a straightforward chronology in *An American Childhood*. This is not to say the writing is simple or unadorned. Like the river she uses as a unifying metaphor, each mile forward brings with it several more of meandering among serendipitous associations. In one, Dillard does the impossible: explaining the family private jokes without deadening their infectious good humor. There are meditations on the family's linguistics, on the portents of the nearby branch library, on the day of a huge snow, on the character of solid Presbyterianism, on an insect collection, on the dancing class's final exam.

In elaborations and playful, poetic digressions lie high stakes and heavy risks. Only a self-assured writer dare intentionally violate the commandment "Thou shalt not digress." Dillard does it, and manages to induce the reader not to get impatient. And to feel sad that it must come to an end.

An American Childhood is neither an adult's paean to romanticized memories nor the opposite sort of retributive memoir most readers would wish the writer

never committed to paper. Dillard has not flinched at capturing the private
fears alongside the rapturous joy, the humble alongside the grand, the com-
forting rituals alongside the bedeviling puzzlements, the intellectual alongside
the sensual. For an autobiographer to comprehend such a wealth of memory
with such balance and understanding shows remarkable maturity, and for a
writer to share it is an act of singular generosity.
  —Catherine Petroski, "Childhood Relived," *Chicago Tribune—Books* (13 September 1987):
  1, 12

NOEL PERRIN

Annie Dillard is one of ⟨William⟩ Blake's company. She may or may not see
auras—but she invariably sees *something* beyond what is just there. In the med-
itative book *Pilgrim at Tinker Creek*, she saw the coming of God in the attempt of
three Canada geese to land on her frozen duck pond. She continues to see
beyond the visible in her autobiography, *An American Childhood*. This woman is
either unusually sensitive or prone to exaggeration, the reader thinks. Both
things are true. ⟨. . .⟩

  The book is Ms. Dillard's equivalent of Wordsworth's *Prelude*. The full title
of that work is *The Prelude; or, Growth of a Poet's Mind: An Autobiographical Poem*. Ms.
Dillard has written an autobiography in semimystical prose about the growth
of her own mind, and it's an exceptionally interesting account. She is one of
those people who seem to be more fully alive than most of us, more nearly
wide-awake than human beings generally get to be. (Thoreau once said he had
never met a man who was fully awake—but he was forgetting about women,
and he hadn't met Ms. Dillard.) She is a stunning observer. There is a passage
in this book, a rather long one, in which she talks about adult skin as perceived
by a child. She begins with an event: herself as a little girl, pinching up the
skin over one of her mother's knuckles, and watching in fascination as it stays
ridged up instead of instantly returning to smooth shapeliness as a child's hand
does. The passage grows into a meditation on how parents (in her case, very
young and very good-looking ones, though she didn't know it then) physically
appear to a child. It seemed to me, reading it, that skin had never been ade-
quately described before.

  She thinks about time, about death, about Pittsburgh streetcars doomed to
their tracks, about herself probably doomed to a future in the Junior League
and a good Pittsburgh marriage. The year she was 13, she notes, "I was reading books on drawing, painting, rocks, criminology, birds, moths, beetles,
stamps, ponds and streams, medicine." She's also looking through a microscope at her own urine, having complicated fantasies and night fears, being
reckless in cars, idolizing aristocratic youths, telling jokes in the expert way
her parents taught her. It makes lively reading, all these things with their auras.

And yet, *An American Childhood* is not quite as good as it at first promised to be. By choosing to make the book an account of the growth of her mind, an inner rather than an outer narrative, Ms. Dillard almost necessarily forfeited plot. Except at the end, the book does not build; there is no continuous narrative. And though scores of people appear, only two of them are real characters: Annie Dillard herself and, for one wonderful chapter, her mother.

Also, the mystic's heightened prose can become mere mannerism, and from time to time in this book it does. I believed easily, reading *Pilgrim*, that Ms. Dillard felt the presence of God in the flight of those three geese; she made me feel it too. Or at least she made me feel a great power and intensity in the occasion. But when in *An American Childhood* she describes her first encounter with formal philosophy at age 16, and refers to "Platonism as it had come bumping and skidding down the centuries and across the ocean to Concord, Massachusetts" (it was on its way to meet Emerson), skepticism comes unbidden to the reader's mind. Plato's thought? Bumping and skidding? Fine, vivid language, certainly—but would it be either more or less true to say that his ideas tip-toed daintily down the centuries, or walked in galoshes through the Dark Ages, carrying an umbrella?

In short, isn't Ms. Dillard overwriting here? I think the answer is yes. It's the romantic's temptation, and she is an extreme romantic. Still, overwriting and all, *An American Childhood* remains a remarkable work. Blake overwrote too.
—Noel Perrin, "Her Inexhaustible Mind," *The New York Times Book Review* (27 September 1987): 7

Judy Schaaf Anhorn

Holy the Firm is tripartite, its shape and movement a Christian paradigm. "Newborn and Salted," Part I, is the book of mortal creation, a celebration of the "one world, bound to itself and exultant" (30). Its central image is that of a golden female moth in flame. This first part is also about human creativity, especially about writing. "God's Tooth," Part II, is the book of the fall to knowledge. It opens with the description of an airplane falling like a singed moth, a plane that "snagged its wing on a tree, fluttered in a tiny arc, and struggled down" (35). The central image is the crash's victim, a "little flamefaced child" (61), seven-year-old Julie. The emergency siren invokes the ancient response, causing the people "to halt, in pity and terror, wondering which among us got hit, by what bad accident, and why" (37). "Holy the Firm," Part III, is the book of communion, of transcendence, about the ascent, through sacrifice, to spiritual illumination. Dillard asks that oldest question, about the purpose of human suffering; and she offers an answer. The fiery central image this time is of the artist who "sets on fire" his world by lighting "the short string of his gut" to make his face a "flame like a seraph's, lighting the kingdom of

God for the people to see" (72). The moth, the child, and the artist aflame express the text's moral. "Julie, who looks somewhat like Dillard, . . . has come to know the experience of the artist, the experience of Rimbaud, with his burnt-out brains, and of Dillard" ⟨William Scheick, "Narrative Fringe," 1985, 58⟩. Exchange the names Julie and Dillard, and I agree.

In Part I, Dillard recalls an experience two summers past, when she retreated to recover her creativity, making for its sake a classically pastoral journey: into solitude, self, the past, nature. Actually, she camped, alone, in Virginia's Blue Ridge Mountains:

> I had hauled myself and gear up there to read, among other things,
> James Ramsey Ullman's *The Day on Fire*, a novel about Rimbaud that
> had made me want to be a writer when I was sixteen; I was hoping it
> would do it again. (14–15)

The novel doesn't perform that miracle; something else does, a night on fire. The "figure Moth" illuminates that night. "I saw it all" (16), claims Dillard, reporting a vision that compelled her sight just as had those of the giant water bug and the Polyphemous moth, but this time to positive effect.

Dillard directs her metaphor deliberately, intently. She's talking about the life of the writer. In the "golden female moth," the golden-haired woman sees, especially, herself. As writer, she's both sacrificed and purified. The moth burns violently, losing her wings, her six legs, and her head, with its antennae and "heaving mouth parts," which "crackled like pistol fire" (16). Here is a metaphor for mystical experience, so non-rational the head "jerks in spasms" at its contact, and so truly ineffable the useless "mouth parts" report their protest like pistols.

Then Dillard wonders at the meaning, asking herself the two questions most interesting to the woman who is an artist: "Had she mated and laid her eggs, had she done her work?" (17). The work of reproduction is an important subject in *Tinker Creek*; the work of writing, of illuminating manuscripts, is the vital subject of *Holy the Firm*—writing manuscripts that light "the kingdom of God for the people to see" (72). Appropriately, *Holy the Firm* fills with medieval images, saints aflame and manuscripts illuminated (the obvious instance is the book on Rimbaud). *Holy the Firm* names, barely concealing her in the burnt child, the mystic Julian of Norwich, whose penultimate of sixteen visions preceded a nightmare of hellfire, from which she woke to the stench of smoking flesh, her own mouth parts heaving to deliver the last holy vision of the *Revelations of Divine Love*.

"In the Middle Ages, I read," says Dillard, "'the idea of a thing which a man framed for himself was always more real to him than the actual thing itself.' Of course. I am in my Middle Ages; the world at my feet, the world through the window, is an illuminated manuscript whose leaves the wind takes, one by one, whose painted illuminations and halting words draw me, one by one, and I am dazzled in days and lost" (23–4). When Julian experienced her "shewings" in May of 1373, she was thirty and one half years old (and thus had been born on a day in November). Writing *Holy the Firm*, Dillard is almost exactly the same age. A "middle aged" woman of the world of "senselit" (43) but not sense-less days, she takes that world as holy text, illuminating its images with her own halting words, and the text itself "draws," or illuminates, her. This is "cor-respondence" of a new sort—or, at least, it's not the thing of the romantic or transcendental traditions. And perhaps Dillard writes, as one critic fears, for "an age reluctant to accept her kind of distinctly female voice and visionary naturalism" ⟨David Lavery, "Noticer," 1980, 270⟩.

—Judy Schaaf Anhorn, "Lines of Sight: Annie Dillard's 'Purified Nonfiction Narration,'" in *Cross-Cultural Studies: American, Canadian and European Literatures: 1945–1985*, ed. Mirko Jurak (Ljubljana, Yugoslavia: University of Ljubljana, 1988), 146–47

B I B L I O G R A P H Y

Pilgrim at Tinker Creek. 1974.
Tickets for a Prayer Wheel. 1974.
Holy the Firm. 1978.
The Weasel. 1981.
Living by Fiction. 1982.
Teaching a Stone to Talk: Expeditions and Encounters. 1982.
Encounters with Chinese Writers. 1985.
An American Childhood. 1987.
On Nature: Essays on Nature, Landscape, and Natural History (editor, with Edward Hoagland and Daniel Halpern). 1987.
The Writing Life. 1989.
Beginnings (with Elaine S. Furlow, Rachel Carson, Sue Hubbell, Douglas Chadwick, and Mercie Hans). 1989.
The Living: A Novel. 1992.
Unarmed but Dangerous: Withering Attacks on All Things Phony, Foolish, and Fundamentally Wrong with America Today (with Hal Crowther). 1995.
Mornings Like This: Found Poems. 1996.
Modern American Memoirs (with Cort Conley). 1996.

JANET FRAME

b. 1924

JANET FRAME was born in Dunedin, New Zealand, in August of 1924, the middle of five children. Because her father, George Frame, worked as a railroad engineer, the family moved frequently, living in several small, isolated towns in southern New Zealand. By 1930, the Frame family had moved back to Oamaru, a town Janet's paternal grandparents had helped build in the middle of the 19th century. Janet's mother, Lottie Clarice Godfrey, was an avid reader and writer who sold her own poetry door to door to help support her family during the Depression. Although the rest of Oamaru had recovered financially by the end of the decade, the Frames continued to live in poverty on the outskirts of town.

Of her siblings, Janet was the first to attend high school, where her performance put her at the top of her class. Although her sisters, Myrtle and Isabella, soon joined Janet in school, the Frame girls did not socialize with other students but lived a rich private life of fantasy and literature, modeling themselves upon the Brontës. When Janet was a young teenager, Myrtle drowned; 10 years later, Isabella did as well, in tragically coincidental circumstances. This second tragedy— as well as Janet's struggles with the conformist requirements of the society around her—precipitated her voluntary entrance into a mental institution at the age of 23. She would spend eight years of her life in institutions, where she was diagnosed as schizophrenic and received electric shock therapy.

In 1951, Frame published her first short story collection, *The Lagoon*, in many ways a transfiguring response to her tragic family life. Released from the hospital, she met New Zealand author Frank Sargeson, who recognized her talents and need of support and who offered to let her live in a small house on his property. There she wrote numerous stories and poems and her first novel, *Owls Do Cry* (1957). Prompted by Sargeson, she applied for, and received, a State Literary Fund grant. With the money she traveled.

In London, Frame again had herself committed—but now she was found to have been misdiagnosed with schizophrenia and was, on the contrary, advised to write rather than try to conform. This discovery launched her most prolific period of writing, yielding *Faces in the Water* (1961), *The Edge of the Alphabet* (1962), and *Scented Gardens for the Blind* (1963). She was at work on *The Adaptable Man* (1965) when she returned to New Zealand upon the death of her father. In New

Zealand she was treated as a celebrated writer and was awarded the Robert Burns Fellowships at the University of Otago. Since then, Frame has published a volume of poetry and numerous short story collections and novels, which have continued to win her fellowships and awards, including the 1989 Commonwealth Writers Prize for *The Carpathians* (1988), her latest novel.

The first volume of Frame's autobiography, *To the Is-Land*, was published in 1982. It was soon followed by *An Angel at My Table* (1984) and *The Envoy from Mirror City* (1985). Her fiction, however, had already received a great deal of biographical criticism—often to the irritation of the author, who has, in her rare interviews, insisted upon the distinction between the truth of fiction and the truth of fact. Although her autobiographies contain many incidents alluded to in her fiction, they are ostensibly more straightforward and contain few of the experiments of her fiction. Nevertheless, in an interview with Elizabeth Alley (*Landfalls* 45, 1991), Frame has said that she is "always in fictional mode, and autobiography is found fiction."

CRITICAL EXTRACTS

JANET FRAME

In our later years at High School my sisters and I ⟨. . .⟩ set to work on our novels, with the titles carefully chosen: *There is Sweet Music, Go Shepherd,* and *The Vision of the Dust,* which I had chosen because I was currently anti-shepherd, anti-sweet music, seeking the poetry in 'the heart of the unobvious' by writing about such topics as cellophane paper, factories, ditches, slums, ugliness. There were tragic happenings in our family. Sometimes when it seemed to us that our family was doomed, we would console ourselves by remembering the Brontes and drawing between them and us a grandiose dramatic parallel which could not harm, though it might have amused, them, but which may have harmed us into believing that we three girls held, by right, 'silk purses' of words. With a background of poverty, drunkenness, attempted murder and near-madness, it was inevitable that we should feel close to the Brontes, once we had read their books and knew the story of their lives. My younger sister (who later died when she was twenty) was assigned the role of Emily; I, more practical and less outwardly 'passionate' became Charlotte, while my youngest sister, shy, overshadowed in many ways by our 'glory', became Anne.

Then, when my own private world became more demanding and I no longer cared to confide in 'Emily' or 'Anne' I spent my spare time writing my diary addressed to the ruler of my Land of Ardenue. I lived increasingly in this imaginary world whose characters were drawn from objects and people I met in my daily life, with occasional intrusion of characters from fiction—from Dostoyevsky, Daudet, Hardy. My home task of milking the two cows enabled me to spend hours on the hills around Oamaru talking to and exchanging opinions with my characters while I persuaded the cows (which I milked in the paddocks) to 'let down' their milk. Or I made poems in my head and wrote them when I came home.

The channels of poetry were strengthened and deepened. Those needs and longings which, during childhood, had been stacked in a tremendous slow-moving mass, like a picturesque glacier seen in the distant mountains of the high country, had begun to thaw, in the spring of adolescence. One always remembers vividly those chilling crashing immense movements of the spirit as the long-frozen ideas found their life and course and merged one with the other in their flow to the sea.

People began asking, What are you going to do with your life? I'll be a teacher, I said, writing in my diary the same evening, I'm going to be a poet.

I left home to attend Training College and University in Dunedin. I looked for the poets. Where were the poets? I spent my free time in the North Dunedin Cemetery, sitting on the tombstones, dreaming, or walking along St Clair beach, by the lupins and the sandhills. One day I wrote a story, sent it to the Listener, and to my surprise it was published, with illustrations. I was very proud of my story. Though it was published only under my initials, someone traced it to me and added to my self-esteem by remarking,—The Listener's hard to get into. Secretly, I was more proud of the illustration by Russell Clark than I was of the story, for the scene depicted a dark-haired attractive schoolgirl in the kitchen of a typical New Zealand home, such a contrast to the home I'd been describing, my own, which had never been 'typical', which had none of the furniture and ornaments portrayed by the artist. The schoolgirl in the smart gym frock was a flattering picture of myself. If I had been able to draw I would have made a 'true' picture, far from the pleasantly romantic etching.

As it was becoming impossible for me to reconcile 'this' and 'that' world, I decided to choose 'that' world, and one day when the Inspector was visiting my class at school I said,—Excuse me, and walked from the room and the school, from 'this' world to 'that' world where I have stayed, and where I live now.

—Janet Frame, "Beginnings," Landfall 19, no. 1 (March 1965): 44–45

P. D. EVANS

No one approaches Janet Frame's writing for an evening of light entertainment. The atmosphere of her work is almost unrelievedly dark; its texture thick with imagery and allusion: its plots full of deceits engineered to trick the reader; its significance half-stated and often obscure, as if the process of writing has not fully released the impulses which have brought it about. It is this last quality which I wish to discuss in this essay: the sense gained by any copious reader of her work that it represents a recurring engagement with the business of writing itself, with the relationships of words and things, and with the limiting nature of the things we attempt to discuss with words, rather than being a process of steadily expressing a vision that is largely preconceived.

In discussing this, as will be evident, I have broken the rule which states that a writer's life has nothing to do with a writer's art. I break it because it does not fit the writer: Janet Frame seems to me to dictate a different critical approach because, as anyone familiar with the details of her life will know, she constantly places herself at the center of her own writing. ⟨. . .⟩

⟨This⟩ is done to a certain extent by all artists, who turn the surrounding world into metaphors which embody their vision. But few so distinctively focus the metaphors on their own special plight; few operate such a gravitational pull on the objects of their fictional worlds, drawing everything towards a central sensibility but refusing subsequently to force them back out again much transformed. Her tendency to do these things in her writing is present from the first collection of short stories, *The Lagoon*, which was written during her early years in a hospital. The personal nature of these stories and their subsequent tendency towards autobiographical parable can only be explained by an understanding of the importance of the events that immediately preceded her admission to a hospital in the fall of 1947.

Frame entered the hospital voluntarily, with the aim of turning herself into a professional writer. The most interesting thing she tells us about herself during this time is that she carried a copy of Rilke's *Sonnets to Orpheus* with her wherever she went. These sonnets had been written in response to the death of the daughter of a friend, a talented dancer whose sudden demise Rilke attempted to understand and to accept in a long sequence of poems about art, life, and death that were based on the classical myth of Orpheus and Eurydice. What must have fascinated Frame was the similarity of Rilke's situation to her own: just before her entry to the hospital she had lost her younger and favorite sister, Isabel, who had drowned at Picton, the beach resort home of the Frames' maternal grandparents, during a late summer holiday taken with the writer. ⟨. . .⟩

⟨. . .⟩ Although no one could deny that the stories in *The Lagoon* ⟨1951⟩ are insistently about death, there is an equally undeniable sense in them of the writer circling about a subject that both fascinates and repels her. The title story of the collection, for example, is set at the scene of Isabel's death, but conceals fact with a layer of fiction. The way in which this is done is worth noting. "The Lagoon" begins with its young female narrator returning in late adolescence to the scene of her happy childhood holidays to find that the little township as well as her favorite lagoon on the beach are far smaller and shabbier than she remembered them. She recalls her beloved grandmother, who has recently died, and especially remembers the old woman's ability to weave stories about everything in Picton except the lagoon, which "never had a proper story." Now that the old woman has gone, the girl's aunt reveals the "proper story" at last: "Your great grandmother was a murderess. She drowned her husband, pushed him in the lagoon." The girl's grandmother never mentioned the murder, as the aunt explains, because, "The reason one talks farthest from the heart is the fear that it may be hurt" (p. 11).

This sentence is the most crucial in the entire collection. It draws attention to the dishonesty possible in storytelling, to the ease with which writers may manipulate facts and thereby control the responses of their readers. The process of storytelling is one of the things this story is about: the grandmother's ability to tell stories about things is one of its subjects, as is the ability (conjectured by the aunt later in the story) of Dostoevsky and popular journalists to do the same. Bringing the inventedness of fiction before the reader, particularly by means of a sentence which speaks of avoidance and hurt, inevitably draws attention to the inventedness of the story itself, and it invites the reader to plunge beneath its surface in order to examine the processes of fictionalization. Aware as we are of the actual events behind the story, we are better placed than most readers to see how Frame forms life into parable. Just as the lagoon is sullied by the invading seawater, she seems to say, childhood is sullied by adult life, especially by its diminution of the transforming imaginative power we have when we are innocent. But that is not all that pollutes the lagoon of childhood: violent death, a death in the family, has contaminated it too. This is the nearest the writer comes to mentioning the incident which has hurt her heart; this, and the clear reference to the invading seawater which in fact carried her sister's life away.

This process of "talking farthest from the heart" becomes a staple of Janet Frame's fiction, a technique in which actual events, and particularly this one event (which becomes melded from time to time with the almost identical loss of her older sister, also by drowning, in 1937), are turned into fiction, but in

such a way that the reader is always made aware of the fictitiousness of the fiction.
—P. D. Evans, "'Farthest from the Heart': The Autobiographical Parables of Janet Frame," *Modern Fiction Studies* 27, no. 1 (Spring 1981): 31, 33–35

LAWRENCE JONES

For the New Zealand literary autobiographer, "There is one story only." The story appears in its simplest symbolic form in Janet Frame's earliest tale (told to her family when she was three):

> Once upon a time there was a bird. One day a hawk came out of the sky and ate the bird. The next day a big bogie came up from behind the hill and ate up the hawk for eating up the bird. ⟨*Beginnings*, 1980, 27⟩

Like most good symbolic stories, this one is open to several interpretations, but for the literary autobiographer the relevant one is Robert T. Robertson's version:

> In a provincial society, the hawk is both the society and untamed nature; and the bogie is the art which eats up both for eating up the bird of inspiration or imagination in an unimaginative society. ⟨"Bird, Hawk, Bogie," 1972, 192⟩

The story, then, is of the artist's struggle to find a "place" (often literal as well as figurative) in a hostile provincial environment: it is a story of defeat and persecution but also of victory in the achievement of art (even if the art succeeds only in holding up a mirror in which the society could see its unlovely self if it chose to look).

But if there is one story, there are two ways of telling it. The first is realistic, attempting to be objective, concerned primarily with the outward environment and the making of a place within it (the story of a career), literal and chronological in method. The second is impressionistic, openly subjective, concerned primarily with the inner self and the development of a sensibility and a sense of psychological place, metaphorical and moving nonchronologically as the memory moves back and forth through layers of time. Given the fixed sexual roles of New Zealand society, the first method tends to be masculine, the second feminine; the first tends to be dominant, the second scarcely recognized as a tradition. ⟨. . .⟩

⟨. . .⟩ Janet Frame's "one story" is not yet complete. The first two volumes of her proposed three-volume autobiography ⟨To the Is-land and An Angel at My Table⟩ take her from her birth in 1924 to 1956 when, Owls Do Cry completed, she set off for Europe. She is thus left on the verge of achieving her first taste of fame, at about the same point in her career as ⟨Sylvia⟩ Ashton-Warner then was (Spinster and Owls Do Cry appeared within a year of each other), but at a much earlier stage in her life. Nonetheless the emerging pattern is clear: the sensitive, naturally imaginative child as the "little bird"; the terrible hawk appearing as Death, taking two of her sisters, and as a conformist society imprisoning her from without and attempting to undermine her from within; then the bogie of imagination and art beginning to come forth in rescue. Art and imagination in Janet Frame's world cannot control Nature (and its agents, Time and Death), but they can see it in all its beauty and terror, with something like "the point of view of angels" (Angel, p. 153). Likewise, art and imagination cannot control society, but they can help one to see it, including its lies and deceptions, and gain a kind of revenge on it by pointing out that the king really is naked, or that the consumer world of "permanent" waves and "permanent" pleats is no defence against Time and Death, for only the cycle is permanent, not its subjects. ⟨. . .⟩

The way of telling this story is impressionist, as befits its inward focus. That is not to say that the books do not present the external world, for it is vividly and vitally there in the literal imagery ⟨. . . .⟩ ⟨M⟩ost of the formative influences Frame mentions are writers of different modes: psychological novelists such as Joyce, Woolf and Faulkner; symbolist poets such as Eliot, Yeats, Rilke, Dylan Thomas, and George Barker (those ubiquitous influences on New Zealand literature in the 1940's and 1950's); theorists such as Coleridge on Imagination, Frazer on myth, Freud and Jung on psychological symbolism. And readers of Frame's fiction will recognize, in less extreme form, many of her characteristic devices for presentation of the inner life. There is in the early sections of To the Is-land the insertion of children's vernacular to capture the child's sense of the experience—"with all the relations dressed up and speaking in their high-up voices," "that same twisty railway journey" (pp. 67–68). There is the self-reflexiveness, the reminders that all of this is filtered through one sensibility: the metaphor comparing memories rising to the surface at a whirlpool, "with different memories rising to the surface at different times and thus denying the existence of a 'pure' autobiography" (Is-land, pp. 235–36); the explicit acknowledgement that "Time confers privileges of arrangement and rearrangements undreamed of until it becomes Time Past" (Angel, pp. 14–15); the description of autobiography as "a looking across or through" as well as a "looking back," with "the passing of time giving an X-ray quality to the eye" (Angel, p. 69); the description of how "the future accumulates like a weight upon the past" so that, for the autobiographer "the weight upon the earliest years is easier to remove to let that time spring up like grass that has been crushed," while with later years the mass has grown and presses harder so "the time beneath . . . lies bled of its green in a new shape with those frail bloodless sprouts of another, unfamiliar time, entangled one with the other beneath the stone" (*Angel*, p. 13). Many of these reflexive passages point to the most characteristic aspect of the way of telling, its symbolic and metaphoric quality. Some of the literal images become symbolic, such as the various rail journeys, especially the one that ends *To the Is-land*, or the sea-journey that ends *An Angel at My Table*, or the silkworms that Frame gives to Sargeson, or the "pine trees in the cool of the evening." And, although they are not woven into as elaborate patterns as in the fiction, metaphorical images abound. Metaphor, combined with pun and allusion, characterizes the titles of both volumes and many of the section and chapter titles. It is also used frequently to capture inward experience, the sense of the death of Frame's parents being compared, for example, to the removal of two trees "between us and wind, sea, snow," a removal that "might expose us but. . . . would also let the light in from all directions, and we would know the reality instead of the rumour of the wind, sea, snow, and be able to perceive all moments of being" (*Angel*, p. 163). As in the fiction, many passages that stick in the memory are the metaphorical ones.

    —Lawrence Jones, "The One Story, Two Ways of Telling, Three Perspectives: Recent New Zealand Literary Autobiography," *Ariel 16*, no. 4 (October 1985): 127–28, 142–43, 147–48

ELIZABETH ALLEY

⟨The following is made of two interviews, one recorded in 1983 and the other in 1988.⟩

Elizabeth Alley: In the autobiography you seem more willing than in the fiction to open some of the doors about yourself and your life—to correct some of the myths that surround you.

Janet Frame: I wanted to write my story, and you're right of course, it is possible to correct some things which have been taken as fact and are not fact. My fiction is genuinely fiction. And I do invent things. Even in *The Lagoon* which has many childhood stories, the children are invented and the episodes are invented, but they are mixed up so much with part of my early childhood. But they're not quite, they're not the *true*, stories. *To the Is-Land* was the first time I'd written the true story. For instance, *Faces in the Water* was autobiographical in the sense that everything happened, but the central character was invented.

But with the autobiography it was the desire really to make myself a first person. For many years I was a third person—as children are. 'They', 'she' . . . and as probably the oppressed minority has become, 'they'. I mean children are forever 'they' until they grow up. ⟨. . .⟩

Elizabeth Alley: In some of your earlier novels I suppose what the critics call the dark side, the pain prevails. But in *To the Is-Land* it's the joy and humour and the fun that is prevalent. And really, humour and satire have always been very important to you, haven't they?

Janet Frame: In *To the Is-Land* I wrote the story of my life. My story, and this is me which comes out. There is pain, things happen, but whatever comes out is ordinary me without fiction or characters.

Elizabeth Alley: How do you react to the critics who so often talk about that dark vision, that's too narrow to share?

Janet Frame: Well, a novelist is subjected in reviews to the blurring of the fine distinction between the writer's work and the writer's life. Extreme views based on the content of a book might even pass judgement on what is assumed to be the outlook of the writer herself. ⟨. . .⟩

The critical references to me and my supposed personal views, I think they're simply a failure of the art of literary criticism. Well, they're an impurity of response which I suppose is natural, but who said literary criticism should be natural? The critic reminds me of the film *The Fly*, where the scientist, immersed in his experiment, doesn't realise that a fly has accompanied him to the cabinet. When he emerges, his work finished, he's part-man, part-housefly. I mean the critic has the sort of little impurity, but the writer works within the limitations or framework of her personality, although the outlook and the view over the territory of time and space and human endeavour is endless. But writing also is a kind of job. You ask about the dark side, well, if I'm a plumber and I find there is a certain amount of work to be done in a certain street, exclusively with, say, the pressure of the household water supply, then you can't assume that I'm not qualified also to fix your sewer or install a shower, or a swimming pool.

If, as a writer I happen to work in a street where a few disasters occur, this is no foundation for the belief that I'm interested only in disasters. Similarly, if I write of a dark side, it doesn't mean that I'm not interested also in the whole view. You must be.

—Elizabeth Alley, "An Interview with Janet Frame," *Landfall* 45, no. 2 (June 1991): 155, 157–59

SIMON PETCH

"Myth" is a charged term in Frame's autobiography, indicating a mode of perception or a way of knowing which is creative and transforming. In its refusal to let the past die, in its consciousness of the incompleteness of the present, and in its manifestations of desire as a way of giving life to the future, this autobiography is always moving towards myth. Writing of her memory of raspberry-picking, in adolescence, in Central Otago, Frame powerfully reinforces this mode of perception in her recreation of it. She responded to the river Clutha as to "an ally" that "would speak for me," an elemental force of liberation with which she "greedily" claimed identification, and eagerly acknowledged its power as part of her life. As Frame describes her love-affair with the landscape, her writing appeals strongly to myths of nature, fertility, innocence, and initiation. Frame, herself "flamed with sunburn" and "stained with raspberry blood," saw the pickers "like goddesses," and the farmers' sons "like younger gods" as she glanced "briefly but often at the bulge, the snowball bedded in snowgrass, between their legs" (*Angel* 34–35). With characteristic tough-mindedness Frame reminds us of "the invisible boundaries" between the human and the natural ("we were not rivers"), but in this mythologizing memory of sun and sexuality, these boundaries are blurred. The writing combines myth-making and memory, forging links between the human and the natural 〈. . . .〉

Myth-making is an imaginative process that is central to Frame's writing of herself. What she calls "my place" is a place of memory and imagination, a *locus* of which she is herself the *genius*, a hoard of secret identity through which she transcends her social being. Such a sense of affinity and belonging is usually associated with nature: the vivid memory of the wind in the telegraph wires, "my first conscious feeling of an outside sadness" (*Is-Land* 16), *lacrimae rerum*; the delicious secrecy among the trees by the creek in Glenham (*Is-Land* 18); and, in a startling act of manipulation by which memory creates a focus for itself, the pine trees of Ibiza:

> Not an unusual scene but . . . it touched the antenna reaching from childhood, just as childhood contains its own antennae originating in conception and the life of the dead and the newly begun; and feeling the sensation at the nerve-ending and its origin in the past among the pine trees and sky and water and light, I made this scene a replacement, a telescoping with the trained economy of memory, so that from then and in the future the memory of this scene contains the collective feeling of those past, and now when I listen to pine trees by water, in light and blue, I feel the link, the fullness of being and loving and losing and wondering, the spinning "Why was the world?" that haunted me in childhood, the shiver of yesterday, yet I remember the pine trees of Ibiza. (*Envoy* 68–69)

The rhythms and repetitions of Frame's prose establish memory as a collective rather than a recollective faculty. Such self-conscious mythologizing of memories is a fictional integration of significant experience, and the meanings created focus identity and give the self a sense of its own unity. In Frame's "economy of memory," the pine trees of Ibiza grow out of Glenham, Southland; and the island of Ibiza belongs to the archipelago which contains the Is-Land of the first volume of her autobiography: "That year I discovered the word *Island*, which in spite of all teaching I insisted on calling Is-Land . . . . In the end, reluctantly, I had to accept the ruling, although within myself I still thought of it as the Is-Land" (*Is-Land* 41).

The conventional and accepted pronunciations of the word force a consideration, as crucial in Frame's book as in anyone's experience of language, between a socially-conferred and agreed meaning, and a meaning privately given and understood by the individual. The private meaning is valued for its uniqueness, and the mind holds to it as a significant reference point, as to the pine-trees of Ibiza. All such meanings denote a system of personal myth, though which Frame negotiates the progress of her relationship with the world, and gives shape and significance to her sense of self. In the case of *Is-Land*, the meaning introduces a complex sense of selfhood: Is-Land insists on presence, by turning the first syllable into a verb, but it writes out the identity submerged in the anti-pun of I-Land. Public and private meanings intermesh to establish the self along a complicated network of public and private, the elusive private self hidden in the interstices of a public network of discourse.

 —Simon Petch, "Janet Frame and the Languages of Autobiography," *Australian and New Zealand Studies in Canada* 5 (1991): 60, 61–62

SIMON PETCH

Janet Frame began to menstruate in August 1939, shortly before the outbreak of the Second World War. The schoolgirl's acquisition of "a new relationship to blood" was mediated by institutions, for it was reinforced by the "sexual languor of the many hymns steeped in blood" which were sung at school, and "made strange by the repeated reference to the spilling of blood in wartime, and the everlasting preoccupation with blood in a country that based its economy on the killing and eating of farm animals" ⟨*To the Is-Land*, 1987, 154⟩. Frame's remembrance relates her personal development as a woman to her country's religion, to its economy, and to the war which signified her country's relationship to Britain. Her writing compacts these several levels of cultural relevance by a process which she describes as "telescoping with the trained economy of memory" ⟨*The Envoy from Mirror City*, 1987, 68⟩. ⟨. . .⟩

If the First World War establishes the patriarchal and imperial context from which Frame's identity and values emerge, the site of the Second World War was her own mind and body. "At the beginning of the month when I was to celebrate my twenty-first birthday, my coming of age, the War was suddenly over, having pursued me through all the years of my official adolescence, as part of the development of my body and mind, almost as an ingredient of my blood, leaving its trace everywhere, even in my hair and my (picked or bitten) fingernails" ⟨*An Angel at My Table*, 1987, 60⟩. The grammatical uncertainty about whether "leaving" is governed by "war" or by "blood", or by both, works the war into the blood. The traces of blood in the hair are ancestral as well as menstrual and martial, for the frizziness of Janet's hair (if not its redness) came from her paternal grandmother. Because her Scottish Grandma Frame sang songs of the American Deep South, Janet "assumed that Grandma Frame was African and had been a slave in America". This fictitious assumption of ancestral enslavement was supported by a fictitious identity based on a fiction of slavery. "The book that everyone was talking about in our house was *Uncle Tom's Cabin* . . . and I was being called Topsy because my hair was frizzy" (*I* 15). As a child, and throughout her adolescence, Janet was baffled by her hair which, by growing the wrong way, seemed to cause alarm and pose a threat to those around her; for no-one had hair like hers "except Fijian and African people in faraway lands" (*I* 138). The threat which her hair represented was both defused and mocked by the nickname Fuzzy, but the phrase about Fijian and African people brings the racial tensions of her colonial culture to bear on her growing sense of identity. Frame's frizzy hair and the traces of blood it holds is a sign of subjugation and oppression. It is also a sign of difference and rebellion, of Frame's need, undirected while she was at school, to define herself against the conformist colonial culture of New Zealand.

Frame charts her relationships to the institutions that formed her by writing of her blood, her hair, and her teeth. Her decaying teeth are a synecdoche for the colonising take-over of her person by the normalising pressure of the medical institutions of New Zealand. Just as the fancy dress of schizophrenia had once masked, for Frame, the horror of decaying teeth, so in her autobiographical narrative the dental implicitly figures the mental. After having her teeth out in Christchurch public hospital "I woke toothless and was admitted to Sunnyside Hospital and I was given the new electric treatment, and suddenly my life was thrown out of focus" (*A* 95). The conjunction along which the sentence is structured masks the mysterious and sinister logic which it implies. Loss of teeth was almost inevitable in a country whose Social Security System provided no dental care beyond primary school, but "the general opinion in New Zealand then was that natural teeth were best removed anyway, it

was a kind of colonial squandering, like the needless uprooting of forests"
(A 80). Susan Stanford Friedman has said that women, historically, "have been
the gathered, the colonised, the ruled", and Frame's knowingly post-colonial
use of the colonisers' rape of the environment as a figure for her dental treatment gestures, in its clear identification between body and landscape, to her
own need or desire for such indigeneity as she can claim.

This qualification is necessary because the forthright clarity of Frame's
simile obscures a complex of issues about the place of a settler woman in a col-
onized environment, which are summed up by Robin Visel: "Although [the
white settler woman] . . . is oppressed by white men and patriarchal structures,
she shares in the power and guilt of the colonists" 〈"A Half-Colonization,"
1988, 39〉. The nexus between the white woman in the colony and the structures of imperialism and patriarchy is a major source of disturbance in Frame's
autobiography, a disturbance which suggests the need for discrimination
between the categories of race and gender. The voices of Frame's autobiography are most unsettled in those autobiographical moments in which they
declare or reveal their complicity with the cultural forces, both patriarchal and
imperial, against which they are rebelling, forces with which they contend but
which have also shaped them, and given them their language. Frame's
acknowledged fictions of alterity (beginning with Topsy) are serious if hesi-
tant gestures, arising from a felt need for indigeneity while acknowledging
that her right to claim it is a limited one. They were the necessary means to
Frame's anxious exploration of her position as a white woman growing up in
the settler culture of New Zealand.

—Simon Petch, "Speaking for Herselves: The Autobiographical Voices of Janet Frame,"
Southerly 54, no. 4 (Summer 1994–95): 44, 46–48

KARIN HANSSON

Regarding the search for identity and the definition of humanity from a
Darwinian aspect, Erich Fromm's statement is noteworthy: "Man may be
defined as the animal that can say 'I', that can be aware of himself as a separate
entity." Fromm also argues that man cannot remain sane without this sense of
'I', and that he is driven to do almost anything to acquire it. Frame's novels
offer numerous examples of the mania and obsession pertinent to such a struggle for identity. 〈. . .〉

〈. . .〉 There is, however, also the opposite strategy as regards identity: the
longing for dissociation from self, for escaping or dissembling the vulnerable
"I", "the lonely nude I" 〈Daughter Buffalo, 103〉. This attitude is exemplified in the
autobiographical volumes where Frame states that as a young woman she felt
that if she were to keep her true identity it had to be concealed efficiently. The

necessary adaptation that her environment demanded turned Frame into "almost a nothingness, like a no-woman's land" ⟨*An Angel at My Table*, 27⟩. As a consequence she frequently makes the distinction between "that" world, where she herself chooses the conditions of her individuation process and personal development, and "this" world, where other authorities set the rules and insist on adaptation and conformity. Like some of her main characters, according to her autobiographical books, she, too, is looking out at "this" world through an "I-shaped window" to borrow an expression from *Living in the Maniototo* (61).

The temptation to choose the easy way out of this predicament by unconditionally surrendering one's selfhood, letting "that" world be swallowed up by "this" world, is expressed in *Daughter Buffalo*: "How good it is to be not-I" (*DB* 176). Here and elsewhere ⟨. . .⟩ the letter "I" for identity is strongly foregrounded. As Patrick Evans argues, "we have no writer who writes the letter 'I' so firmly on the face of the void" ("The Case of the Disappearing Author" 16). Thus an itemized list of "I"s ("I, the Reverend Aisley Maude . . . I, Russell Maude, dentist, stamp-collector . . .") introduces the several dramatis personae in the prologue of *The Adaptable Man*. But at the same time as the notion of identity is accordingly emphasized, the list indicates the utter loneliness and lack of contact and relationship between the separate characters and between their individual worlds. The catalogue of isolated 'I's and their respective feelings of guilt, or private, mutually exclusive dreams in life, ends with the earth itself contemplating its adaptability and its struggle for survival:

> I, the earth, fairly submissive, my seasons arranged beforehand;
> lifeless but hopeful of the overflowing conceit and concern of man
> which spill life and feeling into my shell. Man insists that I weep,
> groan, vomit, laugh; man reminds me that living is not much fun.
> But who wants fun?
> I, I, I, I, I . . . . (6)

Recurrent word-play as in I-land, island, Is-land, Was-land, not only in the title of *To the Is-land*, but also in expressions such as "this island terror" ⟨*A State of Siege*, 63⟩, "the natural exiling power of islands" (*SS* 40), and in numerous contexts in *Living in the Maniototo*, merits notice because it emphasizes the common plight of man and earth wanting to escape the implications of true selfhood.

—Karin Hansson, *The Unstable Manifold: Janet Frame's Challenge to Determinism* (Lund, Sweden: Lund University Press, 1996), 29–31

BIBLIOGRAPHY

The Lagoon. 1951.
Owls Do Cry. 1957.
Faces in the Water. 1961.
The Edge of the Alphabet. 1962.
Scented Gardens for the Blind. 1963.
The Reservoir. 1963.
Snowman, Snowman. 1963.
The Adaptable Man. 1965.
A State of Siege. 1966.
The Pocket Mirror. 1967.
The Rainbirds. 1969. (Published in the United States as *Yellow Flowers in the Antipodean Room.*)
Intensive Care. 1970.
Daughter Buffalo. 1972.
Living in the Maniototo. 1979.
To the Is-Land. 1982.
An Angel at My Table. 1984.
The Envoy from Mirror City. 1985.
The Carpathians. 1988.
You Are Now Entering the Human Heart. 1992.

MARTHA GELLHORN
b. 1908

MARTHA ELLIS GELLHORN was born in St. Louis, Missouri, in 1908, to George and Edna Fischel Gellhorn. Her 60-year career as a journalist, fiction writer, and dramatist began after three years at Bryn Mawr College, when she became part of the pacifist youth movement in Europe. Her first novel, *What Mad Pursuit* (1934), fictionalizes this experience but attracted little attention. In *The Trouble I've Seen* (1936), Gellhorn again drew upon her experiences, this time as an investigator for the Federal Emergency Relief Administration during the Depression, to depict the lives of once-respectable people who have become destitute. Most critics acclaimed the work, noting Gellhorn's incisive, journalistic writing style.

In 1937 Gellhorn left for Madrid with $50 and a knapsack to report on the Spanish Civil War. There she met war correspondent Ernest Hemingway and photographer Robert Capa and learned the basic techniques of writing about warfare. She submitted articles to *Collier's* and was a correspondent for the magazine from 1937 through 1945. As Hitler rose to power in Germany and the Fascist movement gained control in Italy, Gellhorn went to Finland to report on the 1939 Russo-Finnish war. In her next novel, *A Stricken Field* (1940), she describes Prague just before Germany defeats the Czechoslovakian forces.

The Heart of Another (1941) is a collection of nine short stories that was well received by reviewers, who noted its more mature and polished prose and detected the influence on Gellhorn's work of Ernest Hemingway, to whom she was married from 1940 to 1945. During this period Gellhorn continued her work as a correspondent for *Collier's* in China, England, Italy, France, Germany, and Java; she also continued to draw upon her diverse experiences to write fiction. *Liana* (1944), written while Gellhorn lived with Hemingway in Cuba, is a story of racial and sexual inequality: a Caribbean mulatto woman, forced by her destitute family to marry a wealthy white man, is ostracized by both races and eventually commits suicide. *The Wine of Astonishment* (1948) is a powerful story of two American soldiers, one a bigoted officer, the other his Jewish driver, Jacob Levy, after the Battle of the Bulge. The novel was praised for its powerful dramatization of the plight of the individual caught in politics and warfare.

Gellhorn next published two volumes of short fiction that were well received by critics: stories in *The Honeyed Peace* (1953) describe the shattered European communities struggling to survive after the devastation of World War II; in *Two by Two* (1958), a collection of four novellas, Gellhorn's spare prose excavates the pleasures and problems of marriage. She received an O. Henry Award in 1958 and continued to develop her writing in the 1960s and 1970s, publishing *His Own Man* (1961), *Pretty Tales for Tired People* (1965), *The Lowest Trees Have Tops* (1967), and *The Weather in Africa* (1978).

Gellhorn's war reports from the Spanish Civil War, Finland, China, Europe in World War II, and in Java appear in *The Face of War* (1959), which has been updated and republished with Gellhorn's observations on the wars in Vietnam and Central America. She was a war correspondent for the London newspaper *The Guardian* in Vietnam in 1966 and in Israel in 1967. Although she has sometimes been criticized for her unsympathetic portrayal of Palestinians living in Israel, she has been praised for her coverage of Adolf Eichmann's trial in Jerusalem and for her essays on the McCarthy era and the war in Vietnam. *The View from the Ground* (1988) collects various peacetime reports on inhuman conditions around the world and the fears of nuclear war.

In addition to her fiction and journalism, Gellhorn also wrote lighter nonfiction: *Travels with Myself and Another* (1978) is an often humorous autobiography and travelogue about her most interesting trips to Asia, the Caribbean, Russia, and China. In several accounts she is accompanied by an "Unwilling Companion," who is accepted to be a fictional representation of Ernest Hemingway. Although having had a relationship with him was of great fascination, she never capitalized upon it in her writing—and she was caustic in her criticism of those, like Lillian Hellman, who did.

C R I T I C A L   E X T R A C T S

EDITH H. WALTON

In 1936 Martha Gellhorn published a moving and excellent book, *The Trouble I've Seen*. Based on her experiences as an investigator for the Federal Emergency Relief Administration, it proved not only that she was an exceptionally good reporter but also that she had real qualities of imagination and insight. Fiction though they were, her tales of the stubborn, self-respecting unemployed had an accent of truth that was almost unbearable. Since then Miss Gellhorn has branched out more widely. She has been in Spain, she has been in Czecho-Slovakia; currently, she has been writing a series of articles on Finland, which rank among the best commentaries from that scarred and snowbound front.

Knowing this background, one cannot very well miss the flavor of autobiography in Martha Gellhorn's new novel. *A Stricken Field* has as its scene Czecho-Slovakia—more specifically, Prague—just after the Munich pact. The story is told, moreover, from the viewpoint of an American, Mary Douglas, who so obviously stands for the author that a disguise seems superfluous. A journalist—young, sleek, beautiful, precociously experienced, but with an impulsive and pitying heart—Mary descends upon Prague from the Paris plane with hardly any conception of what she is going to find there. Simply, she has been told to get a story—as have the other ambulance-chasers of disaster, her fellow-correspondents, whom she meets and drinks with presently in Prague's hotels. She has no idea that within the space of a week she is to be so torn, so shaken, so terribly disturbed.

The Prague which Mary finds is a city tense, nervous, desolate, bitter with regret because its battle is unfought. Wistfully, it feeds on memories of how fine its army was, wonders if war itself could have outmatched the shameful present.

As for the plot of *A Stricken Field*, it is almost nonexistent. What there is of it concerns a German Communist, Rita, whom Mary tries futilely to save and befriend. It is through Rita—who has found, in exile, a brief security and love—that Mary is introduced to the underground movement and to the heartbreaking efforts of the Sudeten refugees to establish some kind of a shelter, however perilous. Because she sees, thanks to Rita, so much that is both ghastly and gallant, it is impossible for Mary to be as detached as the other journalists from the suffering all about her. ⟨. . .⟩

Largely because it wavers so on the borderline of fiction and non-fiction, *A Stricken Field* is a hard book to appraise. Considered as a novel it is something of a failure—lacking as it does most of the elements that give a novel pith and point—yet its material is so poignant and so well handled that one cannot dismiss it lightly. Miss Gellhorn, as she has previously proved, is an admirable reporter. She has intelligence, feeling, a seeing eye, and she writes a clean, contemporary prose which depends for its effect upon understatement. Why she did not tell this story in the first person, and as a record of her own experience, I really cannot imagine. All that is weak and theatrical in it springs from her effort to go beyond good journalism into a field as yet alien to her. *A Stricken Field* is at its best a compelling book and a moving one, but as a novel it is weak. Miss Gellhorn has done better in her articles.

—Edith H. Walton, "In Prague," *The New York Times Book Review* (10 March 1940): 6–7

HERBERT MITGANG

Derived from her articles over the years in *Collier's* magazine, Martha Gellhorn's *The Face of War* is a brilliant anti-war book that is as fresh as if written for this morning. Seldom can a correspondent assemble past writings from various locations and watch a clear pattern emerge, yet her pieces fall into place in a grand design. Her opinions, because they are rooted in these finely drawn scenes from four wars, deserve to be read by many people.

Her point is this:

> The world's leaders seem strangely engaged in private feuds. . . .
> Their talk sounds as if they believed nuclear war to be a thing that
> can be won or lost, and probable. . . . I believe that memory and
> imagination, not nuclear weapons, are the great deterrents.

The author's memories of war are vivid ⟨. . . .⟩ Her first report is from Madrid in 1937, her last from Dachau in 1945. The names and datelines tell their own story.

Battles are ephemeral, but the people about whom Miss Gellhorn reports survive. There are the bomb-wounded children of Barcelona ("In Barcelona, it was perfect bombing weather"), the firemen dousing the flames in Helsinki ("War started at 9 o'clock promptly"). She was in an airplane over Chungking ("From the air you would not know how these smashed houses looked or sounded as they collapsed"); with the Frenchmen on the Italian front on the way back to Paris ("They are fighting for the honor of France, which is not just a phrase but the personal, undying pride of every one of them"); with the Americans in the Battle of the Bulge ("The bodies of Germans were piled on the trailer like so much ghastly firewood").

Her reporting and writing have the novelist's emotional skill. In Dachau, the meaning of these events of the Thirties and Forties all seemed to coincide in horror. The face of war was and is ugly—and this is a stirring editorial.

—Herbert Mitgang, "A Message for Today," *The New York Times Book Review* (22 March 1959): 10

THE TIMES LITERARY SUPPLEMENT

[*The Face of War*] is another despairing cry from one who has seen many of the facets of war at close quarters. Mrs. Gellhorn acted as a war correspondent for *Collier's* and wrote her descriptive pieces from Spain in 1938 and from most of the fronts except the Russian during Hitler's war. Much of what she wrote she has now resurrected and bound together into a book by means of explanatory introductions and protesting comments. She justifies it all with the remark that what is wanted to-day is "memory and imagination, not nuclear weapons or the deterrents."

Hers was good reporting to begin with. Its pictures of the beastliness and tragedy of war are honestly matched with balancing experiences of what soldiers and airmen and Red Cross workers endured. ⟨. . .⟩

"War," she says in one of her comments, "was always worse than I knew how to say." That, of course, is the feeling of all sensitive people who have had to come close to it. It oppressed many a one who had had to endure the filth and futility of sodden trenches in the Kaiser's war. It so oppressed them that they came back fully persuaded that mankind would never condemn itself to a repetition, and some of them wrote all the misery into their books. Yet a generation was enough to bring something like a repeat performance.

Now Mrs. Gellhorn begins her attempt to keep memory green and to stimulate imagination by confessing that "wars are to be expected." But her point to-day is that then it was the "same nameless tragedy" of the present whether it was in Madrid or Helsinki or Chungking, whereas men now have the means to destroy the future as well and contemplate doing it "for the sake of freedom." She asks: whose freedom?

A pacifist from her youth, she does not deny or try to exclude hate. Her articles confess her hate of those German legions that forced their terror into France, of the torturers that made beastly the underground tunnels of Ivry and made sacred for the French the nearby cemetery. ⟨. . .⟩ All this revived evidence of what war entails does at least enable her to declaim: "Let us not think anyone can use frightfulness in a good cause." And for her the zenith of modern frightfulness would consist in the use of nuclear weapons.

Her arguments, thus backed by the tales she told all those years ago, are powerful. Only her belief that men must by now have learnt the lesson of self-interest vitiates her thesis. She admits that mankind in the lump, however prudent, however humanitarian, has found no way to do the leading and to make sure it shall not lead to war. We who remember the horrors and can imagine worse, she says, are the led, the governed, the nameless victims. And there the case against the right of any leader to condemn the future rests.

—N.A., "The War to End War," *The Times Literary Supplement* (11 September 1959): 515

NIGEL NICOLSON

[*The Face of War*] is a collection of dispatches from four recent wars—Spain, Finland, China and the European end of the Second World war. They were first published in *Collier's* ⟨. . . .⟩ [Gellhorn's] business was to get herself to the war, and to say what war felt like, how it affected the attackers, the defenders and the innocent. She could have made a new book about her experiences, lifting the better phrases from her past articles. She spurned the idea. She has courageously reprinted the articles themselves, tidying the hurried syntax a bit, but damaging none of their immediacy. Undoubtedly she was one of the best correspondents whom the War produced, and today her articles are as fresh as striped shirts returned from the wash.

War-reports like Miss Gellhorn's appear to write themselves. You have only to go to a front-line position, on board a hospital ship, to a prison camp, or on patrol in a fighter-bomber, and make a mental note of the details observed and the remarks made, to become, as Miss Gellhorn describes herself, 'a walking tape-recorder with eyes'. ⟨. . .⟩ How can you go wrong? You can go wrong by indiscretion, by overwriting, by attributing false motives, by the misuse of the dangerous literary device of understatement, by making your word-pictures unbelievably neat or heroic. She made none of these mistakes. She only erred when she came to point morals.

Her moral is, 'War is a crime against the living and always has been'. It is a dangerous platitude, and one which Miss Gellhorn herself contradicts. War is not always a crime. For if a people are living under a tyranny, or are threatened by one, it can be noble to overthrow it by force. She was in no doubt whatever that the Spanish Republicans were right to fight. So were the Finns, the Chinese. The Second World War, she writes in a concluding passage, was waged to abolish Dachau and everything that Dachau stood for: her only qualification of the rightness of that war is that we should have started it three years earlier, in Spain. So in her view war can be a legitimate means of defending the living, as well as a crime against them.

Her book is not a No against all war. It is one of the loudest Yesses yet pronounced. She does not see her soldiers and airmen as unwilling instruments of politicians, but as thinking human beings making a splendid personal choice. She willed them on by her pen. But the other side, whether they were Spanish fascists, Japs, Russians (when fighting in Finland), or Germans, particularly Germans, were almost without exception mean, brutal and despicable. 'Cologne,' she could write, 'is a startling sight. We are not shocked by it'; and then, as if a little ashamed of herself, she adds, 'which only goes to prove that if you see enough of anything you stop noticing it'. She does herself discredit: she never stopped noticing misery. The reason why she did not grieve over Cologne was because it was German. Similarly she admires patriotism, but not German patriotism: 'They were simply not people like us; there was no common place where we could meet'. But there was: the battlefield, and the beastly emotions induced on it. When the GIs during the Battle of the Bulge told her that the Ardennes was 'wonderful Kraut-killing country', she did not flicker an eyelid. The Germans were simply obstacles to be removed, like road-blocks, and the process was not horrible because it demanded great courage on the part of her friends.

This is all very well, and was perhaps necessary at the time. But does it become a great No against war when reprinted fifteen years later? I do not think it does.

—Nigel Nicolson, "A Woman at the Wars," *New Statesman* 58, no. 1492 (17 October 1959): 517–18

EMILY HAHN

Martha Gellhorn is a gentleperson. For 42 pages ⟨in *Travels with Myself and Another*⟩ she writes about an Unwilling Companion on her trip into China's interior in 1941, always referring to him as U. C. and never mentioning that he was in fact her husband, Ernest Hemingway. This—at a time when to have been Hemingway's wife ⟨. . .⟩ seems excuse enough to publish every possible remembrance of the great man—entitles Miss Gellhorn to a medal, at least. But her excellence does not stop there. She renders U. C. justice: she makes him a sympathetic as well as amusing figure, although perhaps a wee bit maddening. ⟨. . .⟩

U. C. apart, Miss Gellhorn can be exceedingly funny on her own. Often, reading of her travels—in China of course, the Caribbean ⟨. . .⟩, Russia and Israel, to name the headliners—I chuckled in a ladylike, repressed manner, but sometimes I had to stop to laugh really loud. Not that Martha Gellhorn is merely entertaining. She is a thoughtful woman with a lot of serious opinions, and whether or not one agrees with her, as I often didn't, it is worth reflecting on her reflections.

—Emily Hahn, "Moving Lady," *The New York Times Book Review* (23 September 1979): 15

BRETT HARVEY

In 1978, Gellhorn published a book called *Travels with Myself and Another* that has to be one of the funniest travel books ever written. Its conceit is "horror journeys" and it includes trips to Africa, Moscow, the Caribbean, and Israel, as well as the trek she and Hemingway made into China in 1941. This piece is a glowering, Perelmanesque chronicle of heart-stopping flights over mountains in tiny, rickety planes, bone-jolting jeep rides through jungles, terrifying journeys on ancient Chriscrafts, and rooms which feature planks for beds, overflowing toilets, and clouds of malarial mosquitoes. "I wish," says the author in one such room, "to die." Hemingway, although referred to throughout as U. C., or "Unwilling Companion," emerges as a splendid fellow traveler—patient, unflappable, able to see comic possibilities in the most appalling conditions. This is the only thing I've ever read that made me think it might have been *fun* to be married to Hemingway.

Travels with Myself and Another is such a hoot it's really a shame she didn't do more of this kind of writing. But then Gellhorn wouldn't be Gellhorn if she weren't contrary. Her contradictions endear her to me. She's a pacifist who could never stay away from war, indeed seemed driven to push in as close as she could get to every battlefront. She's a feminist with a blind spot about women. She fought hard to subdue her ambition and hunger for excitement, and squash herself into the role of helpmeet to the most celebrated writer of her day. She tried to be a wife, but she simply couldn't stay home. And finally she had the sense and the guts to buck the prevailing stand-by-your-man-no-matter-what-especially-if-he's-a-Genius ideology, and carve out an independent life for herself. For a woman with an appetite for fun and booze and comfort and good conversation, Gellhorn has spent a hell of a lot of time in terrible places, with wretched accommodations, recording people's misery and suffering. She may not be a *great* writer, but she never bores, especially if you read her work in the context of her singular life. I like knowing there's a Martha Gellhorn in the world. I like her style.

—Brett Harvey, "Being There," *Voice Literary Supplement* 61 (December 1987): 12–14

KIRSTY MILNE

This collection of Martha Gellhorn's peacetime journalism ⟨*The View from the Ground*⟩ spans six decades ⟨. . . .⟩ In these pages she watches Adolf Eichmann being tried in Jerusalem for the murder of European Jewry; joins peaceful protests in Washington against the Vietnam war; puzzles over communist economics in Poland; and holds her breath with Spain after the death of Franco.

That one person in a lifetime could bear witness to all this gives *The View from the Ground* the burnished status of a historical document. But there's nothing here of the fossil; Martha Gellhorn's writing is spiked with intelligence, individualism and moral indignation.

She celebrates private heroism in the torture rooms of El Salvador and the muddy tents of Greenham Common. Subjects where melodrama or sentiment might lurk get direct and fearless treatment. Visiting Italian orphanages after the war, Gellhorn does not avoid the obvious poignancy of children left homeless, injured and sometimes deranged by the bombing of Italian cities. But she digs beneath the pathos to pinpoint a buried social problem: how to heal the terrible scars left by the war on the coming generation.

Very occasionally, her genuinely felt anger congeals into a righteous sarcasm and her powers of perception are directed to proving a point—nowhere more obtrusively than on a tour of Palestinian refugee camps in Jordan and the Gaza strip before the 1967 war. In championing Israel she, who elsewhere deals so forcefully in the uniqueness of suffering, seems determined to deny the Palestinians theirs. Because the Poles are cultured and rueful, they command her admiration and her sympathy; but when Palestinians complain loudly about their statelessness, Gellhorn hears only self-pity and invention—a rare blindspot in the vision of a humane and independent-minded woman.

—Kirsty Milne, "An American Cassandra," *New Statesman & Society* 2, no. 67 (15 September 1989): 36

JEREMY HARDING

⟨In *The View from the Ground*⟩ Gellhorn's pact with conscience seems to adjourn some lengthy trial of her own, in which the writer who has practised journalism, as a form of political intervention for 25 years acknowledges defeat—defeat in Spain, in Czechoslovakia, at Dachau, none of them quite redeemed by the Allied victory—and accepts that her case against oppression and injustice, having failed to change the world, will now have to rest largely on personal conviction. In fact, the court never convenes for a full session again, for Gellhorn is quickly bored by questions of personal motivation. Instead, she makes a run for it, returning to the fray with all her former anger and energy. On handguns in America, the war in Vietnam, the miners' strike, El Salvador, the approach is more or less unaltered. Similar conclusions about the ills of American imperialism, the follies of government and the evils of poverty are drawn. Regimes commit the same crimes, the powerful are still cowards and abusers, the poor are still pushed around. From pasture to pasture in Martha Gellhorn's extensive grazing, there is no such thing as greener grass.

What emerges instead is a set of archetypes for 20th-century politics, disposed like figures on a ground: from Spain, Czechoslovakia, Vietnam and Central America comes the stooping refugee; from the Depression, the 'basement' of the Great Society and the dole queues of London at the end of the Seventies comes the poor man in the developed capitalist state; from a bestiary of bad or indifferent leaders—Franco, Hitler, Ronald Reagan, Margaret Thatcher—comes the bully. Finally there is the figure of technology, the only abstract on display, which has haunted Gellhorn ever since she saw the effects of German armaments in Spain and which remains for her an instrument used by the powerful to punish the poor. In her writings from the Seventies and Eighties, these archetypes have solidified in the collieries of South Wales, the prisons of El Salvador and the homes of the unemployed in London, but seldom does the work feel like a rehearsal of old preoccupations. It is wholly attentive to the matter in hand.

—Jeremy Harding, "Her Guns," *London Review of Books* 12, no. 5 (8 March 1990): 14

B I B L I O G R A P H Y

What Mad Pursuit. 1934.

The Trouble I've Seen. 1936.

A Stricken Field. 1940.

The Heart of Another. 1941.

Liana. 1944, 1987.

Love Goes to Press (with V. Cowles). 1947.

The Wine of Astonishment. 1948; published as *Point of No Return*, 1989.

The Honeyed Peace. 1953.

Two by Two. 1958.

The Face of War. 1959; revised and enlarged, 1967, 1986.

His Own Man. 1961.

Pretty Tales for Tired People. 1965.

Vietnam: A New Kind of War. 1966.

The Lowest Trees Have Tops. 1967, 1969.

Travels with Myself and Another. 1978.

The Weather in Africa. 1978, 1980.

The View from the Ground. 1988.

Point of No Return. 1995.

LILLIAN HELLMAN
1905–1984

LILLIAN HELLMAN was born in New Orleans on June 20, 1905, to Max and Julia Newhouse Hellman, native southerners. The family moved to New York City, where Lillian attended public schools, New York University, and Columbia University. From 1924 to 1925 she read manuscripts for the publishing house of Horace Liveright and came into contact with many literary figures. At the age of 20 she married playwright Arthur Kober. Hellman, who had been writing fiction since her youth, now began to write book reviews and press releases and became a play reader and Hollywood scenarist. Hellman and Kober were divorced in 1932, however, after Hellman began an intimate friendship with the novelist Dashiell Hammett, a relationship that would continue until his death in 1961.

During the 1930s, Hellman began writing plays. It was Hammett who encouraged her to write what would become her first major literary achievement, *The Children's Hour*, produced in 1934. Set in a girls' boarding school, the play tells the story of two schoolteachers who are destroyed when a malicious child accuses them of lesbianism. *Days to Come* (1936) is about a strike; *The Little Foxes* (1939) portrays a ruthless southern family's struggle to retain its wealth and power; *Watch on the Rhine* (1941), about an anti-Nazi who, with his American wife, commits a murder in a fight against Nazism, and *The Searching Wind* (1944), about the family of a former U.S. ambassador in wartime Washington and prewar Europe, are indictments of the selfishness of the Versailles Treaty generation. *Another Part of the Forest* was produced in 1946; *The Autumn Garden*, a Chekhovian drama about middle-aged people trying to regain a sense of youth, appeared in 1951. *Toys in the Attic* (1960) is set in New Orleans and treats the theme of miscegenation. Although much of her work is intensely political, Hellman's realistic dialogue keeps her characters from becoming merely didactic figures espousing her views.

In addition to creating her own dramatic work, Hellman interpreted and translated that of others. She translated Jean Anouilh's *The Lark* in 1955 and collaborated with Richard Wilbur on a musical adaptation of Voltaire's *Candide* in 1957. In 1963 she adapted Burt Blechman's novel *How Much?* to the stage as *My Mother, My Father, and Me*. She edited Anton Chekhov's *Selected Letters* in 1955 and a collection of stories and short novels by Dashiell Hammett, *The Big Knockover*, in 1966.

Hellman's autobiographical writings were published in three volumes: *An Unfinished Woman* (1969), *Pentimento* (1973), *Maybe* (1980). In *Scoundrel Time* (1976) Hellman recounts her experiences during the McCarthy hearings and her own appearance before the House Un-American Activities Committee. Her memoiristic works received strong and mixed criticism, and she herself speculated frequently on the forms and reliability of memory.

Lillian Hellman died of a heart attack on June 30, 1984, at Vineyard Haven, Martha's Vineyard, Massachusetts.

CRITICAL   EXTRACTS

MURRAY KEMPTON

⟨*Scoundrel Time*⟩ is the third of the meditations of Miss Hellman's memory. Its single theme is her summons by the House Committee on Un-American Activities in 1952, her decision to refuse to yield up the names of Communists she had known, the worse trouble with the Hollywood blacklist that followed that trouble, and the dignity and the shrewdness that carried her through both.

Miss Hellman has developed a style for these discourses very close to the ideal style for letters, say, from an aunt who is envied for her experience of the world and enjoyed for her candor and her comic sense whenever they are directed at persons other than oneself—always a comfortable majority of the cases—amusing, affecting, persuasive, entirely charming, if you don't too much mind being hectored now and then.

Her nieces seem somehow luckier than her nephews. Nieces, I suspect, read her letters for that feminine wisdom condemned to be misunderstood as womanly folly: the sensibility that armors itself with a Balmain dress for the ordeal by the Committee on Un-American Activities, the taste that notices the habit awkward social occasions have of being accompanied by bad food, the gaiety that conquers dread with shopping sprees. It is hard for nephews to find that much unforced pleasure in Miss Hellman; they have to be wary of possible disapproval.

I have never quite understood upon what altar Miss Hellman's moral authority was consecrated, but that authority is there, was there even before the apotheosis of her risky yet grand appearance before the Committee on Un-American Activities. ⟨. . .⟩

Miss Hellman's strength of character is great, but of a kind that is hard to comprehend apart from its candid snobbishness. When she searches for the

core of the self that enabled her to resist and left Clifford Odets naked to sur-
render to the House Committee on Un-American Activities, she can return
with no discovery more useful than: "It is impossible to think that a grown
man, intelligent, doesn't have some sense of how he will act under pressure. It's
all been decided so long ago, when you are very young, all mixed up with your
childhood's definition of pride or dignity." Or elsewhere:

> Many [American intellectuals] found in the sins of Stalin
> Communism—and there were plenty of sins and plenty that for a
> long time I mistakenly denied—the excuse to join those who should
> have been their hereditary enemies. Perhaps that, in part, was the
> penalty of nineteenth-century immigration. The children of timid
> immigrants are often remarkable people: energetic, intelligent, hard-
> working; and often they make it so good that they are determined to
> keep it at any cost.

Observations of that tenor somehow suggest that for strong spirits like
Miss Hellman's, the Sunday family dinner is material for rebellion in childhood, comedy in middle age, and attitudes in final maturity. What is here inti-
mated is some doctrine of predestination by growing up with servants in the
kitchen, but it is not easy to think such a notion prepossessing and impossible
to find it serviceable as a measurement for moral development.
—Murray Kempton, "Witnesses," *New York Review of Books* (10 June 1976): 22

JOHN HERSEY

Lillian Hellman has long been known as a moral force, almost an institution of
conscience for the rest of us—but my view is that her influence, and her help
to us, derive rather from something larger: the picture she gives of a *life* force.

It is the complexity of this organism that stuns and quickens us. Energy,
gifts put to work, anger, wit, potent sexuality, wild generosity, a laugh that can
split your eardrums, fire in every action, drama in every anecdote, a ferocious
sense of justice, personal loyalty raised to the power of passion, fantastic legs
and easily turned ankles, smart clothes, a strong stomach, an affinity with the
mothering sea, vanity but scorn of all conceit, love of money and gladness in
parting with it, a hidden religious streak but an open hatred of piety, a yearn-
ing for compliments but a loathing for flattery, fine cookery, a smashing style
in speech and manners, unflagging curiosity, fully liberated female aggressive-
ness when it is needed yet a whiff, now and then, of old-fashioned feminine
masochism, fear however of nothing but being afraid, prankishness, flirtatious
eyes, a libertine spirit. Puritanism, rebelliousness.

Rebelliousness above all. Rebelliousness is an essence of her vitality—that
creative sort of dissatisfaction which shouts out, "Life ought to be better than

this!" Every great artist is a rebel. The maker's search for new forms—for ways of testing the givens—is in her a fierce rebellion against what has been accepted and acclaimed and taken for granted. And a deep, deep rebellious anger against the great cheat of human existence, which is death, feeds her love of life and gives bite to her enjoyment of every minute of it. This rebelliousness, this anger, Lillian Hellman has in unusually great measure, and they are at the heart of the complex vibrancy we feel in her.

But all the attributes I have listed are only the beginnings of her variousness. She has experienced so much! She has had an abortion. She has been analyzed. She has been, and still is, an ambulatory chimney. She drinks her whiskey neat. She has been married and divorced. She has picked up vast amounts of higgledy-piggledy learning, such as how to decapitate a snapping turtle, and I understand that as soon as she completes her dissertation, said to be startlingly rich in research, she will have earned the degree of Doctor of Carnal Knowledge. This is in spite of the fact that during a long black period of American history she imposed celibacy on herself. She will admit, if pressed, that she was the sweetest-smelling baby in New Orleans. As a child she knew gangsters and whores. She has been a liberated woman ever since she played hookey from grade school and perched with her fantasies in the hidden fig tree in the yard of her aunts' boarding house. She is so liberated that she is not at all afraid of the kitchen. She can pluck and cook a goose and her spaghetti with clam sauce begs belief. She can use an embroidery hoop. She knows how to use a gun. She cares with a passion whether bedsheets are clean. She grows the most amazing roses which are widely thought to be homosexual. She speaks very loud to foreigners, believing the language barrier can be pierced with decibels. She scarfs her food with splendid animal relish, and I can tell you that she has not vomited since May 23, 1952. She must have caught several thousand fish by now, yet she still squeals like a child when she boats a strong blue. I know no living human being whom so many people consider to be their one best friend. ⟨. . .⟩

We must come back around the circle now to the rebelliousness, the life-force anger, with which Miss Hellman does live, still growing every day. There was a year of sharp turn toward rebelliousness in her, when she was 13 or 14. By the late 1930s or early '40s, she had realized that no political party would be able to contain this quality of hers. Yet the pepper in her psyche—her touchiness, her hatred of being physically pushed even by accident, her out-of-control anger whenever she feels she has been dealt with unjustly—all have contributed in the end to her being radically political while essentially remaining outside formal politics. Radically, I mean, in the sense of "at the root." She cuts through all ideologies to their taproot: to the decency their adherents universally profess, but almost never deliver. "Since when," she has written, "do you have to agree with people to defend them from injustice?" Her response to McCarthyism was not ideological, it was, "I will not do this indecent thing. Go jump in the lake." Richard Nixon has testified under oath that her Committee for Public Justice frightened J. Edgar Hoover into discontinuing illegal wiretaps. How? By shaming.

Lillian Hellman is popular now, and needed now, because her stern code touches the national nerve at just the right moment—after Nixonism . . . before what?

Important as this is, our need for her, as I suggested at the outset, is far larger than that. In her plays, in her writings, out of memory, above all in her juicy, resonant, headlong, passionate self, she gives us glimpses of *all* the possibilities of life on this mixed-up earth. In return we can only thank her, honor her, and try to live as wholeheartedly as she does.

—John Hersey, "Lillian Hellman," *New Republic* (18 September 1976): 25–27

ALFRED KAZIN

Lillian Hellman's *Scoundrel Time* has been more than a big seller: it has convinced the generation that has grown up since the Fifties that the author was virtually alone in refusing to name past or present Communist party members to the House Un-American Activities Committee, that the only issue in 1952 was whether you were personally a baddie instead of a hero like her great love Dashiell Hammett. Hammett went to jail for refusing to name the donors of a fund set up to support Communists, the Civil Rights Congress.

It was not only the young who adored *Scoundrel Time*: it was that great body of liberal Americans who are either inattentive to historical facts or have never known them. Studs Terkel said of Hellman, "Let it be recorded that she is merely great." The many adoring reviews of *Scoundrel Time*—most of them quoting Hellman's remark "I cannot and will not cut my conscience to fit this year's fashions"—were ignorant and simpleminded; Hellman's celebration of herself and Hammett was accepted uncritically. The book was sentimental and evasive in its portrait of Hammett. It was totally in error in stating that the documents in Whittaker Chambers' famous pumpkin that nailed Alger Hiss were of no significance. (The pumpkin contained microfilms—two of them reproductions of State Department memoranda to which Hiss had access—plus copies of cables initialed by Hiss.) Hellman obfuscated the fact that H.U.A.C. dismissed her after a little more than an hour because she took the Fifth Amendment when there was no need to: she steadfastly denied ever having been a Communist party member, so there would have been no legal force to her naming anybody. And the book featured a historical introduction by Garry Wills, formerly an extreme rightist and a proponent of war against the

Communist forces of evil, who now acclaimed Hellman as the greatest woman dramatist in all American history and, with the same discrimination, proceeded to blame the cold war and McCarthyism entirely on Truman. ⟨. . .⟩

The success of *Scoundrel Time* is due in part to Hellman's long-standing grievance against government in America. This cannot but please a generation sickened by Vietnam, Watergate, governmental snooping, taxation on every civic level. The young, unlike old leftists and ex-leftists now in their seventies, have no interest in Russia but are understandably suspicious of their own government, so overgrown, unwieldy, secretive, demanding, hideously costly. ⟨. . .⟩ Lillian Hellman has been dramatizing herself ever since she stopped writing plays. She can dramatize anything about herself and she has done herself, Dashiell Hammett, her old retainers, the many people she hates, with a Broadway skill that is a mixture of social snottiness and glib liberalism. A large audience—if it includes many people who disagree with her if they ever think about it—finds her so-called memoirs irresistible.

If you wonder how a nonfiction book can have so much dialogue and why there should be so many baddies in her innocent life, the answer is that Broadway will rewrite anything. ⟨. . .⟩

Hellman is easy on herself and Hammett, exquisitely nasty to those with whom she disagrees. Henry Wallace didn't seem to know that Communists were running his 1948 campaign until she told him. What she does then is mark him down for being dumb; pushes him down even more for being a stingy rube in restaurants; scorns his wife for serving a ridiculous supper of one egg on shredded wheat. She then caps the performance by explaining to Wallace that the Communists running him "'don't . . . mean any harm; they're stubborn men.' 'I see,' he said, and that was that." But it isn't. *Scoundrel Time* is historically a fraud, artistically a put-up job and emotionally packed with meanness. Oh, these ancient positions and position takers! These glib morality plays about goodies and baddies in a world where millions have died, will go on dying, for not taking the correct "line"!

It cannot be said of Lillian Hellman, as was said of Henry James, that she has a mind so fine that "no idea can violate it." She is full of ideas. So, in another bad time, her book has pleased all those who think that Stalin lived in the time of Ivan the Terrible and that her taking the Fifth Amendment in 1952 gives political sanction and importance in the 1970's to her self-approval and her every dogged resentment.

—Alfred Kazin, "The Legend of Lillian Hellman," *Esquire* (August 1977): 28, 30, 34

KATHERINE LEDERER

A generation of theater-goers and theater students have been conditioned to associate the name Hellman with the terms "well-made play," "melodrama," "social protest." If this cultural reflex persists, then Hellman's metaphor of fashion in the theater will continue to describe her critical reputation.

An unnecessary stumbling block to a fresh perception of Hellman is the "political" label. Although, as Jacob Adler comments, "to one assessing her as an artist, politics—particularly her political problems in the Fifties—seems almost entirely beside the point," political partisanship is not likely to subside in the foreseeable future.

The Hellman vision is nonetheless moral, not political. Robert Corrigan and John Gassner arrived independently at the same judgment: Gassner said, "Miss Hellman concerns herself generally with damnation as a state of the soul, and a case might be made out for saying that her real theme, whether she knew it or not, is 'original sin' in a modern context, which brings her closer to such contemporary Catholic writers as Mauriac than to Bernard Shaw or Karl Marx." Corrigan concluded that "she cannot be considered, as she so often is, a social writer; rather, she is interested in showing damnation as a state of the soul, a condition that cannot be reformed out of existence or dissolved by sentimentality or easy optimism."

Murray Kempton said that Hellman's behavior before the House committee was partly determined by her sense of how things would look in due course. For "in due course" substitute the "days to come" of the Old Testament, days determined by human actions today. Engagement, commitment, self-knowledge, and self-acknowledgment of responsibility are the virtues Hellman urges on her audiences and readers. If the memoirs had never been written, the moral vision is clear in play after play.

As critics of the memoirs have pointed out, Hellman's moral vision is inseparable from the ironic vision and voice. Though obviously more overt in the memoirs, the voice is there in the plays. And, "[a]s soon as an ironic voice has been used to any extent in any work of any kind," says Wayne Booth, "readers inevitably begin to take interest and pleasure in that voice—in the tasks it assigns and the qualities it provides; it thus becomes part of whatever is seen as the controlling context."

In *The Context and Craft of Drama*, James Rosenberg raises a pertinent question: "why must generic classification necessarily degenerate into a game of hierarchies? Is it not enough to perceive that there are various modes of perception . . .?" What we should recognize is "a way of seeing, not a trick of writing."

Any final judgment must include a perception of Hellman as ironist, with a way of seeing, and seeing again. This is not to say that such an awareness will necessarily cause a reader to prefer Hellman to other major American playwrights. But it should prevent one's judging her by inapplicable criteria. To "rank" Hellman in a Williams-Miller-Odets-whoever list is, as she might put it, "a losing game." In the modern American theater Lillian Hellman is *sui*

generis, and a careful reading of her plays reveals that those generally considered her best (*The Little Foxes, The Autumn Garden, Toys in the Attic*—to which list
might be added *Watch on the Rhine* and *Another Part of the Forest*) are the most fully
ironic (and novelistic). By the same criteria, *Pentimento,* in which Hellman most
completely employs fictional techniques and a controlling ironic voice, is the
superior memoir.

D. C. Muecke has described irony as "intellectual rather than musical,
nearer to the mind than to the senses, reflective and self-conscious rather than
lyrical and self-absorbed," having the qualities of "fine prose rather than . . .
lyric poetry." Readers and audiences with no predilection for irony will perhaps prefer Arthur Miller's pathos of the common man, or perhaps Tennessee
Williams' poetry of the sensitive, bruised soul. There will always be those,
however, who will turn to Lillian Hellman for a view of life trenchantly
expressed, often moving, frequently funny, uncomfortably accurate in its
ironic vision of the fools met in the forest—and the fools *those* fools meet. In
judging Lillian Hellman's work, critics might abandon the automatic genre
labeling and examine her way of seeing and her appraisal of things seen,
remembering that there is more than one valid way of looking at a blackbird.
And a writer.

    —Katherine Lederer, "An Ironic Vision," *Lillian Hellman* (1979), excerpted in *Twentieth-Century*
    American Literature, ed. Harold Bloom (New York: Chelsea House Publishers, 1986), 1790

MARTHA GELLHORN

Miss Lillian Hellman⟨'s . . .⟩ memoir *An Unfinished Woman* ⟨AUW⟩ I read with
unfathomed amazement. Goodness to Betsy, I said to myself, what an *important*
lady. How marvelous for Miss Hellman to be Miss Hellman. This book reads
like a novel, I thought, and then found that *Pentimento* reads like excellent short
stories. In my specialized study of apocryphism, Miss Hellman ranks as sub-
lime. ⟨. . .⟩

⟨. . .⟩ My favorite apocryphal story ⟨. . .⟩ begins on the last line of p. 63,
AUW: "I liked Ernest." Hemingway had not "just come out of Spain" (p. 64,
AUW). He had sailed from New York on the Champlain two days ahead of
me; in that pre-historic past, we tried steadily though in vain to be discreet.
On p. 65, AUW, Miss H. writes: "Hemingway and Parker, who did not like
each other but who in those weeks were trying hard to mask it from the
Murphys." We are meant to think that Hemingway spent night after night
with Miss H., Dottie ⟨Parker⟩ and Alan ⟨Campbell⟩ "in those weeks." "I don't
remember that Martha Gellhorn joined us, perhaps she was not in Paris." I was,
and with Hemingway; we had six merry hiding days and did our chores for the
return to Spain.

One day Hemingway felt he had to call on Dottie Parker as some sort of anti-gossip ploy. He went alone (more discretion) for an evening drink; Herbert Matthews and I met him in the lobby of their hotel—the Meurice according to Miss Hellman—to go to dinner. He loped toward us, closely resembling a horse that has escaped from a burning stable, with a smear of lipstick on his collar. I went to Le Lavandou to swim for a few days and returned to Paris. Hemingway and I left for Spain on September 6, arriving in Valencia on September 7. Spain was the focus of his life then, not auld lang syne. He never mentioned seeing them after that one drink-time meeting; but I cannot prove how he passed three nights at the beginning of September. So much for Miss H's buddyhood with Hemingway "in those weeks."

Miss H's story picks up speed on p. 65, AUW: "One night after dinner, when we usually parted, the Campbells and I, led by Ernest moved around Paris," etc., Miss H., feeling "drunk and headachy," returned to her hotel room. After she had been asleep for two or three hours, Hemingway pounded on her door (what was the night concierge at the Meurice thinking of?) with whiskey and a package, the proofs of *To Have and Have Not*. Thereafter Hemingway sat in her room all night, while Miss H. read the proofs. When dawn came she made some highly perceptive but rather critical remarks about the ending of the book, which annoyed Hemingway. In the hotel hall, on his way out, he said, "I wish I could sleep with you but I can't because there's somebody else. I hope you understand." Furious at this presumption, Miss H. woke Mrs. Parker who, bright as a button in the dawn's early light, spoke knowingly but improbably about Max Perkins and Hemingway's bad cutting to shorten the book, and soothed Miss H's wrath over the half-offer of sexual intercourse. As dawn conversations go, it is a winner. This anecdote runs from p. 65 through p. 67. It ends: "The next day I left for Moscow, changing trains in Berlin."

Now turn to *Pentimento*, p. 108: "I left a note for them ⟨Dottie and Alan⟩ saying I was leaving early in the morning and would find them again after Moscow . . . Now I lay down, determined that I would not sleep until I had taken stock of myself . . . In any case, I slept through the night and rose only in time to hurry for the early morning train." Turn next to p. 112, *Pentimento*; "I think I have always known about my memory; I know when it is to be trusted and when some dream or fantasy entered on the life, and the dream, the need of dream, led to distortion of what happened . . . *But I trust absolutely what I remember about Julia.*" (My italics.)

Which Miss Hellman shall we believe, if any?

—Martha Gellhorn, "Close Encounters of the Apocryphal Kind," *Paris Review* 23, no. 79 (Spring 1981): 286, 290–91

LINDA WAGNER-MARTIN

If autobiography is at once a personal and a fictional mode, as William Spengemann has recently suggested, then Lillian Hellman's last four books provide apt illustration of the conflict inherent in that description. *An Unfinished Woman* (1969), *Pentimento* (1973), *Scoundrel Time* (1976), and *Maybe, A Story* (1980) tell and retell the story of parts of Hellman's life, but one telling may differ from the account told elsewhere. Clearly, Hellman is using the process of autobiography both to explore her memories and to challenge the notion that recollection is a means to truth (or, in the words of James Olney, autobiography is a "monument of the self as it is becoming"). Hellman writes with recognition of this exploration in *Maybe, A Story*: "What I have written is the truth as I saw it, but the truth as I saw it, of course, doesn't have much to do with the truth . . . . It's no news that each of us has our own reasons for pretending, denying, affirming what was there and never there. And sometimes, of course, we have really forgotten. In my case, I have often forgotten what was important, what mattered to me most, what made me take an action that changed my life. And then, in time, people and reasons were lost in deep summer grass."

The progression from her first memoir, *An Unfinished Woman*, through *Pentimento* and *Scoundrel Time* to the "story" of *Maybe*, helps the reader chart Hellman's search for personal truth, and for a means of recording it. *An Unfinished Woman* seems to be conventional autobiography, at least the first two-thirds of it. Hellman appears at its center; she is on stage throughout, and she also interprets happenings so that "truth" and "meaning" are in some episodes translated for the reader. ⟨. . .⟩

⟨. . .⟩ By the time of *Maybe*, Hellman would have relinquished the well-turned phrase for the sense of reality—groping, confusion, dismay—which might have made this particular set of memories more effective. Until a third of the way through *An Unfinished Woman*, the reader is bothered by the feeling that there is too much finish.

Once the chronology of the memoir becomes fragmented (Hellman's memories of the 1930s and 1940s coalesce around her relationship with Dashiell Hammett, about whom she seldom speaks directly, and her stays in both Spain and Russia), the style begins to fit the experience in a way different from that of the opening section. The accounts of Spain and Russia are given as journal entries, scene leading to scene, and the presumption seems to be that the reader knows the contexts of the trips. The textures and tone of the experience is the valuable focus, not mere facts and dates. ⟨. . .⟩ Hellman by the very mode of telling her story emphasizes the insignificance of factual information. Poem-like, the whole of *An Unfinished Woman* asks the reader to believe that the juxtapositions, the breaks in narrative, the sense of timeless-

ness (scene fused with scene, Hellman's personality recognizable as fragile, dependent yet rebellious, regardless of time) are all calculated to bring the life of Lillian Hellman into comprehension, even if partial. Throughout these books, Hellman ducks the role of author as oracle. In her narrative method of setting scene beside scene, she more nearly assumes the role of observer: here it is; remember the image; appreciate it. And perhaps later, on your own, experience these fragments as a whole. The "knowledge" of Lillian Hellman, both subject and observer, is—and must be—limited.
    —Linda Wagner-Martin, "Lillian Hellman: Autobiography and Truth," *Southern Review* 19, no. 2 (April 1983): 275–77

TIMOTHY DOW ADAMS

Distinctions between historical reporting and personal narrative, as well as between true and false, fiction and nonfiction, are inherently complicated, without reversals of previous political positions, the encroachment of time, deliberate and accidental falsity of memory, and the differing requirements of veracity in various genres. Halfway through *Maybe* Hellman wrote: "It goes without saying that in their memoirs people should try to tell the truth as they see it or else what's the sense? Maybe time blurs or changes things for them. But you try, anyway" ⟨*Maybe*, 1980, 50⟩. But this assertion of trustworthiness—which includes a rhetorical appeal to veracity by admitting the possibility of failure of execution of the intention to tell the truth—occurs within a book that is labeled "A Story." *Maybe*'s generic situation is further confused by its physical appearance as a book: the standard paperback edition continues the color scheme of *Three*—black cover, title in gold accented with red stripes—making it seem to be part of the same package. Hellman posits her attempt at telling the truth in her autobiographical trilogy as being different from what she had done in *Maybe*:

> In the three memoir books I wrote, I tried very hard for the truth. I did try, but here I don't know much of what really happened and never tried to find out. In addition to the ordinary deceptions that you and others make in your life, time itself makes time fuzzy and meshes truth with half truth . . . . What I have written is the truth as I saw it, but the truth as I saw it, of course, doesn't have much to do with the truth. ⟨*Maybe*, 50–51⟩

    Hellman's distinction between her subjective version of truth and the absolute truth of "what really happened," her contrast between the first three books and the last in terms of "history" and "personal history," is unnecessary according to ⟨Marcus K.⟩ Billson, who persuasively argues that all *memoirs* are subjective: "The memorialist's real intention, despite all claims to being an objective observer, is to use this source for subjective ends—to embody his own moral vision of the past. It is not the memorialist's desire to present men and events as they were (although he invariably thinks he is doing so), but rather to represent them as they appeared to him, as he experienced them, and as he remembered them" ⟨"The Memoir," 1977, 264⟩.

The contentions of her most antagonistic critics that Hellman is, at best, a tricky and disingenuous simplifier, at worst, a fraudulent liar should be addressed with the understanding that her four autobiographical works are literary documents, works of art that combine a variety of life-writing's forms (autobiography, biography, memoir, and diary). The major charges against her autobiographies can be summarized: she obscures her life by chronological discontinuity and a tendency toward reticence; she lies by omission because of her elliptical style and her too-meticulous attention to surface finish; she is falsely modest and naive, manipulating her position in history so that her political faults are diminished, her personal heroism augmented; she misrepresents her historical position before the House Committee on Un-American Activities (HCUA) and the split between anticommunists and anti-anticommunists; and most damning, she makes herself look heroic by claiming to aid "Julia" when actually she took the idea for "Julia" from another person's life. Although there are times in her autobiographies when Hellman is less than forthcoming, misleading, annoyingly moralistic and exasperatingly mean spirited, ultimately her autobiographies are exceptionally authentic portraits of America's greatest woman playwright, a woman whose life story has significance far beyond its literal events.

Because her major adverse critics have been political analysts, writing with a historian's approach, rather than literary critics well versed in contemporary autobiographical theory, her autobiographical writing has generally been misinterpreted, primarily because those who have criticized her have misunderstood her tone, failed to consider her four books as one unit, and overlooked the subtitles of her autobiographical performances. Those who have written favorably of Hellman's memoirs are primarily novelists and playwrights like Marsha Norman, who said of Hellman, "I am not interested in the degree to which she told the literal truth. The literal truth is, for writers, only half the story" ⟨New York Times, 27 August 1984⟩.

—Timothy Dow Adams, "'Lies Like Truth': Lillian Hellman's Autobiographies," in *Critical Essays on Lillian Hellman*, ed. Mark W. Estrin (Boston: G. K. Hall, 1989), 197–98

PAMELA S. BROMBERG

For Hellman to overcome her despair and attain ⟨. . .⟩ integrity in her private life, which *Scoundrel Time* celebrates in her public one, she must accept and affirm her past with all its blemishes and failures. In *Maybe* she struggles toward that accommodation by portraying herself in a far less complimentary light than she had in the earlier memoirs. She reveals her neurotic fear of her own body and sexuality, a humiliating instance of Hammett's many sexual infidelities and the pain those betrayals caused her, the real indignities of her heavy drinking, and a series of loveless relationships with people of whom she now disapproves. And throughout *Maybe* there is the fear of ending that becomes so clear at the book's close.

But, despite her efforts at truth and honesty, Hellman still engages in a misleading bit of pretense and denial. As if to shield herself against the pain of self-examination, she writes with an almost parodic toughness and disregard for the niceties of diction. Her style functions self-protectively, as a way of distancing the explosive material in *Maybe*, and also dramatically. Taking up where Dashiell Hammett left off, Hellman speaks with the slangy, hard-bitten voice of a detective who presents this part of her life as a mystery in need of solution: *"What I have written is the truth as I saw it, but the truth as I saw it, of course, doesn't have much to do with the truth. It's as if I have fitted parts of a picture puzzle and then a child overturned it and threw out some pieces"* ⟨*Maybe*, 51–52⟩. The subtitle "a story" is as much a clue to *Maybe*'s genre as it is a reflection of Hellman's concern about the relation of truth to fiction in autobiography.

The solution of the mystery in a detective story restores at least a degree of order and intelligibility to the often shabby, decadent world it portrays. The detective, therefore, despite his knowledge of evil and his ability to camouflage himself within the dark world of his prey, is in truth a figure of moral integrity and honor, a knight who slays the dragons of social corruption and individual depravity. For Hellman to write *Maybe* as a detective story without even the possibility of a solution is then to suggest that in reality good does not triumph over evil, that, as she suggested in *Scoundrel Time* in a more narrowly political context, intellect and knowledge, all the brightness of learning and liberalism, may be no match at all for the mystery and tenacity of evil. *Maybe* is disturbing not so much for its revelations about Hellman's neuroses or for its apparent disjunctiveness and coldness, but for its pessimism, its loss of faith in the power of memory and the recovery of the past. Even more sweepingly, it denies the possibility of any discovery at all, of the restoration of meaning and rightness to the world through the detective writer's quest to solve the mystery. Thus *Maybe* lacks narrative closure in a more profound sense than *An Unfinished Woman* and *Pentimento*, which promise either sequels or at least infinite rereadings of the past. *Maybe* records Hellman's discovery that the "missing pieces" are "black," at least concerning Carter Cameron. She cannot know the Camerons because they are elusively connected with evil and hence unreceptive to the order and salvation of understanding. But to resolve her crisis of despair the writer must accept and affirm the darkness of her past as well as the triumphs of love and honor that she celebrated in her earlier memoirs.

In *Maybe* Lillian Hellman explores a self that did not fit into the earlier memoirs or the selves she created in them. In a radical act of penitence, or pentimento, she reveals a hidden self that she had heretofore scrupulously guarded, and in so doing gives voice to the private struggles that characterize women's autobiographies as a genre. *Maybe* reveals at least some of the conflict and anxiety that Hellman suffered as a woman who defied socially prescribed roles. While Hellman may still be too quick to blame herself, *Maybe* can be read as an inchoate critique of the society and values that made her so frightened and guilty about her body, so vulnerable to misogyny, and so dependent on men's approval and acceptance.

—Pamela S. Bromberg, "Establishing the Woman and Constructing a Narrative in Lillian Hellman's Memoirs," in *Critical Essays on Lillian Hellman*, ed. Mark W. Estrin (Boston: G. K. Hall, 1989), 126–27

B I B L I O G R A P H Y

The Children's Hour. 1934.

Days to Come. 1936.

The Little Foxes. 1939.

Watch on the Rhine. 1941.

The North Star: A Motion Picture about Some Russian People. 1943.

The Searching Wind. 1944.

Another Part of the Forest. 1946.

Montserrat (adapted from E. Roblès). 1950.

The Autumn Garden. 1951.

The Lark (adapted from J. Anouilh). 1955.

Candide (adapted from Voltaire, with R. Wilbur, L. Bernstein, J. La Touche, D. Parker). 1957.

Toys in the Attic. 1960.

My Mother, My Father, and Me (adapted from B. Blechman, *How Much?*). 1963.

An Unfinished Woman. 1969.

Pentimento. 1973.

Scoundrel Time. 1976.

Three. 1979.

Maybe. 1980.

VIOLET HUNT
1866–1942

ISOBEL VIOLET HUNT was born in 1866 in Durham, England. As the daughter of landscape painter Alfred William Hunt and novelist Margaret Raine Hunt, she grew up among the pivotal artists and poets of the Pre-Raphaelite movement, including Robert Browning, Edward Burne-Jones, Ford Madox Brown, John Ruskin, and Christina and Dante Gabriel Rossetti, who would later be the subject of her highly acclaimed biography, *The Wife of Rossetti* (1932).

While in her early teens, Hunt studied painting at the South Kensington Art School and wrote poetry and fiction, mentored by Christina Rossetti. At 17, she met Oscar Wilde, shortly after he arrived in London. They developed a special friendship rumored to have culminated in Wilde's proposal of marriage. Although Hunt even as a young girl possessed what her mother called the "savoir vivre of a woman of 50," the association with Wilde marked her true coming of age, a 10-year relationship recorded in Hunt's unpublished essay "My Oscar."

In her early 20s, Hunt wrote a column for the *Pall Mall Gazette* and regularly contributed to other popular Victorian periodicals. A feminist who resisted conventional social mores and sexual repressiveness, Hunt created protagonists who were largely autobiographical— although the heroine of her first novel, *The Maiden's Progress* (1894), does eventually yield to convention and marry. Later novels, such as *Unkist, Unkind!* (1897) and *The White Rose of Weary Leaf* (1908), would delve into the female psyche and the complexities of sexual politics.

Hunt's artistic and sexual lives coalesced in her numerous love affairs with literary men, including W. H. Hudson, W. Somerset Maugham, and Oswald Crawford. She met Ford Madox Ford at *The English Review* in 1908, and the two began a long affair that produced several collaborative accomplishments, including the short story collection *Zeppelin Nights* (1916) and the discovery of young novelist D. H. Lawrence. Ford left Hunt in 1918, however, when he became involved with her friend Stella Bowen. The majority of Hunt's novels were written during this 10-year period, including *The Governess* (1913), which was begun by her mother and finished by Hunt.

In writing her later novels, *Their Lives* (1916) and *Their Hearts* (1921), Hunt drew much of the conflict from the difficult relationships she had with her two sisters, who opposed her sexually free lifestyle. In *The Flurried Years* (1926), an intimate memoir, Hunt used her novelistic abilities to portray vividly her insider's perspective on English literary society and her friendships with contemporaries like W. Somerset Maugham, Henry James, May Sinclair, Rebecca West, and H. G. Wells.

Until her death from syphilis on January 16, 1942, Hunt continued to live at the center of England's cultural elite, writing and remaining an active feminist.

CRITICAL   EXTRACTS

FREDERIC TABER COOPER

The White Rose of Weary Leaf, by Violet Hunt, is best defined as a sort of modern *Jane Eyre* story, possessing all the defects of the Charlotte Brontë school and few of its merits. It is sensational, melodramatic, often crude in construction and in character drawing—and nevertheless there is a certain relentless sincerity in the story of the central character, a certain poignant tragedy in her fate that make it a book difficult to lay aside, in spite of one's frequent sense of exasperation, and equally difficult to forget after finishing it. The Jane Eyre of this story is not an inexperienced young girl, but a sad, disillusioned woman, who has long looked the world in the face and expects nothing from it but injustice. The Mr. Rochester has been married, not once, but twice; the surviving wife is not crazed, but simply a self-satisfied little fool. The spectacular tragedy is not a fire, but a railroad wreck, and even here the wife, though badly hurt, insists upon recovering, in spite of the doctor's assurances that she will die. The man, however, allows the other woman to believe that the wife is dead; and from this initial wrong the story moves strongly on to a double expiation, told in a spirit of grim fatalism. It is astonishing that a book so faulty should here and there show streaks of such undeniable merit.

—Frederic Taber Cooper, [Review of *The White Rose of Weary Leaf*], *The Bookman* (August 1908): 578–80

MAY SINCLAIR

⟨Among Violet Hunt's novels⟩ there are five outstanding ones. These compel you to remember them: *White Rose of Weary Leaf, Their Lives, Their Hearts, Tales of the Uneasy,* and *Sooner or Later.* This last I should place a little lower than the other four. *White Rose,* even while remembered, can be read again and again with pleasure.

The others must be slightly forgotten to renew their appeal. They should be read separately with a stretch of time between. Taken as the critic must take them, one on the top of the other, their effect is a little stifling. There is a want of perspective and relief. It is like listening to a person with a fixed idea; like looking at repeated portraits of the same figure. There never was such a gallery of English *demi-vierges*.

To be sure, their demi-virginity is purely mental. They are betrayed first by their own minds. There is a *naïveté* about them, an innocent uncertainty. Rosette and Christina offer themselves to their lovers, but they only half know what they are doing; it is partly because they desire to know that they do it. Their passions are too exalted, too pathetic, too foredoomed to count as sensual. Their senses are dumb, unawakened, or superseded. It is their hearts that clamour, unsatisfying and unsatisfied. That is the trouble with them all. One burst of honest sensuality would have settled their business for them and left them calm. But no; they are too subtle for their own or their lovers' satisfaction. They are born to torture and be tortured. ⟨. . .⟩

Scenes repeat themselves. Passion, foreboding, reproach, recrimination, repudiation, despair, and more passion. A vicious circle. These figures have no background that counts. Wherever they are, the effect is always the same, of naked passions played out on bare boards before a dark curtain. They may be walking on the Yorkshire moors, or by the bracing north-eastern sea, in woods smelling of damp moss and earth, in gardens by the Solent, and instantly the air is changed; it becomes sultry with passion; it is the air of a stuffy bedroom with the windows tight shut; there is a smell of hair-brushes, cigarette smoke, and warm sachet.

We are least aware of it in *White Rose of Weary Leaf*, because the dominant character, Amy Stephens, is a higher and healthier type. The atmosphere is cleared by conflict, by the beating of her wings as her will resists her lover.

White Rose is perhaps the best book Violet Hunt has written yet; the finest in conception, in form and technique. It is a surprising piece of psychology, male and female. There is no important character in it that does not live, from the amazing and complex Amy Stephens to the too simple and degenerate Dulce Dand, who will go mad if she is not married. Jeremy Dand, Amy's middle-aged married lover, is the one entirely successful male figure that Violet Hunt has created. It is more than a portrait; a portrait is painted in the flat, as are the figures of Robert Assheton and Euphan Balfame, in the two dimensions of brutality and sensual passion. Jeremy Dand is a three-dimensional form that we can walk round; he is not drawn, but hewn, chiselled faithfully in his many-sided detail. He is the average sensual man, but he is never brutal like Assheton and Balfame; Violet Hunt has abandoned the fallacy of the ruling passion and presented him as he is, with all his inconsistencies; selfish and unselfish, generous and mean, faithful and faithless, a human battlefield, till in the end his passion for Amy masters him. Whatever he is at the moment, he is given with an unfaltering rightness. All his mental processes are inevitable.

And the drawing of Amy is as masterly. Nothing she does and feels and says could have been done or felt or said differently. This intricate, utterly feminine soul is laid bare to its last throbbing nerve, its ultimate secret thought. We have the whole of it, all the wonderful detail, its courage, its recklessness, its pity, its scrupulousness, its essential decency, its all but indestructible loyalty, its strength and the infinite pathos of its weakness.

The tragedy is worked out to its end with unrelieved, unrelenting gloom. Every line has the effect of rightness, of a flawless finality. It is so far beyond anything that mere cleverness can do. *White Rose of Weary Leaf* alone should have placed Violet Hunt high in the ranks of the tragic realists.

—May Sinclair, "The Novels of Violet Hunt," *The English Review* 34 (January to June 1922): 108–11

LADY DOROTHY MILLS

Miss Violet Hunt's flurried years, 1908–1914, included the women's suffrage movement, the founding of the *English Review*, of which Mr. Ford Madox Hueffer was the first editor, her personal relations with him, and much family trouble concerning these relations, and also concerning her administration of the affairs of her mother. The object of the book is not to give a detailed account of the facts. As Miss Hunt writes, "There are some things no one tells, some things that no woman tells, some things I cannot tell, but people know them"; and those who do not know them will not learn them very clearly from this book. It is not easy, indeed, to say what is the object of the book. It is not an *apologia*; but just in so far as it is obviously an outlet for the author's feelings, this, like any other intimately personal book, makes the reader feel uncomfortable. Its claims upon attention will be found, perhaps, to be two: first, that the story brings in several great figures in English literature who were Miss Hunt's friends; and secondly, that the story and the characters have laid hold upon the novelist in her. What she has written is the material for a very interesting novel of the literary life. It seems a pity that she has been content with the material and did not write the novel. The additional labour would have refined away a good deal of the soreness and the fretfulness that were inevitable in a book of this nature. We should have seen the heroine under the influence of other things than persecution. And there would still have been enough memories of Henry James, of Conrad, of Hudson, to be worth putting in an autobiographical work of a tone other than this.

Still, it is worth while reading through a distressing book because amid these materials *pour servir* there are many very good things.

⟨. . .⟩ And Miss Hunt can tell brilliantly a delightful story of how James read to her his article for Mme. Duclaux's Book of France, how she accused him of being "passionate," how he glared, searched for the *mot juste*, and found it:—

> He turned on me an eye, *narquois*, reflective, stork-like, a little devilish, calmly wise—the Henry James eye, in fact—and, with a little pompous laugh . . . the male warding off any attack that the persevering female might possibly be contemplating against his supreme bachelordom:
> "Ah madam, you must not forget that in this article I am addressing—not a Woman, but a Nation!"

Of that kind of reminiscence—sharp, irreverent, but not unkind or belittling—there is plenty; and this novelist-daughter of a painter and a novelist has known many men and women worth recording. There are flashes, too, of shrewd and sensible criticism of popular idols and others. The book's other claim upon attention cannot be illustrated by quotation. It is in its very spirit, as well as in its material, that it exhibits—sometimes more clearly than its author knew—the incompatibility between ordinary life and what Miss Hunt calls genius, but is perhaps more safely called the temperament possessed by some novelists, dramatists, and poets, whose reality is not the reality of the world in general.

—Lady Dorothy Mills, [Review of *The Flurried Years*], *The Times Literary Supplement* (18 February 1926): 111

GEOFFREY ROSSETTI

That there are but few examples of good biography proves how extremely difficult it is to tell the story of a person's life so as to be faithful at once to art and to truth. ⟨. . .⟩ In Miss Violet Hunt's life of Elizabeth Siddall her novelist's imaginative talent comes first and her sense of fact follows very half-heartedly in the rear. The documentation for many hitherto unpublished details in the lives of the well known figures who occur in her book is meagre. The story of the piece of paper which Ford Madox Brown found on the nightdress of Mrs. Rossetti when she was dead surely should receive some documentation. There is probably little doubt that Miss Hunt was told this very interesting detail by someone else. But why is the source not referred to in a foot-note?

Miss Hunt's obvious sympathy with her heroine hardly allows for the fact that Miss Siddall was playing with fire the whole time. From the experience she had had before she married Rossetti, Miss Siddall must have known that he was an odd creature. Indeed she seems to have been no less odd herself, and certainly far more fractious and disagreeable. ⟨. . .⟩

But this biography undoubtedly reveals that Miss Hunt has a very strong sense of melodrama. In Sir Hall Caine's biography of Rossetti, and now in Miss Hunt's biography of his wife, there is a strong tendency to exaggerate the melodramatic and the sensational. Nevertheless, we must confess we are becoming a little tired of those "great flares by night in the cemetery" when the coffin was being exhumed, and the anguish of the poet before the dead body of his beautiful young wife. Miss Hunt's story will touch those who are touched by this sort of thing, but to those who are most anxious to know exactly what did occur, and have no wish that any true fact should be concealed, this book will be somewhat disappointing.

Yet it must not be thought that Miss Hunt has produced a worthless or uninteresting piece of work. Her accounts of the Bohemian life led by the various members of the Pre-Raphaelite group are most entertaining.

—Geoffrey Rossetti, [Review of *The Wife of Rossetti*], *The Bookman* (October 1932): 56

THE NEW YORK TIMES BOOK REVIEW

The Blessed Damozel, as all persons who are acquainted with the story of the Pre-Raphaelite Brotherhood know, was Elizabeth Eleanor Siddall, long the model of Dante Gabriel Rossetti and for a briefly tragic period his wife. Like that other Dante's Beatrice, of whom the world knows little, she was the inspiration of one of the great sonnet-sequences of the world, the "House of Life" series, and her story is indelibly set forth in "The Wife of Rossetti," by Violet Hunt. 〈. . .〉

Let us start the picture as Violet Hunt starts it. "Models! Models! and more models!" This, she tells us, was the constant cry of the painters in the early '50s, especially the younger painters, among whom was one Walter Howell Deverell 〈. . . who〉 found The Sid and carried the news of her wondrous beauty to his brother artists, who were already calling themselves Pre-Raphaelites. Elizabeth Eleanor Siddall, that being her full name, was in the employ of a millinery establishment whence had come more than one model. But she, with her chaste and stand-offish air—how was she to be approached? Young Deverell (there was no impecuniousness there) induced his mother to go to the shop, buy herself several bonnets and tactfully approach the girl on the question of posing. This she did, with the result that The Stunner (later she was The Sid) gave her consent. Rossetti singled her out for his own, and although she posed, as time went on, for several of the brotherhood, under the code she was the especial property of Rossetti. With the moment of their meeting began one of the most unusual and the most poignant of stories, a story not unlike, yet vastly dissimilar to, the story of Robert Browning and Elizabeth Barrett; alike, because it is a story of the love of artist for artist, and dissimilar because on the man's side there was nothing of gallantry, and on the woman's the artist was negligible. Moreover, it was the man who postponed marriage, not the woman.

And here we touch on what underlies the volume by Violet Hunt. The author everywhere adumbrates rather than specifies, and the reader is not always certain that her implications are what they appear on the surface. But it would seem, without the mention of Freud, that it is Miss Hunt's thesis that any study of Dante Gabriel and Elizabeth Siddall should be made from the Freudian approach if any satisfactory conclusion is to be arrived at. If the reviewer is right, then, in this book, extensively and intensively complete, and documented at every point, but never pedestrian in its narrative, is all the material for that study, the key to which would be that Rossetti demanded of Miss Siddall, although most of the time housed with her, a rigid observation of chastity, not from any ethical motive, but in order that he might preserve toward her a rigidly esthetic attitude. A strange tale indeed, if we read the biographer aright in it, and one offering not merely startling conclusions, but conclusions from which one instinctively shrinks. For if Rossetti commanded of The Sid this cloistral existence, he himself led anything else but; and it would appear to be the thesis that it was this self-repression, while at the same time she was forced to suffer the humiliation of Rossetti's disaffection—had the two been married one would call it infidelity—which gradually wore her down. When Rossetti eventually married her, ten years after their first meeting, she was wan and emaciated, far gone in a hopeless malady which may have been tuberculosis, incapable of bearing living children. She used laudanum daily. When she died from an overdose of the drug the coroner's jury, after an examination of witnesses, cleared her of the stigma of suicide, although with many the thought will not down that she willed her death; though she may not deliberately have brought it about. ⟨. . .⟩

⟨. . .⟩ But her pathetic story is brilliantly told by Violet Hunt. Indeed, so brilliantly told is her story, with such an assimilation of fact and rehabilitation of fact as few biographers attain, that "The Wife of Rossetti" is one of the most expertly executed biographies of recent years. Miss Hunt has done for Elizabeth Eleanor Siddall what "The Barretts of Wimpole Street" did for Elizabeth Barrett, or "Ariel" did for Shelley.

—N. A., "That Tragic Figure, Rossetti's 'Blessed Damozel,'" *The New York Times Book Review* (30 October 1932): 3

EDA LOU WALTON

The experience of reading this biography is very much like spending a week end with a houseful of famous artists and writers, most of whom are strangers to you. You find yourself in a large roomful of people who know each other intimately. You hear first one bit of gossip, then another. Women and men address each other by first names and nicknames. You cannot quite fix any of them at first. All seem to have lived very complicated lives. There are hints of scandal and frequent gossip about a certain tragic suicide—Gabriel's wife—yes. Motives are suggested, then dropped.

You strain your ears trying to determine something about this story. After a few hours of desperate listening you come to the conclusion that every one in the room is just a little mad, after the manner of artists, and that you, yourself a very commonplace person, may turn mad too if you linger long in this fascinating and exotic company. You soon realize that you cannot quite believe all you hear, that tales are contradictory. These people are given to ghosts, too, and hallucinations. How to piece it all together! Truly this is a brilliant gathering. The women in their rich, full, clinging gowns are beautiful in the golden light of the late afternoon. The men, perhaps a little given to eccentricities of manner and egomania, are men of genius. ⟨. . .⟩

⟨. . . It⟩ is from memory and from the gossipy notebooks and letters of these people, that Miss Hunt reconstructs the innumerable amazing scenes in the lives of the Rossettis and of their many famous friends. The result is a biography which is really a kind of moving picture with sound in which expert photography has caught every gesture, every expression—expert recording, every quality of the voice, even every half-spoken phrase or whisper. The book is tremendously alive, much more dramatic than most more conventionally written biographies. And if the reader is sometimes a little sceptical, a little suspicious of the author's exaggerated sensibility to all that she saw or heard or read about the P. R. B., it is nevertheless this very heightened imagination that makes possible the recapturing of the words, the feelings, the dramatic attitudes of every actor in this most un-Victorian group. ⟨. . .⟩

"The Wife of Rossetti" is an absorbing memoir devastatingly analytical at times, richly embroidered in all kinds of carefully searched out details, now and then a little sensational because of its author's superstitious and morbid interest in her heroine. One feels that Violet Hunt might well have been one of these Pre-Raphaelite women herself, she interprets them with such romantic and yet satirical accuracy. They are not pictures to her, they are living women capable of creating glamour, frustration, and bitterness. She understands them even better than she does their more famous husbands. She can follow them into their bedrooms where they giggle and chatter while their husbands argue academically in the studio. Here they all are, tall, full-throated, with heavy-lidded eyes, dressed much alike in the "unstayed" fashion their painter husbands thought medieval and therefore beautiful.

And here, too, presented with a little less penetration, perhaps, are their husbands and lovers, all men obsessed by Art and by themselves, the sensual and yet sensitive Rossetti, the impotent and business-like Ruskin, the strong and slightly inhuman Browning; the weakling Swinburne; the gentle Hunt; the reticent, and wise Allingham, the clumsy Morris. And all these men, being artists, are from a woman's point of view, inept as husbands, and, for the most part, incapable as business men. And so when the week end—on the reading of this memoir—is over, one feels as if one knew every character in this famous Brotherhood and Sisterhood, for it was that, too, almost too intimately, as if one would choose to get off alone for a while and think them over, these people who are bound to haunt one's dreams.

—Eda Lou Walton, "Pre-Raphaelite House Party," *New York Herald Tribune* (30 October 1932): 1, 6

ROBERT AND MARIE SECOR

⟨As⟩ an historian of the social implications of the Pre-Raphaelite period, Violet Hunt may have left her mark not in her biographical books and essays, but in her fiction. Perhaps nowhere can we find what it meant to be a young woman born into Pre-Raphaelite society as convincingly depicted as it is in her auto-biographical novels, *Their Lives* (1918) and *Their Hearts* (1921). Important early readers recognized the value of these novels. May Sinclair praised them for "the naked thoughts, the naked lives of people we have known" ⟨*English Review*, February 1922⟩. Ford Madox Ford claimed that *Their Lives* had "the character of the work of history. It *is* history—and it makes it plain" ⟨"Preface" to *Their Lives*, 1918⟩. Rebecca West said *Their Lives* gave "a cold white vision of reality that recalls Maupassant; it is a valuable historical document . . . It is a study of girl-hood which is worth the entire two volumes compiled by Professor Stanley Hall on 'Adolescence,' and which is worthy to stand beside Dostoevsky's 'A Raw Youth.'" Over sixty years later, Rebecca West still remembers the novel fondly. ⟨. . . .⟩

Their Lives tells the story of Christina, Virgilia, and Orinthia Radmall, daughters of a respected if not properly honored Pre-Raphaelite painter. Like other Pre-Raphaelite women and children, who frequently served as models and ideals for artists' visions of vulnerable beauty, the Radmall girls were expected to play their parts in homemade dresses of peacock blue serge and in bonnets of medieval shape. The roles assigned to them keep the girls in sexual ignorance. The novel evokes well a society where young girls are humiliated when their "stomachs" are alluded to in public, and even the word "love" is to be circumvented when applied to real people rather than characters in books. ⟨. . .⟩

Christina refuses to be like either the conventional Virgilia or the repressed Orinthia. Blessed with literary ability and an independent spirit, she seems to be born between two worlds, too late to be a Pre-Raphaelite "stunner" and too soon to be a "New Woman." She is driven by a desire to leave behind the powerless world of childhood and exploits her position as eldest to distance herself from her two sisters. ⟨. . .⟩

Their Lives develops the shaping influences on the Radmall sisters from their Pre-Raphaelite childhood to the marriage of Virgilia; *Their Hearts* shows the consequences of that childhood upon them as they become fully adult. Here is no sensitive young man coming to terms with his environment, no artist on the brink of achievement, no successful struggle for identity and independence. Such masculine dreams of fulfillment are impossible for Victorian girls like the Radmall sisters. Instead Violet Hunt's young women, conditioned by their Pre-Raphaelite upbringing, struggle separately and with each other to define their feminine roles in the context of ordinary life. Their lives consist of weddings, courtships, births, deaths, and family tensions, rather than extraordinary achievement, and their hearts are engaged in the pursuit of sexual and social adjustment. ⟨. . .⟩

Unlike the submissive Orinthia, Christina in *Their Hearts* is a woman with a latch key, a symbol of liberation from Victorian parental supervision. She moves into the Bohemian world of artists and journalists, where laws of chaperonage are relaxed and "there were no proposals, strictly speaking—you did not speak strictly in Bohemia, where everyone was in love with Christina almost as a matter of course" (*TH*, p. 126). Here Christina is noticed, admired, and regarded as a pleasant attraction in otherwise drab offices. She comes and goes as she pleases, muddies her skirts and her reputation, and succumbs to the facile charm of her editor, Euphan Balfame. She is, however, neither proposed to nor taken seriously as an artist, and she does not take her own career very seriously. Despite herself she is a victim of what Rebecca West calls "the Victorian order of things," where for a young girl:

> There was no escape from this inadequate society into intellectual
> activities, for the pre-Raphaelite and the aesthetic movements
> described here with such gentle malice had nothing more to do with
> a woman than put her on a brocade settee with a sunflower. So all a
> girl could do was sit up in the "Trust" position till a husband was
> given one, and one could drop into the happy relaxation of "Paid
> For."

—Robert and Marie Secor, "Lives and Hearts in Pre-Raphaelite England: The Autobiographical Novels of Violet Hunt," *The Pre-Raphaelite Review* 2, no. 2 (May 1979): 60–64

ROBERT SECOR

We have no evidence that Wilde's proposal to Violet Hunt was more than legend, although in her later life Hunt herself insisted to friends like Douglas Goldring and Rebecca West, in her published memoirs, and even in her autobiographical novels, that she had "as nearly as possible escaped the honour of being Mrs. Wilde." In her unpublished papers and diaries, Hunt claims she met Wilde shortly after he arrived in London in 1879, and that for most of his stay before he left on his American tour she saw him regularly, once a week. There is among these papers a curious fragment of a book she contemplated writing, tentatively titled "My Oscar." The pages we have tell us a little about Wilde, more about Hunt, and a great deal about the disparate Victorian figures and images which Hunt's maddeningly associative and retentive mind assimilated: the artists and the poets, the great men and the beautiful women, the fools and the scoundrels, as well as the lines of verse, the snatches of song, and the images of paintings which formed the milieu of Violet Hunt's England. A record of the popularity and significance of even minor characters on the Victorian scene, "My Oscar" tells us what it meant for Hunt to grow up Pre-Raphaelite as she basks in the attention given her by the conquering hero of Aestheticism. ⟨. . .⟩

Hunt was destined to become a close friend of literary giants over the years. As "My Oscar" reveals, she grew up in the Victorian society of her parents' friends, who included all the major artists and writers of their generation; but she would also become the confidante of Henry James ("I used to enjoy shocking him") and the dinner companion of Arnold Bennett. She was the earliest champion of D. H. Lawrence and the self-proclaimed wife of Ford Madox Ford. Still, her published memoirs and fiction as well as her unpublished papers show that she always attached special importance to her friendship with Wilde, for it represented the first time she had made a conquest of her own. Ruskin gave her fatherly advice, and Millais and Burne-Jones treated her kindly when she accompanied her father to their studios, but Oscar Wilde called her "the sweetest Violet," and she was sure he meant something by it the others in their compliments did not. Wilde represented her coming of age. ⟨. . .⟩

⟨But by⟩ 1889 Wilde has ⟨. . .⟩ been transformed in Hunt's eyes from the gallant young conqueror to an ambitious and cynical young man on the move, armed with "courteous manners and splendid sins." But at the same time, she kept undisturbed the image of their meeting at Bellevue House, when to her romantic imagination he was Prince Charming ready to carry Cinderella away from her parents' house. At some point, Hunt thought of writing a book springing from this moment so fixed in her mind, when the last daughter of

Pre-Raphaelitism monopolized for two hours Letitia Scott's "afternoon's lion," the swaggering Aesthete just down from Oxford. Ranging far from the moment, backwards and forwards, Hunt writes about her Victorian world like nobody else, as her fine intelligence gives point and coherence to her rapid shifts and private associations. The meeting between the Pre-Raphaelite and the Aesthete becomes for Hunt an occasion to draw up accounts, and although she fully understands what Wilde and Whistler owed to Rossetti and his followers, Hunt is willing to choose between them. Awed as she was by the young conqueror, she still prefers "the Turkey reds of Rossetti and Morris to the greys and whites of Whistler."

—Robert Secor, "Aesthetes and Pre-Raphaelites: Oscar Wilde and the Sweetest Violet in England," *Texas Studies in Literature and Language* 21, no. 3 (Fall 1979): 396–400

BIBLIOGRAPHY

The Maiden's Progress. 1894.
The Celebrity at Home. 1894.
A Hard Woman. 1895.
The Way of Marriage. 1896.
Unkist, Unkind! 1897.
The Human Interest. 1899.
Affairs of the Heart. 1900.
Sooner or Later. 1904.
The Cat. 1905.
The Workaday Woman. 1906.
The White Rose of Weary Leaf. 1908.
The Wife of Altamont. 1910.
The Doll. 1911.
Tales of the Uneasy. 1911.
The Celebrity's Daughter. 1913.
The Desirable Alien. 1913.
The Governess. 1913.
The House of Many Mirrors. 1915.
Their Lives. 1916.
Zeppelin Nights (with Ford Madox Ford). 1916.
The Last Ditch. 1918.
Their Hearts. 1921.

The Tiger Skin. 1924.
More Tales of the Uneasy. 1925.
The Flurried Years. 1926.
The Wife of Rossetti: Her Life and Death. 1932.

ZORA NEALE HUR/TON

c. 1891–1960

ZORA NEALE HURSTON, although she gave her birthdate as 1901 or 1903, was probably born on January 7, 1891, in America's first all-black incorporated town, Eatonville, Florida. Her father, John Hurston, was a sharecropper who became a carpenter, preacher, and three-term mayor of Eatonville. Her mother, Lucy Hurston, died in 1904. As a child, she recounts in her autobiography, she listened to the "lying sessions" of the men on a storefront porch "straining against each other in telling folks tales. God, Devil, Brer Rabbit, Brer Fox, Sis Cat, Brer Bear, Lion, Tiger, Buzzard and all the wood folk walked and talked like natural men." The richness and singularity of black folklore would permeate all her work.

In her teens, five years after her mother's death, Hurston left Eatonville to work as a maid and wardrobe girl for a traveling Gilbert and Sullivan troupe. Some biographers have conjectured that she was married during this period, but no evidence supports or disproves it. In 1917, her travels brought her to Baltimore, where she enrolled at the Morgan College Preparatory School. She graduated in 1918 and entered Howard University, from which she received an associate's degree in 1920. The following year, her first published story, "John Redding Goes to Sea," appeared in the college literary magazine *The Stylus*. "Drenched in Light" (1924) and "Spunk" (1925) were published in *Opportunity*, the magazine edited by Charles S. Johnson, who subsequently urged Hurston to come to New York. She arrived, as she tells it, with "$1.50, no job, no friends, and a lot of hope."

Hurston also had brilliance and scholarly ambitions, however. In 1925, she won a scholarship to Barnard College to study with the anthropologist Franz Boas, and two years later, she undertook anthropological field research in Alabama, Louisiana, the West Indies, and Eatonville, Florida. She received her B.A. in 1928. She meanwhile continued to write: a play, *Great Day*, was published in 1927, followed in 1930 by "Dance Songs and Tales from the Bahamas" and the third act of *Mule Bone: A Comedy of Negro Life in Three Acts*, a play written in collaboration with Langston Hughes; "Hoodoo in America" was published in 1931.

In New York City, at the center of the Harlem Renaissance in 1926, Hurston published "Muttsy" and, with Langston Hughes and Wallace Thurman, founded the avant-garde literary magazine *Fire!!* "The Gilded Six-Bits" appeared in 1933, and her first novel, *Jonah's*

Gourd Vine, loosely based on the life of her parents, was published the following year. With a Rosenwald Fellowship in 1934, Hurston traveled throughout the South collecting folklore. The result of her research was the publication of *Mules and Men* (1935), an anthropological study of black American folklore that was praised as a major contribution but criticized for its lack of political perspective. Guggenheim Fellowships in 1936 and 1938 enabled Hurston to study folklore in the West Indies, and she is the first black American woman to have collected and published such work. In later years, her interest in anthropology took her to several Caribbean and Latin American countries, including Jamaica, Haiti, and Honduras.

Hurston's most artistically successful fiction is *Their Eyes Were Watching God* (1937), a novel about a woman who tells a story of identity and love. In 1939, Hurston published *Moses, Man of the Mountain;* her autobiography, *Dust Tracks on a Road*, was published in 1942 and won the 1943 Annisfield Award. She also wrote many articles during this period, including "Fannie Hurst," "Story of Harlem Slang," "Negroes Without Self-Pity," and "Black Ivory Finale." In 1948, *Seraph on the Suwanee* was published, her final novel and the only one depicting the lives of whites.

Hurston wrote for various magazines in the 1950s, but her increasingly conservative views concerning race relations alienated her from black intellectual circles. A recluse in her later years, she died on January 28, 1960, in a welfare home in Fort Pierce, Florida.

CRITICAL EXTRACTS

ZORA NEALE HURSTON

I can look back and see sharp shadows, high lights, and smudgy inbetweens. I have been in Sorrow's kitchen and licked out all the pots. Then I have stood on the peaky mountain wrappen in rainbows, with a harp and a sword in my hands.

What I had to swallow in the kitchen has not made me less glad to have lived, nor made me want to low-rate the human race, nor any whole sections of it. I take no refuge from myself in bitterness. To me, bitterness is the underarm odor of wishful weakness. It is the graceless acknowledgment of defeat. I have no urge to make any concessions like that to the world as yet. I might be like that some day, but I doubt it. I am in the struggle with the sword in my hands, and I don't intend to run until you run me. So why give off the smell of something dead under the house while I am still in there tussling with my sword in my hand?

If tough breaks have not soured me, neither have my glory-moments caused me to build any altars to myself where I can burn incense before God's best job of work. My sense of humor will always stand in the way of my seeing myself, my family, my race or my nation as the whole intent of the universe. When I see what we really are like, I know that God is too great an artist for we folks on my side of the creek to be all of His best works. Some of His finest touches are among us, without doubt, but some more of His masterpieces are among those folks who live over the creek.

So looking back and forth in history and around the temporary scene, I do not visualize the moon dripping down in blood, nor the sun batting his fiery eyes and laying down in the cradle of eternity to rock himself into sleep and slumber at instances of human self-bias. I know that the sun and the moon must be used to sights like that by now. I too yearn for universal justice, but how to bring it about is another thing. It is such a complicated thing, for justice, like beauty, is in the eye of the beholder. There is universal agreement on the principle, but the application brings on the fight. Oh, for some disinterested party to pass on things! Somebody will hurry to tell me that we voted God to the bench for that. But the lawyers who interpret His opinions, make His decisions sound just like they made them up themselves. Being an idealist, I too wish that the world was better than I am. Like all the rest of my fellow men, I don't want to live around people with no more principles than I have. My inner fineness is continually outraged at finding that the world is a whole family of Hurstons.

Seeing these things, I have come to the point by trying to make the day at hand a positive thing, and realizing the uselessness of gloominess.

Therefore, I see nothing but futility in looking back over my shoulder in rebuke at the grave of some white man who has been dead too long to talk about. That is just what I would be doing in trying to fix the blame for the dark days of slavery and the Reconstruction. From what I can learn, it was sad. Certainly. But my ancestors who lived and died in it are dead. The white men who profited by their labor and lives are dead also. I have no personal memory of those times, and no responsibility for them. Neither has the grandson of the man who held my folks. So I see no need in button-holing that grandson like the Ancient Mariner did the wedding guest and calling for the High Sheriff to put him under arrest. ⟨. . .⟩

⟨. . .⟩ For me to pretend that I am Old Black Joe and waste my time on his problems, would be just as ridiculous as for the government of Winston Churchill to bill the Duke of Normandy the first of every month, or for the Jews to hang around the pyramids trying to picket Old Pharaoh. While I have

a handkerchief over my eyes crying over the landing of the first slaves in 1619,
I might miss something swell that is going on in 1942.
    —Zora Neale Hurston, "Looking Things Over," *Dust Tracks on a Road* (1942, 1970),
    excerpted in *Twentieth-Century American Literature*, ed. Harold Bloom (New York: Chelsea
    House Publishers, 1986), 1950–51

ANN RAYSON

Zora Neale Hurston is a paradox among American black autobiographers. To
begin with, she is, politically, something of an establishment black writer, and
like those who yearn for the establishment she gives up militancy and denies
any racial conflict within herself. Yet she goes beyond a conservative like
George Schuyler, whose autobiography is entitled *Black and Conservative*, by
innovating within the form of black autobiography through the independence, not of her politics, but of her style. Because she is free in a personal
way, she is willing to take liberties with autobiographical form that others
have not. Because of her willingness to be colloquial, she becomes the sophis-
ticated person who uses style for a deliberate effect. And because she is one
autobiographer who is willing to allow the folklore of her race to influence her
work, it has a broader sense of cultural vision, language, and idiom than the
works of her—mostly male—contemporaries. As a result of her attitudes and
influences, then, Hurston's autobiographical style leads away from that of the
traditional self-written accounts of a life reviewed at the end of a successful
career and toward the "as-told-to" oral narration of contemporary black autobiographers like Malcolm X. Since she can use all three stages of class language—colloquial, informal, and formal, although she shies away from the
latter—using the differences without making invidious distinctions, she adds
to the genre a sense of assimilation, a stylistic sense that says, "One is what he
is." Hurston proves that there is no longer any need for painstakingly concen-
trating on being formally "literate." Consequently, where a McKay or a
Hughes autobiographically (in *A Long Way from Home* and *The Big Sea*) emphasizes the independent flair in his lifestyle, Hurston reinforces our sense of her
personal uniqueness not only through action and narration, but also through
prose style.
    Hurston avoids as stumbling blocks the issues of politics and race in her
fiction, and she minimizes their effect on her life in her autobiography.
Perhaps naively, she ends *Dust Tracks on a Road* by saying, "I have no race prejudice of any kind." Going on to deny the existence of a problem, she writes:

> My kinfolks, and my "skin-folks" are dearly loved. My own circumfer-
> ence of everyday life is there. But I see their same virtues and vices
> everywhere I look. So I give you all my right hand of fellowship and
> love, and hope for the same from you. In my eyesight, you lose noth-

> ing by not looking just like me. I will remember you all in my good
> thoughts, and I ask you kindly to do the same for me. Not only just
> me. You, who play the zig-zag lightning of power over the world,
> with the grumbling thunder in your wake, think kindly of those who
> walk in the dust. And you who walk in humble places, think kindly
> too, of others. There has been no proof in the world so far that you
> would be less arrogant if you held the level of power in your hands.
> Let us all be kissing-friends. Consider that with tolerance and
> patience, we godly demons may breed a noble world in a few hun-
> dred generations or so. Maybe all of us who do not have the good
> fortune to meet, or meet again, in this world, will meet at a barbecue.

Said any other way, a comment like this would elicit considerable hostility
from friends and foes alike. But Hurston is such a "character" herself that her
style comes off as being both naively ridiculous and camp in a finely ironic
self-parody. Through style alone she can get away with saying things for
which a straight conservative like Schuyler could never be forgiven.

By beginning the study of Zora Hurston at the end of her own story, one
can immediately intuit her spirit and the form its expression takes; both influence the "truth" of her telling. In a foreword to her book Darwin T. Turner
remarks, "as someone once said, *Dust Tracks* may be the best fiction Zora Neale
Hurston ever wrote."

—Ann Rayson, "*Dust Tracks on a Road*: Zora Neale Hurston and the Form of Black
Autobiography," *Negro American Literature Forum* (Summer 1973): 39–40

ELLEASE SOUTHERLAND

Miss Hurston's insights as a student of folklore influenced the form of all her
works, even her autobiography, *Dust Tracks on a Road*. This work describes techniques of the folklorist, as well as some very real dangers encountered in collecting her material. In Polk County, place of sun, sand, sweat and sawdust,
place where the blues are born, place where they dance the scronch and the
belly-rub and tell great stories, she was almost knifed to death. In explaining
how laughter and death work so closely together, Miss Hurston says, "primitive minds are quick to sunshine and quick to anger." So on the evening she
partied at the jook, enjoying the music, dancing and drinking, the music came
to a sudden halt and a woman, jealous of Zora, faced her with a knife. Zora
had no knife and didn't know how to use one anyway. If a friend, Big Sweet,
had not interfered, it would have meant certain death for the writer. In the
general fighting that broke out, blood already had spilled on the floor and
many people with open switch-blades already had joined the fight when a
friend told Zora to run, shoved her toward the door. And she says she ran all
the way from Polk County to New Orleans.

In New Orleans, there were other dangers, not physical this time. Mind and spirit had to be spent as Miss Hurston studied under all the famous two-headed doctors in order to bring us new and important information on Hoodoo in America. This information is not available to outsiders. One must be initiated. One must learn the ceremonies, herbs, formulas. Miss Hurston did all these things; she fulfilled the most demanding ceremony, calling for a three-day fast during which she was to lie on her stomach, naked, with her navel in touch with a snake skin. During this ceremony, she had five psychic experiences which she said seemed real for weeks. This was under the two-headed doctor, Luke Turner, nephew to the famous Marie Leveau. Her work with him lasted five months.

Despite the stress and the dangers, Miss Hurston's autobiography is filled with the laughter so characteristic of the oral tradition. What is known as "the dozens" in New York is called "playing" in a family situation, "reading," "specifying" or "putting the foot up" in Polk County. Miss Hurston records her friend, Big Sweet, "putting her foot up" on a particular man's stoop and proceeding to tell him that his pa was a "double-humpted camel and his ma was a grass-gut cow, but even so, he tore her wide open in the act of getting born, and so on and so forth. He was a bitch's baby out of a buzzard egg."

The tales and jokes bring a gentler humor. They give new life to Bible passages, slave narratives. ⟨. . .⟩

Three closing chapters of the autobiography deal with love, race and religion. Of race, Miss Hurston says, "Personal benefits run counter to race lines too often for it to hold. . . . Since the race line has never held any other group in America, why expect it to be effective with us?" This was the kind of comment that brought criticism. It led to ideas of Miss Hurston as lacking serious race consciousness. If the statement brings criticism, then her works should correct that criticism; her folklore collections show her love, respect and appreciation for Black art.

—Elleaze Southerland, "Zora Neale Hurston: The Novelist-Anthropologist's Life/Works," *Black World* (August 1974), excerpted in *Twentieth-Century American Literature*, ed. Harold Bloom (New York: Chelsea House Publishers, 1986), 1965–66

ROBERT E. HEMENWAY

Mules and Men is a collection of seventy folk-tale texts, a series of hoodoo rituals, a glossary of folk speech, an appendix of folk songs, conjure formulas, and root prescriptions, plus a personal account of Zora Neale Hurston's collecting experiences. Interspersed among all of this are proverbs, a folk sermon, rhymes, blues lyrics, and street cries. Some of the material had been collected before, and lurid hoodoo stories had appeared in popular magazines. But the book presented mostly new, authentic materials, and presented them in a different context than had previously existed.

Its publication was historically important, the first book of Afro-American folklore collected by a black American to be presented by a major publisher for a general reading audience. ⟨. . .⟩

Aware of the historical importance of her effort, Hurston paid considerable care to the choice of approach for *Mules and Men*, the communication context she would offer the reader. Her decision was to report from a black communal perspective. As the black poet June Jordan has stated, "white America lies outside the Hurston universe . . . you do not run up on the man/the enemy"; in Hurston's work black people put aside the "warrior postures" that enable them to deal with that enemy and adopt the "person postures" that enable them to relax and freely express themselves. Hurston reports on what happens on Clarke's store porch after the day's labors. The tale-tellers at Clarke's store understood the ancient black folk song:

> Got one mind for white folks to see,
> Nother for what I know is me;
> He don't know, he don't know my mind.

The verse affirms identity; the singer knows that there is a *me*, that this person is someone quite different from the stereotypical figure seen from the outside. Even though white possessiveness may seem to consume all, it cannot take possession of the private self. ⟨. . .⟩

Hurston's personal experience of poverty and her commitment to an integrated society were subordinated in *Mules and Men* so that she could address the negative image of the black folk publicly held by most Whites and by some Blacks. (Some of Hurston's strongest opposition came from middle-class black people who thought of the folk heritage as something which should be forgotten, a legacy of ignorance which could be used to justify racism.) The problem was that too many people confused material and ideological poverty. Because the men at Joe Clarke's were sometimes unemployed, often uneducated, occasionally hungry, it was assumed that no significant *ideas*, expressive *forms*, or cultural *creations* could emanate from the store porch. The black folk were placed in a kind of ideological strait jacket that interpreted their responses to the environment as either the product of social pathology, cultural deprivation, or an understandable, but simplistic desire to "protest."

Mules and Men creates a black communal perspective in order to emphasize the *independent* cultural creation of black people. Because Hurston was not a theorist, and *Mules and Men* was meant for the "average reader," her method was presentational. The folklore was expected to speak for itself. It said many things, but one of the most important was that Afro-American culture was not simply a *reactive* phenomenon. Black people's behaviors could not always be interpreted in the light of white oppression. What much of *Mules and Men* demonstrates, to paraphrase Ralph Ellison, is that black Americans are not the creation of the white man. As Ellison puts it, "Negro folklore, evolving within a larger culture which regarded it as inferior, was an especially courageous expression. It announced the Negro's willingness to trust his own experiences, his own sensibilities as to the definition of reality, rather than allow his masters to define these crucial matters for him."

Hurston once told Langston Hughes that he should make a Southern tour and read his poetry in sawmill camps and turpentine stills, on docks and levees: "There never has been a poet who has been acceptable to his Majesty, the man in the gutter before, and laugh if you will, but that man in the gutter is the god-maker, the creator of everything that lasts." Hurston identified with that figure, whom she called the "Negro farthest down"; *Mules and Men* was meant to affirm his place in the artistic universe.

—Robert E. Hemenway, "That Which the Soul Lives By" (originally "Introduction" to *Mules and Men* by Zora Neale Hurston, 1978). Reprinted in *Zora Neale Hurston*, ed. Harold Bloom (New York: Chelsea House Publishers, 1986), 88, 90, 94

ROBERT E. HEMENWAY

Hurston's style, rich and expressive, is a natural by-product of her attempt to represent the oral voice in written narrative, a process that marks the only times that public and private personae come together in the *Dust Tracks* text. Yet even at such moments the famous writer and the young Eatonville girl usually coexist rather than fuse, demonstrating the dual perspective that characterized so much of Hurston's experience. ⟨. . .⟩

Hurston never found a voice that could unify the dualistic vision of *Dust Tracks*. Her style, rich in sensory imagery, always searches for the right image for the expressed emotion, but her voice never quite builds beyond imagery to idea. ⟨. . .⟩ In short, one *sees* Hurston's prose. One also hears it, smells it, and touches it, but primarily one sees it. As she put it, "I am so visual minded that all the other senses induce pictures in me."

Interestingly enough, this admission comes when she is describing her reaction to first reading Samuel Taylor Coleridge's *Kubla Khan*. The adult writer, a professional woman of words, describes the process whereby literature creates its personal effects for the Eatonville novice. If Hurston has a fault in *Dust Tracks*, it may be that she overestimated the power of the image and underestimated her audience's curiosity about what is behind the image.

Hurston's account of men enamored of their own sexuality is visually hilarious: "I may be thinking of turnip greens with dumplings, or more royalty checks, [and] there is a man who visualizes me on a divan sending the world up in smoke." If a lover persists after her momentary ardor has cooled, calling up to remind her of "every silly thing I said," then "it is the third presentation of turkey hash after Christmas. It is asking me to be a seven-sided liar." The image begs for another dimension, for the sources of Hurston's sexual independence, for the trials of chauvinism that she had faced. But we are left only with the image, and the mystery of the woman who can so easily visualize her own amorous exploits as warmed-over turkey hash.

Emphasizing the process of Hurston's vision leads to the twelve visions meant to structure her life for her autobiography. Although intended to explain Hurston's life, these visions do not successfully shape the book. She even forgets about them after a while, so that the twelve visions, each "like clearcut stereopticon slides" that flashed before her as a young girl, end with vision nine in the text.

However, the visions do suggest Hurston's literary dilemma in the autobiography. A conscious literary device, the visions were intended to explain how an imaginative young girl could travel from Eatonville to the horizon, discovering fame and fortune as a nationally known author. But the visions also beg the question of how she got there, a black writer in a white world, a woman who refused the roles men imposed, a southern agrarian who learned her way around the city. The private Zora Neale Hurston of Eatonville, a mischievous child who "used to take a seat on top of the gate post and watch the world go by," never actually becomes one with the famous black novelist and anthropologist whose life story is of sufficient interest to merit an autobiographical statement. How did the transformation take place? Hurston never really explains the inner workings of the metamorphosis. As she admitted about *Dust Tracks*, "I have the feeling of disappointment about it. I don't think that I achieved all that I set out to do. I thought that in this book I would achieve my ideal, but it seems that I have not yet reached it . . . it still doesn't say all that I want it to say."

The paradox of the public and private Zora Neale Hurston, the enigma of a personality who could be culturally nationalistic and politically accommodationist, is never fully explained or explored in the picturesque prose of *Dust Tracks*. In the end, style in *Dust Tracks* becomes a kind of camouflage, an escape from articulating the paradoxes of her personality. Hurston used her talent for visual imagery as a snapshot photographer, not as a serious painter. Her style deflects high seriousness and implies that life is simpler than it is. Finally, though, the style does not deflect enough, and serious questions multiply. As Mary Helen Washington has argued, the chapters on her adult life become a "study in the art of subterfuge."

Dust Tracks fails as autobiography because it is a text deliberately less than its author's talents, a text diminished by her refusal to provide a second or third

dimension to the flat surfaces of her adult image. Hurston avoided any exploration of the private motives that led to her public success. Where is the
author of *Their Eyes Were Watching God?* One is never sure in *Dust Tracks*, even as
we know that the mystery behind the question—who is Zora Neale
Hurston?—will continually send us back to the *Dust Tracks* text for whatever
clues might be wrestled from its enigmatic author.

> —Robert E. Hemenway, "Introduction" to *Dust Tracks on a Road* (1984), excerpted in
> *Twentieth-Century American Literature*, ed. Harold Bloom (New York: Chelsea House Publishers,
> 1986), 1958

HENRY LOUIS GATES JR.

Rereading ⟨*Dust Tracks on a Road*⟩, I was struck by how *conscious* her choices
were. The explicit and the implicit, the background and the foreground, what
she states and what she keeps to herself—these, it seems to me, reflect
Hurston's reaction to traditional black male autobiographies (in which, "in the
space where sex should be," as one critic says, we find white racism) and to a
potentially hostile readership. As Lyndall Gordon says of Virginia Woolf, "the
unlovable woman was always the woman who used words to effect. She was
caricatured as a tattle, a scold, a shrew, a witch." Hurston, who had few peers
as a wordsmith, was often caricatured by black male writers as frivolous, as the
fool who "cut the monkey" for voyeurs and pandered to the rich white women
who were her patrons. I believe that for protection, she made up significant
parts of herself, like a masquerader putting on a disguise for the ball, like a
character in her fictions. Hurston *wrote* herself just as she sought in her works
to rewrite the "self" of "the race." She revealed her imagination as it sought to
mold and interpret her environment. She censored all that her readership
could draw upon to pigeonhole or define her life as a synecdoche of "the race
problem."

Hurston's achievement in *Dust Tracks* is twofold. First, she gives us a *writer's*
life—rather than an account of "the Negro problem"—in a language as "dazzling" as Mr. ⟨Robert⟩ Hemenway says it is. So many events in the book were
shaped by the author's growing mastery of books and language, but she
employs both the linguistic rituals of the dominant culture and those of the
black vernacular tradition. These two speech communities are the sources of
inspiration for Hurston's novels and autobiography. This double voice unrec-
onciled—a verbal analogue of her double experiences as a woman in a male-
dominated world and as a black person in a non-black world—strikes me as
her second great achievement.

Many writers act as if no other author influenced them, but Hurston freely
describes her encounter with books, from Xenophon in the Greek through

Milton to Kipling. Chapter titles and the organization of the chapters themselves reflect this urge to testify to the marvelous process by which the writer's
life has been shaped by words. "The Inside Search" and "Figure and Fancy"
reveal the workings of the youthful Hurston's mind as she invented fictional
worlds, struggled to find the words for her developing emotions and learned
to love reading. "School Again," "Research" and "Books and Things" recount
her formal education, while "My People! My People!"—printed in its original
form for the first time—unveils social and verbal race rituals and customs with
a candor that shocks even today. Hurston clearly saw herself as a black woman
writer and thinker first and as a specimen of Negro progress last. What's more,
she structured her autobiography to make such a reading inevitable.

Here is an example of the verdant language and the twin voices that com-
plement each other throughout *Dust Tracks*: "There is something about poverty
that smells like death. Dead dreams dropping off the heart like leaves in a dry
season and rotting around the feet; impulses smothered too long in the fetid
air of underground caves. The soul lives in a sickly air. People can be slave-
ships in shoes." Elsewhere she analyzes idioms used by a culture "raised on simile and invective. They know how to call names," she concludes, then lists
"'gator-faced," "box-ankled," "puzzle-gutted," "shovel-footed." "It is an every-
day affair," she writes, to hear someone described as having "eyes looking like
skint-ginny nuts, and mouth looking like a dish-pan full of broke-up crockery!"

Immediately after the passage about her mother's death, she writes: "The
Master-Maker in His Making has made Old Death. Made him with big, soft
feet and square toes. Made him with a face that reflects the face of all things,
but neither changes itself, nor is mirrored anywhere. Made the body of death
out of infinite hunger. Made a weapon of his hand to satisfy his needs. This
was the morning of the day of the beginning of things."

Language in these passages is not merely "adornment," which Hurston
called a key black linguistic practice; rather, sense and sound are perfectly balanced. She says the thing in the most meaningful manner without being cute
or pandering to a condescending white readership, as Wright thought. She is
"naming" emotions, as she says, in a private, if culturally black, language.

The unresolved tension between Hurston's two voices suggests that she
fully understood the principles of modernism. Hers is a narrative strategy of
self-division, the literary analogue of the hyphen in "Afro-American," the
famous twoness W. E. B. Du Bois said was characteristic of the black experience. Hurston uses the two voices to celebrate both the psychological frag-
mentation of modernity and the black American. Hurston—the "real" Zora
Neale Hurston whom we long to locate in this book—dwells in the silence
that separates these two voices: she is both and neither, bilingual and mute.

This brilliant strategy, I believe, helps explain why so many contemporary critics and writers can turn to her works again and again and be repeatedly startled at her artistry.

—Henry Louis Gates Jr., "A Negro Way of Saying," *The New York Times Book Review* (21 April 1985), excerpted in *Twentieth-Century American Literature*, ed. Harold Bloom (New York: Chelsea House Publishers, 1986), 1972–73

NELLIE MCKAY

Unlike the solitary but representative hero of male autobiography, Janie Starks and Zora Neale Hurston join voices to produce a personal narrative that celebrates an individual and collective black female identity emerging out of the search for an autonomous self. Although the structure of this text is different, the tradition of black women celebrating themselves through other women like themselves began with their personal narratives of the nineteenth century. Female slave narratives, we know, generally had protagonists who shared their space with the women who instilled pride of self and love of freedom in them. The tradition continued into the twentieth century. For instance, much of the early portion of Hurston's autobiography, *Dust Tracks on a Road*, celebrates the relationship she had with her mother and the lessons she learned, directly and indirectly, from other women in the community. Thus, Hurston's structure for Janie's story expands that already existing tradition to concretize the symbolic rendering of voice to and out of the women's community by breaking away from the formalities of conventional autobiography to make Janie's text an autobiography about autobiographical storytelling, in the tradition of African and Afro-American storytelling. Hurston, struggling with the pains and ambivalences she felt toward the realities of a love she had to reject for the restraints it would have placed on her, found a safe place to embalm the tenderness and passion of her feelings in the autobiographical voice of Janie Crawford, whose life she made into a very fine crayon enlargement of life.

—Nellie McKay, "'Crayon Enlargements of Life': Zora Neale Hurston's *Their Eyes Were Watching God* as Autobiography," in *New Essays on* Their Eyes Were Watching God, ed. Michael Awkward (New York: Cambridge University Press, 1990): 68–69

MAYA ANGELOU

Zora Neale Hurston chose to write her own version of life in *Dust Tracks on a Road*. Through her imagery one soon learns that the author was born to roam, to listen and to tell a variety of stories. An active curiosity led her throughout the South, where she gathered up the feelings and the sayings of her people as a fastidious farmer might gather eggs. When she began to write, she used all the sights she had seen, all the people she encountered and the exploits she had survived. One reading of Hurston is enough to convince the reader that Hurston had dramatic adventures and was a quintessential survivor. According to her own account in *Dust Tracks on a Road*, a hog with a piglet and an interest in some food Hurston was eating taught the infant Hurston to walk. The sow came snorting toward her, and Zora, who had never taken a step, decided that the time had come to rectify her reluctance. She stood and not only walked but climbed into a chair beyond the sow's inquisitive reach.

That lively pragmatism which revealed itself so early was to remain with Hurston most of her life. It prompted her to write and rewrite history. Her books and folktales vibrate with tragedy, humor and the real music of Black American speech.

⟨. . .⟩ Is it possible that Hurston, who had been bold and bodacious all her life, was carrying on the tradition she had begun with the writing of *Spunk* in 1925? That is, did she mean to excoriate some of her own people, whom she felt had ignored or ridiculed her? The *New Yorker* critic declared the work a "warm, witty, imaginative, rich and winning book by one of our few genuine grade A folk writers."

There is, despite its success in certain quarters, a strange distance in this book. Certainly the language is true and the dialogue authentic, but the author stands between the content and the reader. It is difficult, if not impossible, to find and touch the real Zora Neale Hurston. The late Larry Neal in his introduction to the 1971 edition of *Dust Tracks on a Road* cited, "At one moment she could sound highly nationalistic. Then at other times she might mouth statements which in terms of the ongoing struggle for Black liberation were ill conceived and were even reactionary."

There is a saying in the Black community that advises: "If a person asks you where you're going, you tell him where you've been. That way you neither lie nor reveal your secrets." Hurston called herself the "Queen of the Niggerati." She also said, "I like myself when I'm laughing." *Dust Tracks on a Road* is written with royal humor and an imperious creativity. But then all creativity is imperious, and Zora Neale Hurston was certainly creative.

—Maya Angelou, "Foreword" to *Dust Tracks on a Road* (New York: Harper Perennial, 1991), viii–xii

BIBLIOGRAPHY

Color Struck; A Play in Four Scenes. 1926.
Great Day. 1927.
Mule Bone: A Comedy of Negro Life in Three Acts (with Langston Hughes). 1930.
Jonah's Gourd Vine. 1934.
Mules and Men. 1935.
Their Eyes Were Watching God. 1937.
Tell My Horse. 1938.
Moses, Man of the Mountain. 1939.
Dust Tracks on a Road: An Autobiography. 1942.
Caribbean Melodies for Chorus of Mixed Voices and Soloists. 1947.
Seraph on the Suwanee. 1948.
*I Love Myself When I Am Laughing and Then Again When I Am Looking Mean and
    Impressive: A Zora Neale Hurston Reader.* 1979.
The Sanctified Church. 1981.
Spunk: The Short Stories of Zora Neale Hurston. 1984.

HARRIET ANN JACOBS

c. 1813–1897

HARRIET ANN JACOBS was born into slavery around 1813, in Edenton, North Carolina. Her maternal grandmother, Molly Horniblow (named after her previous owner), had been freed in middle age and owned a house in Edenton, where she earned her living as a baker. Both Harriet's parents, however, were slaves: her father was a carpenter; her mother, Delilah, was owned by John Horniblow, a tavernkeeper.

Harriet was orphaned as a child, and at the age of 11, upon the death of her mistress, Margaret Horniblow, she was willed to three-year-old Mary Matilda Norcom, whose family lived near Harriet's grandmother. Dr. Norcom, Mary's father, was a harsh man who subjected the young Harriet to constant sexual harassment. As a teenager, Harriet formed a relationship—and had two children—with a white neighbor, Samuel Tredwell Sawyer, as a form of resistance against Dr. Norcom. She was consequently sent away by Norcom to work on a distant plantation. Fearing to leave her children with Norcom and hoping to force him to sell them, Jacobs ran away, and Norcom did sell the troublesome young pair to their father, Samuel Sawyer. Sawyer allowed them to live with their grandmother. Although he later took their daughter to a free state, he did not keep his promise to Jacobs and emancipate the children.

In hiding, Jacobs was protected by sympathetic black and white neighbors until she took up residence in a tiny crawlspace above a storeroom in her grandmother's house, where she remained for nearly seven years. In 1842 she escaped to the North and was reunited with her daughter. Although Norcom made several attempts to capture Jacobs as a runaway slave, she escaped with her daughter to Boston in 1844. She then moved to Rochester, New York, to join her brother, John S. Jacobs, also a fugitive slave and a lecturer for the abolitionist movement.

In March 1849 Harriet Jacobs began working in an antislavery reading room and bookstore above Frederick Douglass's newspaper, *The North Star*. During this period, she read widely in abolitionist literature. She also became part of a weekly sewing circle of abolitionist women who met for discussion and companionship. Jacobs lived for several months with the Quaker reformers Isaac and Amy Post, developing a close relationship with Amy. The two women maintained a correspondence, and Amy urged Harriet to tell the story of her experience in slavery in order to strengthen the abolitionist cause.

At this point the Fugitive Slave Law of 1850 was passed, and Jacobs faced a renewed threat of capture: indeed, upon Dr. Norcom's death, his daughter Mary Matilda came to seize Jacobs under the provisions of the new law. To ensure Jacobs's freedom, in early 1852 the American Colonization Society bought her for $300. Jacobs, in return, gave serious thought to Amy Post's suggestion that she tell her life story to help the cause generally. Her first published piece, "Letter from a Fugitive Slave," appeared anonymously in Horace Greeley's New York *Tribune*.

In September 1860, writer, editor, and abolitionist L. Maria Child negotiated a contract with a Boston publisher for Jacobs to tell her story fully. When the publisher subsequently went bankrupt, Jacobs bought the printer's plates, and in 1861 *Incidents in the Life of a Slave Girl, Written by Herself*, edited by L. Maria Child, was published. The work appeared the following year in London, entitled *The Deeper Wrong, Or, Incidents in the Life of a Slave Girl*.

The book was promoted by the black and antislavery presses, and Jacobs enjoyed a limited celebrity among abolitionists. She became an agent of the Philadelphia and New York Quakers, working in relief efforts for freedmen in Washington, D.C., Virginia, and Georgia, from 1862 to 1866. During this period Jacobs was able to gain press coverage for fundraising and to publicize conditions in the South.

Harriet Ann Jacobs died in 1897.

CRITICAL EXTRACTS

HARRIET A. JACOBS

Reader, be assured this narrative is no fiction. I am aware that some of my adventures may seem incredible; but they are, nevertheless, strictly true. I have not exaggerated the wrongs inflicted by Slavery; on the contrary, my descriptions fall far short of the facts. I have concealed the names of places, and given persons fictitious names. I had no motive for secrecy on my own account, but I deemed it kind and considerate towards others to pursue this course.

I wish I were more competent to the task I have undertaken. But I trust my readers will excuse deficiencies in consideration of circumstances. I was born and reared in Slavery; and I remained in a Slave State twenty-seven years. Since I have been at the North, it has been necessary for me to work diligently for my own support, and the education of my children. This has not left me much leisure to make up for the loss of early opportunities to improve myself; and it has compelled me to write these pages at irregular intervals, whenever I could snatch an hour from household duties.

When I first arrived in Philadelphia, Bishop Paine advised me to publish a sketch of my life, but I told him I was altogether incompetent to such an undertaking. Though I have improved my mind somewhat since that time, I still remain of the same opinion; but I trust my motives will excuse what might otherwise seem presumptuous. I have not written my experiences in order to attract attention to myself; on the contrary, it would have been more pleasant to me to have been silent about my own history. Neither do I care to excite sympathy for my own sufferings. But I do earnestly desire to arouse the women of the North to a realizing sense of the condition of two millions of women at the South, still in bondage, suffering what I suffered, and most of them far worse. I want to add my testimony to that of abler pens to convince the people of the Free States what Slavery really is. Only by experience can any one realize how deep, and dark, and foul is that pit of abominations. May the blessing of God rest on this imperfect effort in behalf of my persecuted people!

    —Harriet A. Jacobs, "Preface by the Author," *Incidents in the Life of a Slave Girl, Written by Herself* (1861) (Cambridge: Harvard University Press, 1987), 1–2

WILLIAM L. ANDREWS

Incidents is written in a manner to appeal (in both senses of the word) to a woman-identified reader. By this I mean a reader who is capable of identifying, first, with the woman who narrates and plays the central role in this autobiography, and, second, with the community of women to whom the book is addressed as both a criticism and an appeal. The status of this particular female community in *Incidents* is very similar to that of the northern black community in ⟨Frederick Douglass's⟩ *My Bondage and My Freedom*. In both books, a homeless black fugitive creates an autobiography that pictures as a partially realized goal of fulfillment a community on the margins of the perverse American social sphere. For both autobiographers, that community offers a truly familial kind of fellowship untainted by the traditional authoritarianism that puts blacks and women to the service of cognate masters pretending to paternal or patriarchal office. Both autobiographers want very much to qualify themselves for admission into that idealized marginal community. But neither writer seems confident of the existence of such a community unless its rituals and values are articulated and reinforced through the narrative act of autobiography itself. It appears as though Jacobs and Douglass appeal for acceptance into communities, of women and blacks respectively, whose viability depends greatly on declarative autobiographical acts that create historical models for the desired community, and directive autobiographical acts that attempt to recreate the implied readership into a contemporary model of that community. Moreover, the two dimensions of autobiographical action in which this remodeling takes place, namely, the historical and the discursive, gravitate toward an uneasy union in the plot structure of both Jacob's and Douglass's narratives. For both writers, the pattern of the past involves (1) an initiatory separation from the community of home; (2) successive periods of isolation and alienation within oppressive hierarchies, interrupted by brief glimpses of redeeming community; and (3) a final recognition, from the liberating perspective of liminality, of the conditions on which lasting community had to be predicated. *Incidents in the Life of a Slave Girl* was written as much to assert the power and potential of women's community in the South and the North as to denounce the state of commonage under which all resided under the patriarchy of slavery.

Harriet Jacobs's quest for freedom, from chattelism in the South and from the tongue-tying sense of moral unworthiness that was slavery's legacy to her in the North, could not have been successful without the support of women's community. The fugitive slave's revelations about this community in the South and the North furnish an important commentary on what Carroll Smith-Rosenberg has called "the female world of love and ritual" in nineteenth-century America. Rosenberg found access to this world by examining "women's private letters and diaries" wherein she discovered "a very private world of emotional realities" central to women's lives, though often screened off from men's perceptions. This intimate world was "built around a generic and unself-conscious pattern of single-sex or homosocial networks. These supportive networks were institutionalized in social conventions or rituals which accompanied virtually every important event in a woman's life, from birth to death." Rosenberg's sources introduce us to the female support networks that conducted the socializing rituals that white middle-class women underwent in the nineteenth century. *Incidents* unveils for us not just a private but a clandestine set of women's support networks, often interracial in their composition, which presided over perilous black female rites of passage in which the stakes were, quite literally, life and death. The homosocial networks of Smith-Rosenberg's research enjoyed a "complementary" relationship to the male-dominated heterosexual world. The parallel homosocial networks of Jacobs's autobiography are maintained clandestinely outside of male awareness because they are subversive of the patriarchy in varying degrees. This covert

women's community did not document itself through private written sources;
it was knit together by oral means, Jacobs informs us, through the most private and personal of all communications—secrets. Jacobs approaches her
woman-identified reader with a personal history of secrets whose revelation,
she hopes, will initiate that reader into the community of confidence and support that nineteenth-century women needed in order to speak out above a
whisper against their oppression.

   —William L. Andrews, *To Tell a Free Story: The First Century of Afro-American Autobiography,
1760–1865* (Urbana: University of Illinois Press, 1986), 253–54

Jean Fagan Yellin

At first reading, Jacob's narrative of her seven-year self-incarceration suggests
connections with the metaphor of "the madwoman in the attic," that aberrant
alter-ego of "the angel in the house" who inhabits the parlor in popular
nineteenth-century fiction. Unlike this fiction, however, Jacob's narrative
focuses on the woman in the attic; and she is completely sane. Linda Brent
(Jacobs's fictionalized narrator) chooses the space above her grandmother's
storeroom in preference to her master's bed; and her grandmother, the apparently conforming woman in the kitchen below, supports her insurgency. The
goals of Harriet Jacobs's woman in hiding are not destruction and self-destruc-
tion, but freedom and a home.

    This endorsement of domestic values links *Incidents* to what has been called
"woman's fiction." Written by women for a female audience, these works
chronicle (in the words of Nina Baym) the "'trials and triumph' . . . of a heroine who, beset with hardships, finds within herself the qualities of intelligence,
will, resourcefulness, and courage sufficient to overcome them." Ultimately,
however, they identify an unhappy home as the source of evil and a happy
home as the center of human bliss. Like such literature, Jacobs's book
addresses a female audience. Instead of dramatizing the idea that the private
sphere is women's appropriate area of concern, however, *Incidents* embodies a
social analysis asserting that the denial of domestic and familial values by chat-
tel slavery is a social issue that its female reader should address in the public
arena. Jacobs's Linda Brent does not seek to inspire her audience to overcome
individual character defects or to engage in reformist activity within the private sphere, but urges them to enter the public sphere and work to end chat-
tel slavery and white racism. Informed not by "the cult of domesticity" or
"domestic feminism" but by political feminism, *Incidents* is an attempt to move
women to political action.

    In 1849, when Jacobs was in Rochester, the women in her circle were
developing a critique of sexism patterned on the Garrisonian analysis of chat-

tel slavery. Reflecting this model in their rhetoric, these abolitionist-feminists wrote of "the slavery of woman." The most committed, like Amy Post, did not confuse their own experience with the triple oppression of sex, condition, and race to which they knew slave women were subjected. It was nevertheless a sense of their own oppression that spurred freeborn white feminists to identify with a black fugitive slave woman like Jacobs.

In shaping *Incidents*, Jacobs combined this feminist consciousness with the black feminist consciousness she had absorbed as "grandmother's child." Given its closed community split into two warring camps—blacks who oppose slavery and whites who support it—the narrative is surprising. We expect to encounter the supportive black women, both slave and free, as well as the fiendish neighboring female slaveholder and the jealous mistress. But how are we to explain the presence of the white women who defect from the slaveholders' ranks to help Linda Brent? How can we account for the lady who, at the request of the young slave's grandmother, tries to stop her master from molesting her? Even more strange, how can we account for the female slaveholder who hides the runaway female slave for a month? Or the northern employer who entrusts her baby to Linda Brent so that she can flee slavecatchers by traveling as a nursemaid rather than as a fugitive? One explanation is that these women are responding to Linda Brent's oppression as a woman exploited sexually and as a mother trying to nurture her children. A central pattern in *Incidents* shows white women betraying allegiances of race and class to assert their stronger allegiance to the sisterhood of all women.

In her signed preface Jacobs's narrator invites this reading by the way in which she identifies her audience and announces her purpose: "I do earnestly desire to arouse the women of the North to a realizing sense of the condition of two millions of women at the South, still in bondage . . ." Jacobs's book— reaching across the gulfs separating black women from white, slave from free, poor from rich, bridging the chasm separating "bad" women from "good"— represents an attempt to establish an American sisterhood and to activate that sisterhood in the public arena.

—Jean Fagan Yellin, "Introduction" to *Incidents in the Life of a Slave Girl, Written by Herself* (Cambridge: Harvard University Press, 1987), xxxi–xxxiii

BLYDEN JACKSON

It was probably inevitable that at least one abolitionist slave narrative, if not more, would focus on sex and, specifically, on the history of a black woman in bondage to whom the protection of herself from the lust of white men legally empowered to use her body as they might choose had been a matter of prime concern. Such a narrative is *Incidents in the Life of a Slave Girl*, published in Boston in 1861 as the autobiography of Harriet Jacobs, a pseudonym for Linda Brent. The veteran writer and abolitionist Lydia Maria Child edited *Incidents*, a circumstance highly suggestive of Child's translation of recollections dictated to her into a text of her own composition. *Incidents*, however, does seem what it proclaims itself to be, insofar as it does apparently recount, whether or not as originally as claimed, events actually experienced by a female slave in the antebellum South. Jacobs, to adopt the nomenclature of *Incidents*, was apparently the kind of woman ideally, in an imagined scenario, suited to suffer as she claims she did. She was a mulatto of an attractive physique and a house servant often present in her master's eye. According to Jacobs, her seduction became virtually the one driving obsession of that master's whole existence, so much so that, in desperation, she gave herself to another white man, by whom she had a succession of children, in order thus to avoid the even worse degradation of herself she firmly believed submission to her master would have entailed. Incredibly, Jacobs hid for seven years, separated from her children, in an attic and finally accomplished her escape to the North a desperate stowaway at sea. In justice to *Incidents*, it must be said that Jacobs manages, with all of her attention to her problems with white men, also to testify on other aspects of slavery. ⟨S⟩he was a good observer, and so ⟨. . .⟩ her story may be read with profit solely as a thoughtful slave's picture of what slavery had meant to her.

   —Blyden Jackson, *A History of Afro-American Literature, Volume I: The Long Beginning, 1746–1895* (Baton Rouge: Louisiana State University Press, 1989), 155–56

VALERIE SMITH

In *Incidents in the Life of a Slave Girl*, the account of her life as a slave and escape to freedom, Harriet Jacobs refers to the crawl space in which she concealed herself for seven years as a "loophole of retreat" ⟨1973, 117⟩. The phrase calls attention both to the closeness of her hiding place—three feet high, nine feet long, seven feet wide—and the passivity that even voluntary confinement imposes. For if the combined weight of racism and sexism already placed inexorable restrictions upon her as a black female slave in the antebellum South, her options seem even narrower after she conceals herself in the garret, where just to speak to her loved ones jeopardizes her own and their welfare.

   And yet Jacobs's phrase, "the loophole of retreat," possesses an ambiguity of meaning that extends to the literal loophole as well. For if a loophole signifies for Jacobs a place of withdrawal, it signifies in common parlance an avenue of escape. Likewise, the garret, a place of confinement, also—perhaps more importantly—renders the narrator spiritually independent of her master, and makes possible her ultimate escape to freedom. It is thus hardly surprising that Jacobs finds her imprisonment, however uncomfortable, an improvement over "[her] lot as a slave" (117). As her statement implies, she dates her emancipation from the time she entered her loophole, even though she did not cross over into the free states until seven years later. Given the constraints that framed her ordinary life, even the act of choosing her own mode of confinement constituted an exercise of will, an indirect assault against her master's domination.

The plot of Jacobs's narrative, her journey from slavery to freedom, is punctuated by a series of similar structures of confinement, both literal and figurative. Not only does she spend much of her time in tiny rooms (her grandmother's garret, closets in the homes of two friends), but she seems as well to have been hemmed in by the importunities of Dr. Flint, her master ⟨. . . .⟩ Repeatedly, she escapes overwhelming persecutions only by choosing her own space of confinement: the stigma of unwed motherhood over sexual submission to her master; concealment in one friend's home, another friend's closet, and her grandmother's garret over her own and her children's enslavement on a plantation; Jim Crowism and the threat of the Fugitive Slave Law in the North over institutionalized slavery at home. ⟨But⟩ each moment of apparent enclosure actually empowers Jacobs to redirect her own and her children's destiny. To borrow Elaine Showalter's formulation, she inscribes a subversive plot of empowerment beneath the more orthodox, public plot of weakness and vulnerability ⟨"Review Essay," 1975, 435⟩.

I would suggest further that these metaphoric loopholes provide a figure in terms of which we may read her relation to the literary forms that shape her story. Restricted by the conventions and rhetoric of the slave narrative—a genre that presupposes a range of options more available to men than to women—Jacobs borrows heavily from the rhetoric of the sentimental novel. This latter form imposed upon her restrictions of its own. Yet she seized authority over her literary restraints in much the same way that she seized power in life. From within her ellipses and ironies—linguistic narrow spaces— she expresses the complexity of her experience as a black woman.

—Valerie Smith, "'Loopholes of Retreat': Architecture and Ideology in Harriet Jacobs's *Incidents in the Life of a Slave Girl*," in *Reading Black, Reading Feminist: A Critical Anthology*, ed. Henry Louis Gates Jr. (New York: Meridian, 1990), 212–13

KAREN SÁNCHEZ-EPPLER

Jacobs's two-part title, *Incidents in the Life of a Slave Girl, Written By Herself*, reveals more than convention, since the book is as much about the act of writing these incidents of sexual exploitation as it is about the incidents themselves. Jacobs's anxiety over literacy strikingly differentiates her text from the majority of slave narratives, in which command over letters frequently serves as a tool and symbol of liberation. Only rarely does Jacobs celebrate the cunning and skill that permitted Frederick Douglass to write his own pass or reveal the educational bravado with which William Wells Brown tricked white schoolchildren into teaching him letters by showing off the nonsense "writing" he had scratched with a stick into the dirt road. Hiding in her grandmother's attic, Linda does send Dr. Flint taunting letters with misleading Northern postmarks. But in general the trickery and authority of literacy do not remain in her control, for at the very moments that she gains literacy she finds these new skills turned against her. Linda is taught to read and spell by the almost motherly mistress whose written will bequeaths her to the Flints, and when Dr. Flint discovers her teaching herself to write he twists this accomplishment to serve his own plans and begins to slip her threatening and lascivious notes. Thus Jacobs's abolitionist text must also be seen as a site of bondage and sexual degradation. Just as Linda's liaison with Mr. Sands succeeds in challenging the authority of her master at the cost of "womanly virtue," telling her sexual story both emancipates and exploits. The strained relations between the public record of slavery and the intimate whispers of sexuality are reenacted in the scene of writing.

In her introduction to this slave narrative, Lydia Maria Child states that the sexual dimensions of slavery have "generally been kept veiled" but that she, in her role as editor, "willingly take[s] the responsibility of presenting them with the veil withdrawn." In heralding the narrative as a form of undressing, a discursive striptease, Child also records the resistance that awaits the sexual exposure of reading and writing. She explains that her "sisters in bondage . . . are suffering wrongs so foul that our ears are too delicate to listen to them." At work here is not only the solipsism that replaces the suffering of the slave woman with the suffering of her auditor, but also a recognition, even in critique, that the act of narration is itself a sexual act—that though, as Child asserts, Jacobs's experiences may be called "delicate subjects," issues of delicacy are also entailed in their transmission. Urging female readers to the exertion of "moral influence" and exhorting male readers to actively "prevent" the implementation of the fugitive slave laws, Child concludes with a distinctly conservative vision of the gendering of abolitionist response. Out of keeping with her usual feminist posture, Child's insistence that the reading of this slave narrative will work to produce traditional gender norms testifies to her sense of the story's threatening indelicacy—its siege on sexual order and conventional morality (4).

Anxieties over the obstacles to transmission posed by the delicate ears of a Northern audience are directly thematized within Jacobs's text as she repeat-

edly restages the scene of telling: the abusive erotics of narration become the
subject of her narration.

—Karen Sánchez-Eppler, *Touching Liberty: Abolition, Feminism, and the Politics of the Body*
(Berkeley: University of California Press, 1993), 93–94

B I B L I O G R A P H Y

Incidents in the Life of a Slave Girl, Written by Herself. 1861. Published in England
as *The Deeper Wrong, Or, Incidents in the Life of a Slave Girl*, 1862.

ALICE JAMES
1848-1892

ALICE JAMES was born in 1848 in New York City, the youngest child of Mary Robertson Walsh James and Henry James Sr., a Swedenborgian lecturer and writer on religious, social, and literary topics. Alice was the only daughter among four brothers, who included psychologist William James and author and critic Henry James Jr. When Alice was seven the family embarked on a five-year tour of Europe, staying in England, France, Switzerland, and Germany; the children had already learned to speak German and French. It was a cosmopolitan and intellectual household that provided an eclectic education without fixed neighborhood, school, or church affiliations: the chief tenet of the children's education was that they "*be*" something.

Although theirs was a loving family, the high intellectual expectations of Henry James Sr. for his children produced stress. All suffered from degrees of emotional ill health, and Alice from the age of 16 suffered recurrent although seemingly intangible illnesses. She was nervous and hypochondriacal by the time she was 20 and would endure a debilitating depression for the last 14 years of her life. During that time, as she lay dying in a sanatorium, she could express herself only in her private journal. Her letters, though interesting, are not unusual, but in her journals, Alice James takes her place among the great minds of her family.

William encouraged his sister to write, convinced that she, like the rest of the family, had a "book inside." Alice perceived the world in what William called "an unhabitual way" and shared with her brothers a gift for psychological analysis. Influenced and inspired by the writing of her brother Henry, Alice recounted with clinical accuracy and imagination the early history of her nervous malaise.

In 1881 Alice traveled from the family's Boston home to visit Henry in London in the company of a longtime friend, Katharine Loring. Loring seemed to enjoy making her invalid friend's life comfortable and interesting, and the two were constant companions for the rest of Alice's life. In 1890 Alice was diagnosed with breast cancer, which she herself seemed almost to welcome as a "palpable disease."

A few hours before her death, Alice James sent a cable to her brother William, advising him that she was "going soon" and sending "tenderest love." She died in London on March 9, 1892, with Katharine Loring and Henry at her bedside. She was cremated and her ashes buried next to the graves of her parents, in Cambridge, Massachusetts. Her *Journal* was published in 1894; the *Diary*, in 1934.

CRITICAL EXTRACTS

LEON EDEL

The claim of life against the claim of death—this is the assertion of every page of Alice's diary. Even when her strength failed her, she brought a resistance to death that was all the stronger for her having decided long before that she would not take her own life. In her final entry she says she had "almost asked for Katharine's lethal dose," but added "one steps hesitatingly along such unaccustomed ways and endures from second to second." The need to endure beyond the grave was reflected in her worries, even in the final hours, about her prose. This prose had in it many echoes from her father—his quickness to seize on the paradoxical and the contradictory, his double-play between man's glory as a creature of God and man's mundane stupidity. However much she might be exhausted and depressed, Alice's aggressive intellectual strength, her ability to exclaim and to complain—literally to fight disability and the cruelty of her fate—revealed itself in all that she set down. Life is reduced in the diary largely to the simple existential fact—as it was for her. "He didn't fear Death, but he feared dying," she had written in her commonplace book, long before the doctors gave her the final verdict. Yet she chose the act of dying rather than the immediacy of death, and to this act she addressed herself in her pages.

For the rest she had her string of daily facts, her comments on British manners, the crass egotism of the gentry, the misery of the masses, the heroic qualities she saw in Parnell. Her expatriation aided her. ⟨. . .⟩ Only an American, living abroad, could ridicule "the British constitution of things" quite as pointedly as Alice does—the monarchy and "its tinsel capacity," the "boneless church," the "hysterical legislation over a dog with a broken leg whilst Society is engaged making bags of 4,000 pheasants or gloating over foxes torn to pieces by a pack of hounds!" The docility of classes enslaved by respectability, whatever the "good form" of the moment may be; and finally the supine masses ⟨. . . .⟩

That was the bite in Alice's prose, as she looked at the British world through the newspapers: and doubtless there was within it an unpleasant, overly-aggressive side, which her brother caught when he was creating Rosie, the little working-class invalid, in *The Princess Casamassima*. Alice could seize on one of her brother's amusing anecdotes, say his remarks about William Archer, and spend a full page tearing the poor man to pieces. Life had to answer for a great deal to her; and when she could discharge her resentments nowhere else she attached them to a mere bit of gossip, a humble paragraph in the *Standard* or the *Times*. She possessed a vigorous and often belligerent democratic feeling. "She was really an Irishwoman!" Henry exclaimed as he read her, "transplanted, transfigured—but none the less fundamentally natural—in spite of her so much larger and finer than Irish intelligence. She felt the Home Rule question absolutely as only an Irishwoman (not anglicized) could. It was a tremendous emotion with her—inexplicable in any other way—but perfectly explicable by 'atavism.' What a pity she wasn't born there—and had her health for it. She would have been . . . a national glory!"

Henry's tribute to Alice's diary was contained in a long letter written to his brother from Rome on May 28, 1894. The first part expressed his concern at the printing of the four copies, the failure to disguise names and persons, the danger this represented to his privacy and the privacy of others. Then, turning away from his misgivings, he launched into an appreciation of his sister's power as a writer, and here there were few reservations, save in his feeling quite accurately that the diary reflected Alice's confined state. As he put it "she simplified too much, shut up in her sick room, exercised her wondrous vigour of judgment on too small a scrap of what really surrounded her." He felt her opinion of the English might have been modified "if she had *lived* with them more—seen more of the men, etc. But doubtless it is fortunate for the fun and humour of the thing that it wasn't modified—as surely the critical emotion (about them), the essence of much of their nature, was never more beautifully expressed."

—Leon Edel, "Introduction" to *The Diary of Alice James* (1934) (New York: Dodd, Mead & Company, 1964), 17–19

F. O. MATTHIESSEN

"Oh, woe, woe is me!" Alice James wrote in her journal: "I have not only stopped thinning but I am taking unto myself gross fat. All hopes of peace and rest are vanishing—nothing but the dreary snail-like climb up a little way, so as to be able to run down again! And then these doctors tell you that you will die or *recover!* But you *don't* recover. I have been at these alternations since I was nineteen, and I am neither dead nor recovered. As I am now forty-two, there has surely been time for either process. I suppose one has a greater sense of intellectual degradation after an interview with a doctor than from any other human experience." Her special tone is there, with her quizzical self-mockery and her complete lack of self-pity, and the detachment with which she has schooled herself to observe her body as a bad experiment for which she is not responsible, and in which she refuses to let her mind become implicated. ⟨. . .⟩

⟨. . .⟩ Only a few glimpses survive into her deeper troubles. Hardly a month before her death she wrote: "The fact is, I have been dead so long, and it has been simply such a grim shoving of the hours behind me as I faced a ceaseless possible horror since that hideous summer of '78 when I went down to the deep sea, and its dark waters closed over me, and I knew neither hope nor peace, that now it's only the shrivelling of an empty pea-pod that has to be completed." Her father had written Bob at the time of her crisis: "She asked me if suicide, to which at times she felt strongly tempted, was a sin. . . . I told her that so far as I was concerned she had my full permission to end her life whenever she pleased. She then remarked that . . . she could never do it now I had given her freedom . . . she was more than content to stay by my side and battle in concert with me against the evil that is in the world. I don't fear suicide much since this conversation."

She may not have thought actively thereafter of ending her own life, but she was to write of the hushed-up suicide of a friend:

"What a pity to hide it; every educated person who kills himself does something towards lessening the superstition. It's bad that it's so untidy. There is no denying that, for one bespatters one's friends morally as well as physically, taking them so much more into one's secret than they want to be taken. But how heroic to be able to suppress one's vanity to the extent of confessing that the game is too hard. The most comic and apparently the chief argument used against it is that because you were born without being consulted, you would be very sinful should you cut short your blissful career. This had been said to me a dozen times, and they never can see how they have turned things topsy-turvy."

One of the most remarkable things about her was her ability to entertain such thoughts without allowing them to become obsessive. Long after she had come to be regarded as a hopeless invalid, WJ ⟨William James⟩ wrote: "Alice met all attempts at sympathy with jeers and laughter, having her own brave philosophy, which was to keep her attention turned to things outside her sickroom and away from herself." The secret of her philosophy was not unlike the belief in will that sustained WJ, though the only world in which she could deploy her force was the inner world of HJ's ⟨Henry James's⟩ typical heroines. She seems to have found that secret very young:

"How I recall the low grey Newport sky in that winter of '62–63; as I used to wander about over the cliffs, my young soul struggling out of its swaddling-clothes, as the knowledge crystallized within me of what life meant for me, a knowledge simple, single, and before which all mystery vanished. A spark then kindled, which every experience, great and small, has fed into a steady flame which has illuminated my little journey, and which, although it may have burned low as the waters rose, has never flickered out,—'une pensée unique, éternelle, toujours mêlée à l'heure presente.' How profoundly grateful I am for the temperament which saves me from the wretched fate of those poor creatures who never find their bearings, but are tossed like dried leaves hither, thither and yon, at the mercy of every event which o'ertakes them; who feel no shame at being vanquished, or at crying out at the common lot of pain and sorrow; who never dimly suspect that the only thing which survives is the resistance we bring to life and not the strain life brings to us."

She continued to live at home, with occasional oases of fair health, until her parents' deaths. It seemed best for her then to join HJ in England, but her six or seven years there were spent almost entirely in private sanatoriums. In one of these, at Leamington, she undertook the one formulation that gives her a permanent place in this family of minds. Though her letters were lively, they moved, for the most part, within the orbit of the more usual women's letters of her time. It was to be very different with the journal which she started with one sentence in May 1889: "I think that if I get into the habit of writing a bit about what happens, or rather doesn't happen, I may lose a little of the sense of loneliness and desolation which abides with me." Later in that month she made her second entry: "My circumstances allowing of nothing but the ejaculation of one-syllabled reflections, a written monologue by that most interesting being, myself, may have its yet to be discovered consolations. I shall, at least, have it all my own way, and it may bring relief as an outlet to that geyser of emotions, sensations, speculations and reflections which ferments perpetually within my poor old carcass for its sins; so here goes,—my first journal."

—F. O. Matthiessen, *The James Family: Including Selections from the Writings of Henry James, Senior, William, Henry, & Alice James* (New York: Alfred A. Knopf, 1947), 272–74.

JEAN STROUSE

Katharine Loring had four copies of Alice James's diary printed privately in 1894 (by John Wilson and Son, Cambridge)—one for herself and one for each of Alice's living brothers, William, Henry, and Rob. William, who received his copy in March, took it away to New Bedford for a twenty-four-hour vacation from his daily round of teaching, writing, and family life in Cambridge. There, alone, he read it through. "It sank into me with strange compunctions and solemnity," he wrote to Henry a few days later. "The diary produces a unique and tragic impression of personal power venting itself on no opportunity. And such really *deep* humor!" He went on, "Of course the whole thing is less new and odd to you than to me. It ought some day to be published. I am proud of it as a leaf in the family laurel crown, and your memory will be embalmed in a new way by her references to your person . . ."

But the whole thing *was* new and odd to Henry, who received William's letter in Italy. He had just heard of the diary's existence from Katharine, who had mailed his copy to London. He told William that news of the diary came as a "'revelation' to me.—I mean a surprise and agitation. The agitation is a great and sacred impatience to see it—and above all, or also, to know if it was Alice's own design that it be printed, or a pious inspiration of KPL's. I can well believe that it is exceedingly remarkable—for I have never had occasion to express the full impression I received, in the last years of Alice's life, of the extraordinary energy and personality of her intellectual and moral being. There is almost no exhibition of it that would surprise me." He learned from Katharine that the impetus to publish *had* come from Alice, but his anxiety about what the diary might contain remained high.

Finally his copy was forwarded from London to Venice, where he had come on a sad mission. Constance Fenimore Woolson had committed suicide there in January, and he was helping her sister dispose of Fenimore's belongings and literary remains. Of his own sister's literary remains he wrote at first that he found the diary "magnificent . . . rare—wondrous," but that he was preoccupied with Woolson affairs and "terribly scared and disconcerted—I mean alarmed—by the sight of so many private names and allusions in print." He wished Katharine had "sunk" a few names, "put initials—I mean in view of the danger of accidents, some catastrophe of publicity."

Henry James viewed personal publicity as a catastrophe. To thwart the curious future, he burned most of his letters and papers. His autobiography, a rich evocation of the growth of artistic consciousness, adroitly obscures many details of what actually happened. ⟨. . .⟩

In May of 1894, Henry described himself to William as "intensely nervous and almost sick with terror about possible publicity" resulting from the printing, even in private, of Alice's diary. He imagined Robertson and his wife showing their copy around Concord and discussing it "with the fearful American newspaper lying in wait for every whisper, every echo." And he was embarrassed at the thought of people reading what he had said about them in private to Alice, sometimes embroidering the truth for her entertainment: "When I see that I say that Augustine Birrell has a self-satisfied smirk after he speaks—and see that Katharine felt no prompting to exercise a discretion about the name I feel very unhappy, & wonder at the strangeness of destiny. I used to say everything to Alice (on system), that would *égayer* her bedside & many things in utter confidence. I didn't dream she wrote them down." But even that wouldn't have mattered, he said; it would, in fact, have interested him. "It is the printing of these precious *telles-quelles* that disturbs me when a very few merely superficial discriminations (leaving her *text* sacredly, really untouched) wd. have made all the difference."

—Jean Strouse, *Alice James: A Biography* (Boston: Houghton Mifflin Company, 1980), 319–21

JEAN STROUSE

James Sr. constantly stirred up and thwarted his daughter ⟨. . . .⟩ When his children were young, he devoted himself to what he called their "sensuous" education, exposing them to theater, music, art, and books, searching out unusual schools in Europe and America for his four boys, then quickly finding those schools disappointing and dragging the entire family off to a new city or a new continent in search of the perfect education that existed only in his mind. For all his originality on the subject of education, however, James Sr. did not believe in the education of women. He thought his boys would learn to be "good"—to struggle against selfishness and the evils inherent in the universe—through wide intellectual experience and the interesting uses of perception. Girls, however, he thought good by nature: they could dispense with interesting ideas. To be a James and a girl, then, was virtually a contradiction in terms—"in our family group," wrote Henry Jr., "girls seem scarcely to have had a chance" (quoted in Edel, 1953–1972, 2:49). ⟨. . .⟩

For all his opposition to female intellect, however, James Sr. delighted in the quickness of his daughter's mind. He addressed her as "heiress of the paternal wit and of the maternal worth" (HJ Sr. to AJ, n.d.). He encouraged her to read, and they spent long hours together in his study, talking, joking, trading opinions and insults. Her early education, then, was a haphazard mix of encouragement and slight: her father enjoyed sharing knowledge with her piecemeal, but more as a pleasant way to pass time than as a serious effort to train her mind. Ambiguity characterized Alice's lifelong estimates of the female sex and her own mental prowess: toward the end of her life she wondered wryly whether "if I had had any education, I should be more, or less, of a fool than I am" (A. James, 1964, p. 66). She then went on to contradict by example that assertion of foolishness, for the modesty and irony of her remarks present a clear contrast to her father's solemn, inflated rhetoric on the subject of female "didactic dignity": education, she wrote, "would have deprived me surely of those exquisite moments of mental flatulence which every now and then inflate the cerebral vacuum with a delicious sense of latent possibilities—of stretching oneself to cosmic limits, and who would ever give up the reality of dreams for relative knowledge?" (p. 66).

—Jean Strouse, "Alice James: A Family Romance," in *Emotions and Behavior Monographs*, no. 4, ed. George Moraitis and George H. Pollock. *Psychoanalytic Studies of Biography* (Madison, Connecticut: International Universities Press, Inc., 1987), 74–76

GLORIA FROMM

Jean Strouse's biography of Alice James, more perhaps than anything else, is an indictment of the nineteenth-century society that offered so few options to young women. Oddly enough—as in Alice's case—harping on the failure can have the effect of turning it into a form of success or achievement, in that, given the extraordinary handicaps shown as having existed, it becomes a wonder that anything at all was accomplished. Thus Alice's diary can be viewed as something of a *liber mirabilis*, in spite of its frequently turgid, convoluted, coy style. (Surely Henry's praise of the diary, surprised as he was that it even existed, needs some such context.) And Alice herself is made (by Howard Feinstein, for example) as much a casualty of the Civil War as ⟨her brothers⟩ Wilkie and Bob, who—unlike her—*had* to try to make their way in an unsettled postwar world. Granted there may not have been many options for Alice (were there many more for Wilkie and Bob?), but at least she was protected and provided for—and could quite literally command the undivided attention of her parents, while they were alive, and in due course of Henry and Katharine Loring after that. This is not at all to deny Alice's real sufferings, both of mind and body, but to attribute them mainly to her sex—to the fact that she was a girl as well as a James—seems to me to beg the question, which as I see it is, "Why did she exercise so negatively the Jamesian will and force of character she had in such abundance?"

All the evidence indicates that she worked very hard at being ill—or, as she herself put it, at dying ("the hardest job of all")—and one has to wonder why. It seems too easy to accept at face value Henry's explanation—that it was the "only solution" for her to "the practical problem of life." Most commentators have identified the problem as the dual one of being a girl and a James, which is how her own explanation is understood—the well-known passage in the diary describing how at fourteen she "absorb[ed] into the bone that the better part of life [was] to clothe oneself in neutral tints, walk by still waters and possess one's soul in silence." But, as Leon Edel has pointed out in his portrait of Alice, neutrality was impossible for her. Yet in her last years this was how she liked to present herself—in a continuing rejection of the reality that others saw plainly—the harsh reality articulated by Henry as her inability to lead a "reciprocal" life—to give and take in equal measure. This may certainly be true, but again why does everyone seem to have taken for granted that Alice would always find life in the open—as it were—too much for her? Because—or so it begins to appear to me—this was the destiny carved out for her within the James family. You hear it pronounced by all of them: look after Alice; humor her; it won't be for terribly long. Well before her cancer was discovered, both Henry and Katharine Loring said they were prepared to see her through to the end, seeming to imply that the end was not very far off. In the meantime, as Alice herself put it—mingling praise of Henry with her long-standing, undisputed need for "devotion" such as his—he was invariably at her disposal: her nerves were his nerves, she claimed he said; her stomach was his stomach. Certainly no give and take there!

How did such a firm belief grow among the Jameses, especially when repeatedly no organic cause was found for Alice's periodic prostrations? And was the belief basically different from the understanding that came to prevail about Wilkie and Bob—that, in spite of their brave soldiering, they would be perennially childlike and not amount to anything? Of course they did not amount to anything (no matter how sympathetically you describe their lives), forced as they were to contend, practically speaking, with hostility within as well as without. Indeed, having learned to expect it, they even sought it. Or so one might infer from their idealistic efforts to grow cotton in Florida, immediately after the war, using black labor, and from their ventures into what was for them the alien territory of the Midwest. So, too, when Alice—primed for a short life—learned from her last doctor that she could expect to die soon from the lump in her breast, she remarked that her "aspirations" had finally been "brilliantly fulfilled": she had a "palpable disease." They were not as "eccentric"—these aspirations—as Alice would have us believe, but rather an integral part of her life-script, thoroughly absorbed by all the Jameses, who were nothing if not dutiful, every one of them, which is why Wilkie was so shocked at his father's will, and why Alice "worked" at dying, which she not only thought was expected of her but which made her feel connected once again with her parents, especially her father, who had died so unresistingly, so willingly.

Perhaps, then, the ultimate paradox of the James family is the appearance of looseness and freedom (which both Henry and Alice complained so bitterly about) when in reality the children's destinies were preordained.

—Gloria Fromm, "Alice in Jamesland," *The Henry James Review* 10, no. 2 (Spring 1989): 85–86

MARIA ANTONIETTA SARACINO

As ⟨by 1890⟩ her parents were now dead and she had turned herself into a permanent invalid, she chose to move to Europe, where her brother lived. But whereas Henry on landing in Europe had proudly declared: "I take possession of the old world, I inhale it. I appropriate it!" ⟨*Henry James Letters, vol. 2 1875–1883*, 1975, xi⟩. Alice arrived in Europe "suspended . . . like an old woman of the sea round his neck where to all appearances I shall remain for all time" ⟨*The Diary of Alice James*, 1982, 104⟩. From this moment on she spent her life waiting for death, entrusting to the pages of her diary whatever—day after day—fell within her radius of observation. If her invalid condition prevented her from going outside, toward the social, it was the outside, the social, that came to her, in the form of visits, letters, and readings from books and newspapers. Alice devoted special attention to all that happened around her, and in particular she reflected upon the world of politics and the world of the social. And it is through this filter that we find in her diary new and different references to Italy.

In sharp contrast with the haughty attitude of the British monarchy, "the King of Italy seems alone among them all, to have some imagination, and to get some fun out of his limitations," writes Alice ⟨115⟩. She praises the fact that Gladstone knows Italian and can sing Italian songs in a tenor voice. She quotes several passages from the *Memoirs* of the Italian statesman Massimo d'Azeglio in order to point out the difference between democracy and autocracy. And in sharp contrast with what she sees as "the all pervasive sense of pharisaism in the British Constitution of things" ⟨87⟩, she quotes an amusing anecdote which underlines the behavior of the men who run the House of Savoy—who "seem alone to have that sense of the picturesque which lifts them out of the vulgar and flimsy platitude of contemporary monarchs. As the Duke of Aosta lay dying," Alice writes, "he told the priest who was standing by his bedside to go and rest. The old man turned away and a man who was standing among the others stepped forward and took his hand and said "Thanks"—the priest then expressed some sorrow and affection for the duke—when "Thanks" was repeated with much emotion—as the room was dark the confessor said "I don't know who you are?"—"I am his brother." In all the five years that I have been in England," concludes Alice James, "I have never heard or read of a word said by 'our family' which would give one reason for supposing that they had the faintest conception of what they represented, save on its flimsiest side" ⟨83⟩.

In the diary she also makes ironic reference to the way Italians face life: "as soon as an Italian has a pain . . . he not only sobs, but the whole household surrounds him in chorus. Lately . . . [the doctor] was called to a gallant colonel and found a large, handsome man lying on a bed all gorgeous with pink silk and lace draperies, crying his eyes out because his throat was sore" ⟨136⟩.

The whole of Henry James's work—directly or indirectly, in the stories he creates, in the metaphors he chooses, as well as in the language he uses— seems to place at its center the image of the woman. It is to the female world that he mostly directs his attention as a narrator. In the case of Alice James the opposite seems to happen. In the way she looks at the world around her, in the judgments she makes on people and situations, in the readings she selects for herself, she seems to be constantly geared to male models. If in talking about Italy Henry James makes use of metaphors mostly drawn from the female world, Alice does exactly the opposite. In spite of all the descriptions of Italy she assimilated over the years from her brother's correspondence, whenever she refers to this country in her diary she does so in connection with the male world, or rather with what is by definition regarded as a male realm: the world of politics. She observes Italy with an attentive eye, but at the same time her attitude toward the country is rather benevolent. And perhaps it could not have been otherwise, given the affection and the happy memories attached to a place where she seems to have lived one of the few really happy experiences of her life.

—Maria Antonietta Saracino, "Alice James and Italy," in *The Sweetest Impression of Life: The James Family and Italy*, ed. James W. Tuttleton and Agostino Lombardo (New York: New York University Press, 1990), 157–59

BIBLIOGRAPHY

Journal. 1894, 1934.
Diary. 1934.

MAXINE HONG KING∫TON
b. 1940

MAXINE HONG KINGSTON was born October 27, 1940, in Stockton, California, the daughter of Chinese immigrants Tom and Ying Lan Hong, who owned and operated a laundry. Aside from attending school and helping with the family business, Maxine spent her free time reading the literary classics her parents had brought from China and attending movies, mostly Chinese operas, at the local Confucian Church. The Kingstons' tradition of passing down myths and family history profoundly influenced the future author, who would incorporate much of these memories into her novels.

In 1962, Maxine graduated from the University of California at Berkeley with a bachelor's degree and married actor Earll Kingston, with whom she has had one son. She then taught high school English and mathematics in California and Hawaii until the publication of her first book, *The Woman Warrior*, in 1976. At the narrative core of the book is Brave Orchid, a fictionalized characterization of Kingston's mother; the text is in fact populated with numerous characters drawn from the Chinese-American community of Kingston's youth. While critical of Chinese traditions, Kingston also disassembles classic stereotypes of Chinese Americans. At once a novel, an autobiography, a fairytale, and an epic poem, *The Woman Warrior* constitutes a genre unto itself. Its original narrative style and exploration of gender and generational conflicts garnered considerable critical acclaim, culminating with the 1976 National Book Critics Circle Award for nonfiction.

In 1980, Kingston published a companion piece to *The Woman Warrior* called *China Men*, in which men are the chief characters. Beginning with the story of the author's father, the poetic narrative explores themes of emigration, ritual, struggle, persecution, and assimilation. Again her literary talents were lauded, and she received the American Book Award for general nonfiction. Her latest novel, *Tripmaster Monkey*, shows off her unique skill of blending, in the words of Herbert Gold in his review for *Tribune Books*, "the kind of magic realism familiar to readers of Latin American fiction with the hard-edged black humor of flower-epoch comic writers and performers."

Kingston's honors include the Anisfield-Wolf Race Relations Award in 1978, the American Library Association Notable Books List in 1980, and the Hawaii Writers Award in 1983. Her poetry and non-fiction articles have been published in academic and mainstream periodicals, including the *English Journal, Iowa Review, Ms., The New Yorker,* and the *New York Times Magazine.* Kingston has held numerous visiting professorships and continues to lecture at institutions worldwide.

CRITICAL EXTRACTS

SARA BLACKBURN

In this searing, beautiful memoir of growing up as the first-generation American daughter of Chinese immigrant parents, Maxine Hong Kingston illuminates the experience of everyone who has ever felt the terror of being an emotional outsider. It seems to me that the best records of the immigrant experience and the bittersweet legacy it bestows upon the next generation fascinate us because of the insights they provide into the life of the family, that mystified arena where we first learn, truly or falsely, our own identities. It should therefore not be very startling—as it was to me—that this dazzling mixture of pre-revolutionary Chinese village life and myth, set against its almost unbearable contradictions in contemporary American life, could unfold as almost a psychic transcript of every woman I know—class, age, race, or ethnicity be damned. Here is the real meaning of America as melting pot.

Kingston alternates the experiences of her parents and their generation, in China and the Chinatowns of California, with her own. In a starving society where girl children were a despised and useless commodity, her mother had become a physician, then joined her long-ago immigrated husband in America, where she was hence to labor in the laundry which was their survival in the terrifying new land. Their children, raised in the aura of the old myths and their parents' fears for their children and themselves, alternated between revering and despising them. ⟨. . .⟩

In the book's climax, Kingston, now in high school, lashes out at her mother in an extraordinary, liberating tirade in which she claims at last her own shaky identity. And her mother, who once struggled so valiantly for her own, first denies her feelings and then tries to convey the dangers, real and imagined, which have molded her own attitude toward this beloved, maddening stranger. The gap is too wide, for the teenage Maxine has perceived more of her mother's fear than her love, more of her culture's confines than its richness and beauty. The possibilities of love and forgiveness will have to be postponed for the more immediate necessities: the struggles for autonomy, on the one hand, and assimilation on the other. The depiction of these twin struggles is this memoir's great strength.

The Woman Warrior is not without flaws: much of the exquisite fantasy material comes too early in the book, before we're properly grounded in the author's own "reality," and we can appreciate its full impact only in retrospect. There's often a staccato, jarring quality in transition from one scene to another, and we have to work hard placing ourselves in time and event. Prospective readers should not be discouraged by these minor problems. What is in store for those who read on is not only the essence of the immigrant experience— here Chinese, and uniquely fascinating for that—but a marvelous glimpse into the real life of women in the family, a perception-expanding report for the archives of human experience. Praise to Maxine Hong Kingston for distilling it and writing it all down for us.

—Sara Blackburn, "Notes of a Chinese Daughter," *Ms.* 5, no. 7 (January 1977): 39–40

ANNE TYLER

It becomes apparent fairly early in *China Men* that this is a less particularized account than *The Woman Warrior*. The ancestors stand for many other ancestors, for the entire history of Chinese emigration. They farmed cane in Hawaii, built the Central Pacific Railroad across the Sierras ("Only Americans could have done it," officials announced at its completion), or mined gold in Alaska. The author's father entered this country either as a stowaway or as a legal immigrant; both versions are recounted in full, as if they really happened. And there's a chapter on America's Chinese immigration laws from 1869, when this was declared to be a land of "Nordic fiber," through 1978, when at long last the quota system ceased to work specifically against Asians.

But inevitably, the particular triumphs over the general. China, to Maxine Hong Kingston, is "a country I made up." Equally, she makes up her history, her family mythology, coloring it with an artist's eye. Both of her books are nonfiction ⟨. . .⟩ but in a deeper sense, they are fiction at its best—novels, fairytales, epic poems. While the father of the family, preparing to be tested by American immigration authorities, may have had to memorize "another man's life, a consistent life, an American life," his daughter has to memorize a Chinese life. Neither memory, of course, is entirely accurate. Both are creative—sad for the memorizers, perhaps, but all the better for the reader. ⟨. . .⟩

What make the book more than nonfiction are its subtle shifts between the concrete and the mythical. Edges blur; the dividing line passes unnoticed. We accept one fact and then the next, and then suddenly we find ourselves believing in the fantastic. Is it true that when one of the brothers was born, a white Christmas card flew into the room like a dove? Well, possibly; there could be an explanation for that, but . . . . And did it really happen that an uncle lost all his money due to post-hypnotic suggestion—walked the streets in a trance, located a certain stranger in an unfamiliar room, and handed him the contents of his bank account? Does sandalwood grow in phoenix-shaped roots in the caves of lions; does it congeal in the Eastern Ocean as a cicada?

Some of the mythologies are accepted whole from storytelling relatives; others are newly invented by the author's quirky vision. ⟨. . .⟩

The Woman Warrior was startling because of its freshness; it wasn't a book that called to mind any other. *China Men*, of course, lacks that advantage, but it's every bit as compelling as its predecessor. It's a history at once savage and beautiful, a combination of bone-grinding reality and luminous fantasy.

—Anne Tyler, [Review of *China Men*], *The New Republic* (21 June 1980): 33–34

E. M. BRONER

Maxine Hong Kingston has developed a new form. Anthropologists will call it ethnographic. Critics will call it regionalism, the grotesque or gothic. The National Book Award, or the ghost of it, will press it into the category of auto-biography, as they did her first book, *The Woman Warrior*, when it won the NBA. I call *China Men* personal epic.

In the title Hong Kingston uses the pejorative, the patronizing "Chinamen," but she separates the words, perhaps to indicate that this designation is different. These men will not be dealt with pejoratively but heroically as the "binders and builders" of Hawaii and the States. This is a book of men, of male ancestry, a counterpart to *The Woman Warrior*, which was the search for self through the untold and told tales of the Chinese family, through the naming and exorcising of ghosts.

That which must be fought through in both books is imposed silence: the aunt in *The Woman Warrior* who cannot tell her tale, the author who, as a shy child, cannot speak in class. *The Woman Warrior* ends triumphantly with the author speaking out and with reference to the legend of a woman poet. The poet was kidnapped and lived among barbarians, yet sang her own songs. When ransomed, she brought back these songs to her people, and the Chinese still sing her words to their instruments. So, in both books, they, in exile, must still remember the words to sing and Hong Kingston is the instrument.

China Men commences with the angry silence of the father, a laundry worker in the land of Gold Mountain (all immigrants call the States "golden"). The daughter chronicler writes, "I think this is the journey you didn't tell me," and she proceeds to "talk story," to imagine-tell for her father. She tells of the arduous test in China given to prospective scholars, to her father's ordeal and his being selected as minor scholar, village schoolmaster to unappreciative boys. ⟨. . .⟩

As the book begins with the teacher father and his unappreciative students, it ends with the brother, a gentle fellow, a remedial-reading teacher to louts who rip books that he buys for the school library. This brother, like all the China Men, has to take his journey into the world of demons. All who are not their own are demons: immigration demons, employer demons, mortician demons, even garbage demons and movie-usher demons. This brother goes into the demonic world of the war in Vietnam, careful, even in war, not to hurt another. When he returns he cannot tell his tale. His sister writes it for him, gives her brother throat and soaring song.

Although the author mentions, in an aside, attending a conference on oral history, this book is not that kind of documentation—the nondramatic, nonselective form of the oral tale. Her work is kinesthetic memory. She takes data and makes it mythopoetic. Her umbilicus branches, encircles, twines around her ancestors. They sprout through her.

—E. M. Broner, "Stunning Sequel to *Woman Warrior,*" *Ms.* 9, no. 2 (August 1980): 28, 30

ELAINE H. KIM

Kingston says that she wrote *The Woman Warrior* and *China Men* together, having conceived of them as an interlocking story about the lives of men and women. But the women's stories "fell into place," and she feared that the men's were anti-female and would undercut the feminist viewpoint. So she collected and published the women's stories in *The Woman Warrior* first, although the men's experiences are no less important and moving to her.

In *China Men*, the narrator, who is again the daughter, is less involved with the characters and far less concerned with relating how she feels about them; Kingston says that *The Woman Warrior* was a "selfish book" in that she was always "imposing my viewpoint in the stories" through the narrator.

Like *The Woman Warrior*, *China Men* expresses the Chinese American experience through family history combined with talk-story, memory, legend, and imaginative projection. But while *The Woman Warrior* portrays the paradoxical nature of the Chinese American experience through the eyes of an American-born Chinese, *China Men* is a chronicle of Chinese American history less particular and less personal. The distance between the narrator and the characters in *China Men* might be attributed to the fact that Kingston heard the men's stories from women's talk-story: ". . . without the female storyteller, I couldn't have gotten into some of the stories . . . many of the men's stories were ones I originally heard from women" ⟨Timothy Pfaff, "Talk with Mrs. Kingston," 1980⟩. ⟨. . .⟩

Despite what some Chinese American male critics of Kingston have alleged, *China Men* is not anti-male; on the contrary, it is the portrait of men of diverse generations and experiences, heroes who lay claim on America for Chinese Americans and who refuse to be silenced or victimized.

China Men is also about the reconciliation of the contemporary Chinese American and his immigrant forefathers, nourished by their common roots, strong and deep, in American soil.

The men and women of *China Men* and *The Woman Warrior* are vivid and concrete refutations of racist and sexist stereotypes. For every No-Name Woman, there is a Fa Mu Lan; for every Great Grandfather of the Sandalwood Mountains, there is a brother in Vietnam. And for each perspective set forth by Maxine Hong Kingston, there is a myriad of other Chinese American viewpoints.

While immigrant and American-born Chinese are reconciled in Kingston through their mutual claim on America, and while Kingston's men and women are survivors, the reconciliation between the sexes is not yet complete. Kingston demonstrates that Asian American writers can depict with compassion and skill the experience of both sexes. A future task is the bringing together of our men and women, in life and in the literature which reflects it.

—Elaine H. Kim, "Visions and Fierce Dreams: A Commentary on the Works of Maxine Hong Kingston," *Amerasia Journal* 8, no. 2 (Fall/Winter 1981): 154–55, 159

SUZANNE JUHASZ

Maxine Hong Kingston's two-volume autobiography, *The Woman Warrior* and *China Men*, embodies the search for identity in the narrative act. The first text places the daughter in relation to her mother, the second places her in relation to her father; they demonstrate how finding each parent is a part of finding oneself. For Kingston, finding her mother and father is to name them, to tell their stories. Language is the means with which she arrives at identity, first at home, and then in the world. But because a daughter's relation to her mother is psychologically and linguistically different from her relation to her father, so is the telling of these stories different.

Although the two texts are superficially similar, they are generated from different narrative patterns. In *The Woman Warrior* alternating movements toward and away from the mother take place within a textual field in which a linear progression, defining first the mother, then the daughter, takes place. In *China Men* narrative movement goes in one direction only, toward the father. But because this impulse in the latter book is continually diffused into generalization and idealization, it begins over, again and again. Such narrative structures suggest the evolution of female identity, which is formed in relation to the mother through the achievement of individuation in the context of connection, in relation to the father through the understanding of separation, the creation of substitutes for connection. Taken together, *The Woman Warrior* and *China Men* compose a woman's autobiography, describing a self formed at the source by gender experience.

To say this is neither to ignore nor to minimize the question of national identity everywhere present in Kingston's writing. Born in the United States to Chinese immigrant parents, her search for self necessarily involves a definition of home. Is it America, China, or some place in between? For Kingston the question of national identity complicates the search for self. Yet it is possible to understand how gender identity and national identity can be versions of one another, how home is embodied in the mother and father who together stand for the primary source of the self. For Kingston, in fact, who has never been there, China is not so much a physical place as it is a construct used by her parents to define their own identities. America too, especially for her parents, is a psychological state as much as it is a place. My own focus ⟨. . .⟩ on sexual identity is therefore not meant to negate the other dimension of the problem, but rather to reveal sexual and national identities as parts of one another. For it is as a Chinese-American woman that Kingston seeks to define herself.

—Suzanne Juhasz, "Maxine Hong Kingston: Narrative Technique and Female Identity," *Contemporary American Women Writers*, ed. Catherine Rainwater and William J. Scheick (Lexington, KY: University of Kentucky Press, 1985), 173–74

LESLIE W. RABINE

In *The Woman Warrior* this conflictual texture ⟨the narrator's ambivalence toward her mother⟩ provides the internal structuring principle; in *China Men* the relationship to the father forms the external framework in which Kingston molds the lives and thoughts of the men in her family and the immigrant community. In *China Men*, the theme of revenge, which permeates the *Woman Warrior*, becomes secondary to the theme of being exiled from home, precisely the theme of the lost paradise, whose absence in *The Woman Warrior* so marked the structure and the female experience recounted. Both books describe with nostalgia the loving rituals accompanying the birth of boys, and both express bitterness over the silence accompanying the birth of girls. Within the texts, these rituals express parental love and make childhood an Edenic place from which girls are excluded. But there are sociohistoric reasons for this difference as well. In *China Men*, the grandfathers and great-grandfathers, admitted to the United States as agricultural and railroad workers, long to go home because the cruel treatment they receive deprives them of a worthwhile life. But in *The Woman Warrior*, the place Maxine's family calls "home" is the country where families sell their daughters into slavery and where daughters-in-law are tortured. "Home" is a place she does not want to go.

Yet Kingston's writing makes permeable this boundary between the apparently mutually exclusive experiences of men and women. Most of the legends incorporated into *China Men* are about exiles who wander in search of returning home, and, in at least two of these legends, exile is symbolized by the men being transformed into women. To be a woman, whose birth is not recognized by the family, is to be a permanent exile, without any home, without a place. To be a man who loses one's home is to cross over into the feminine gender. *China Men*, about men who have been forced to cross over into the feminine gender, is written by a woman, who, in the act of writing, has also, like the woman warrior, crossed over, albeit voluntarily, into the masculine gender and assumed the voice of the men she writes about.

—Leslie W. Rabine, "No Lost Paradise: Social Gender and Symbolic Gender in the Writings of Maxine Hong Kingston" (copyright 1987 by the University of Chicago), in *Revising the Word and the World: Essays in Feminist Literary Criticism*, ed. Vèvè Clark, Ruth-Ellen Boetcher Joeres, and Madelon Sprengnether (Chicago: University of Chicago Press, 1993), 151–52

KING-KOK CHEUNG

⟨In *The Woman Warrior*⟩ Maxine evolves from a quiet listener to a talker of stories. Having transformed the military warrior into a verbal fighter, she recognizes that she herself is a powerful spinner of yarns and not just a receptacle for her mother's tales. Although many chapters of her autobiography are in a sense collaborations between mother and daughter, the daughter becomes increasingly aware of her own contribution, especially in the last section of the book: "Here is a story my mother told me, not when I was young, but recently, when I told her I also talk-story. The beginning is hers, the ending, mine" (240). It is toward the end of this story that the tone noticeably softens. Unlike Brave Orchid, the mother who would "funnel," "pry," "cram," "jam-pack" the daughter with unabated torrents of words, and unlike young Maxine, who has "splinters in [her] voice, bones jagged against one another" (196), adult Maxine modulates her notes to the music of her second tongue, in the manner of Ts'ai Yen, the heroine of her final tale.

Kingston reinterprets the legend of Ts'ai Yen—a poet amid barbarians—and, as she has done with the stories about the no-name aunt and the woman warrior, subverts its original moral. The Chinese version highlights the poet's eventual return to her own people, a return that reinforces certain traditional and ethnocentric Chinese notions ⟨. . . .⟩ Kingston's version, by contrast, dramatizes interethnic harmony through the integration of disparate art forms.

Ts'ai Yen, Maxine's last tutelary genius, resembles but transcends the various other influential female figures in her life. Like Fa Mu Lan, Ts'ai Yen has fought in battle, but as a captive soldier. She engages in another art hitherto dominated by men—writing—yet she does not disguise her sex, thus implicitly denying that authorship is a male prerogative. Like the no-name aunt, Ts'ai Yen is ravished and impregnated; both give birth on sand. But instead of being nameless and ostracized, Ts'ai Yen achieves immortal fame by singing about her exile. Like Brave Orchid, she talks in Chinese to her uncomprehending children, who speak a barbarian tongue, but she learns to appreciate the barbarian music. The refrain of this finale is reconciliation—between parents and children, between men and women, and between different cultures.

It is by analogy to Maxine—alienated alike from the Chinese world of her parents and the world of white Americans—that Ts'ai Yen's full significance emerges. The barbarians attach primitive pipes to their arrows, which thereby whistle in flight. Ts'ai Yen has thought that this terrifying noise is her nomadic captors' only music, until she hears, issuing night after night from those very flutes, "music tremble and rise like desert wind" ⟨. . . .⟩ Recalling young Maxine's ambivalence toward language (because it is frequently associated with dominance), an ambivalence that is in a sense reinforced by the lethal text on the warrior's back, we can appreciate all the more the poet's alternative mode of expression. The American language, Maxine discovers, can send forth not just terrifying "death sounds"—threats, insults, slurs—but stirring tunes. Caught in a cross-cultural web of Eastern and Western chauvinism, Maxine too conveys sadness and anger through high-sounding words. She does not (and does not want to) return to China, but she reconnects with her ancestral culture through writing. Instead of struggling against her Asian past and her American present, she now seeks to emulate the poet who sings to foreign music. Not only have her Chinese materials and imaginings "translated well," in the course of such creative translation she has achieved an inner resolution. As the lyrical ending intimates, Maxine has worked the discords of her life into a song.

—King-Kok Cheung, " 'Don't Tell': Imposed Silences in *The Color Purple* and *The Woman Warrior*," *Publications of the Modern Language Association* 103, no. 2 (March 1988): 171–72

Amy Ling

Maxine Hong Kingston's *Woman Warrior* was deservedly recognized for its boldness, power, and beauty, its fullness of voice in expressing the hyphenated condition, but this work did not spring full blown from the empyrean. Most of the writers we have examined, despite the Chinese tradition of repression of women, were also outspoken and individualistic. Nearly all their works have been ignored—in many cases, as I hope to have shown, undeservedly so. Looking back, we find that the works that received accolades in their time— Winnifred Eaton's romantic confections, Jade Snow Wong's autobiography— reflected more their audience and its taste than the quality of the books themselves. The frail Japanese or Eurasian heroines romantically involved with dominant Caucasian men in high positions, the Chinese American success story at a time when the United States was at war with Japan, satisfied a public that sought to confirm its own myths, in stories about its superiority, generosity, and openness. It was not particularly interested in learning about the Chinese themselves or in dispelling stereotypes. In fact, to a large extent, it still finds them "inscrutable."

In "Cultural Mis-Readings by American Reviewers," Kingston expresses her frustration that two-thirds of the critics who praised her book could not see beyond their own stereotyped thinking; she cites examples of the painful "exotic-inscrutable-mysterious-oriental reviewing." Here is one example, from the *Chattanooga News–Free Press*:

> At her most obscure, though, as when telling about her dream of
> becoming a fabled "woman warrior" the author becomes as
> inscrutable as the East always seems to the West. In fact, this book
> seems to reinforce the feeling that "East is East and West is West and
> never the twain shall meet," or at any rate it will probably take more
> than one generation away from China. (63)

The inscrutableness, it seems to Kingston and to me, is in the eyes of the beholder, and the unbridgeable gulf as well. Chinese Americans have been explaining themselves for nearly a century, but their voices are either ignored or misunderstood.

A major theme in Kingston's *Woman Warrior* is the importance of articulateness. Finding one's voice and telling one's stories represents power, just as having one's stories buried is powerlessness. From the first episode, "No Name Woman," in which Kingston disobeys her mother's injunction and tells the story of the prodigal aunt whom she calls her "forerunner," through the accounts of her own childhood (her belief that her mother had cut her frenum, her silence in Caucasian school, her terrible bullying of a Chinese American classmate in an effort to make her speak—an act of self-hatred), to the last episode, "A Song for a Barbarian Reed Pipe," Kingston elaborates on this theme. Instead of the confusion and humiliation about her Chinese background that she felt as a child, she now finds, in the stories and customs that set her apart from her Caucasian classmates, her heritage and treasure, her strength and identity. Kingston's work combines the traits of the Chinese American writers who preceded her—protest, storytelling, nostalgia, and experimentation. The effect is one of surprising power and startling beauty.

—Amy Ling, "Chinese American Women Writers: The Tradition behind Maxine Hong Kingston," *Redefining American Literary History*, ed. A. LaVonne Brown Ruoff and Jerry W. Ward Jr. (New York: Modern Language Association of America, 1990), 235–36

SIDONIE SMITH

⟨No⟩ single work captures so powerfully the relationship of gender to genre in twentieth-century autobiography as Maxine Hong Kingston's *Woman Warrior*.

⟨. . . It⟩ is, quite complexly, an autobiography about women's autobiographical storytelling. A post-modern work, it exemplifies the potential for works from the marginalized to challenge the ideology of individualism and with it the ideology of gender. Recognizing the inextricable relationship between an individual's sense of "self" and the community's stories of selfhood, Kingston self-consciously reads herself into existence through the stories her culture tells about women. Using autobiography to create identity, she breaks down the hegemony of formal "autobiography" and breaks out of the silence that has bound her culturally to discover a resonant voice of her own. Furthermore, as a work coming from an ethnic subculture, *The Woman Warrior* offers the occasion to consider the complex imbroglios of cultural fictions that surround the autobiographer who is engaging two sets of stories: those of the dominant culture and those of an ethnic subculture with its own traditions, its own unique stories. As a Chinese American from the working class, Kingston brings to her autobiographical project complicating perspectives on the relationship of woman to language and to narrative.

Considered by some a "novel" and by others an "autobiography," the five narratives conjoined under the title *The Woman Warrior* are decidedly five confrontations with the fictions of self-representation and with the autobiographical possibilities embedded in cultural fictions, specifically as they interpenetrate one another in the autobiography a woman would write. For Kingston, then, as for the woman autobiographer generally, the hermeneutics of self-representation can never be divorced from cultural representations of woman that delimit the nature of her access to the word and the articulation of her own desire. Nor can interpretation be divorced from her orientation toward the mother, who, as her point of origin, commands the tenuous negotiation of identity and difference in a drama of filiality that reaches through the daughter's subjectivity to her textual self-authoring.

Preserving the traditions that authorize the old way of life and enable her to reconstitute the circle of the immigrant community amidst an alien environment, Kingston's mother dominates the life, the landscape, and the language of the text as she dominates the subjectivity of the daughter who writes that text. It is Brave Orchid's voice, commanding, as Kingston notes, "great power" that continually reiterates the discourses of the community in maxims, talk-story, legends, family histories. As the instrument naming filial identities and commanding filial obligations, that voice enforces the authority and legitimacy of the old culture to name and thus control the place of woman within the patrilineage and thereby to establish the erasure of female desire and the denial of female self-representation as the basis on which the perpetuation of patrilineal descent rests. Yet that same voice gives shape to other possibilities, tales of female power and authority that seem to create a space of cultural significance for the daughter; and the very strength and authority of the maternal voice fascinates the daughter because it "speaks" of the power of woman to enunciate her own representations. Hence storytelling becomes the means through which Brave Orchid passes on to her daughter all the complexities of and the ambivalences about both mother's and daughter's identity as woman in patriarchal culture.

—Sidonie Smith, "Maxine Hong Kingston's *Woman Warrior*: Filiality and Woman's Autobiographical Storytelling," *Feminisms: An Anthology of Literary Theory and Criticism*, ed. Robyn R. Warhol and Diane Price Herndl (New Brunswick, NJ: Rutgers University Press, 1991), 1058–59

SHIRLEY GEOK-LIN LIM

What marks Kingston's memoirs as literary is the way in which "naming" or language figures in her work to deconstruct and deny any single reality of Chinese American female identity. What marks it as feminist is its persistent constructions and reproductions of female identity, the continuous namings of female presences, characters, heroines, and figures. No Name Woman is the first of these figures (and behind No Name Woman the storyteller/mother), a victim valorized by the narrator as hero. In this first narrative act, the narrator's self-conscious "writing" is presented as a rescue of the ancestor from the punishment of silence. No Name Woman's name is itself an oxymoron. She has no name, but the narrator in naming her No Name Woman has given her a name. No Name Woman's identity is that of lack, her presence inscribed in her absence. No Name Woman is a figure for woman as that which is displaced by man and from man, a gap in the his-storical memory. But the act of writing is itself not unambiguous; the rescue into memory through writing is after all a testimony to No Name Woman's sins, and the opening chapter closes on the instability of the writer's position in the feminist project of reclaiming a matrilineal genealogy: "My aunt haunts me—her ghost drawn to me because now, after fifty years of neglect, I alone devote pages of paper to her. . . . I do not think she always means me well. I am telling on her" (16).

The ambivalence of relationship between writer and ancestor echoes the ambivalences between narrator/daughter and mother. The maternal discourse informs the daughter, producing such strong female figures as the swordswoman, Fa Mu Lan: "When we Chinese girls listened to the adults talking-story, we learned that we failed if we grew up to be but wives or slaves. We could be heroines, swordswomen" (19). Or the figure of the shaman, the mother as midwife and healer. But it also deforms the daughter: "My mother has given me pictures to dream—nightmare babies that recur, shrinking again and again to fit in my palm" (86). The discourse is disturbingly female, of "nightmare babies," and it is also racial: "To make my waking life American-normal, I turn on the lights before anything untoward makes an appearance. I push the deformed into my dreams, which are in Chinese, the language of impossible stories" (87). Race and gender intersect in the daughter's response to her Chinese mother's talk-stories, as do form and deformity, language and dream, American and Chinese. Chinese is "the language of impossible stories," impossible because the dreams are nightmares, because the language is Chinese in an "American-normal" life, and because the reality of that dream-Chinese language is denied (as No Name Woman was denied) in the American-normal waking life. The mother's talk-stories are in Chinese (Cantonese), and the narrator, head stuffed "like the suitcases which they jam-pack with homemade underwear," is engaged in the project of disburdening herself of them. As with No Name Woman, the narrator is "telling" on her mother who "does not always mean me well."

The narrator's self-consciousness about her writing (storytelling) is a consistent thread in the book which she picks up in various metaphors. One figure is that of the forbidden stitch, that knot of embroidery so fine that in sewing it thousands of embroiderers reputedly lost their sight. The narrator claims: "There was one knot so complicated that it blinded the knotmaker. Finally an emperor outlawed this cruel knot, and the nobles could not order it anymore. If I had lived in China, I would have been an outlaw knotmaker" (163). The knot is what the narrator makes, a figure so tightly and complexly interwoven that its making leads to blindness. The metaphor of the knot covers the making of the mother/daughter relationship in the text, a figure so tightly and complexly tied that the greatest skill will be needed to unknot it. In China the knots were made into buttons, frogs (fasteners), and bellpulls, figures of joining, tying, connection, and sound. The metaphor of the knot leads to the story of the mother cutting the daughter's tongue. The image is of silencing, but it is actually the frenum the mother cuts "so that you would not be tongue-tied" (164). The mother cuts the knot so the daughter can speak, in a figure which paradoxically conveys both silencing and speech; the daughter's desire is to be a knotmaker, a figure for art and affiliation. The daughter's empowerment by maternal action and discourse is expressed in these series of figures, together with the powerful ambivalences of response that these figures produce: "Sometimes I felt very proud that my mother committed such a powerful act upon me. At other times I was terrified. . . . 'Did it hurt me? Did I cry and bleed?' " (164). The mother is informing and deforming power; the rein-

scribing of maternal talk-stories, of oral into written speech, is the daughter's
act of appropriating the power of the maternal discourse for herself.

—Shirley Geok-lin Lim, "The Tradition of Chinese American Women's Life Stories:
Thematics of Race and Gender in Jade Snow Wong's *Fifth Chinese Daughter* and Maxine Hong
Kingston's *The Woman Warrior*," *American Women's Autobiography: Fea(s)ts of Memory*, ed. Margo
Culley (Madison, WI: University of Wisconsin Press, 1992), 261–62

DONALD C. GOELLNICHT

The social and psychological repercussions of the exclusion laws on Chinese
and Chinese American men were tremendous, and they have been documented by a number of historians and sociologists (including Stanley Sue,
Nathaniel Wagner, and Reed Ueda). Elaine Kim has pointed out that with job
opportunities scarce and women absent in the "bachelor" Chinatowns—ghet-
toes where Chinese and Chinese American men were forced to live—some
of these men ended up, against their will, in traditionally "women's" jobs, as
waiters, launderers, servants, and cooks. In "The Father from China" Hong
Kingston presents her father and his partners as engaged in their laundry business for long periods each day—a business considered so low and debased
that, in their songs, they associate it with the washing of menstrual blood,
which links their occupation back to Tang Ao, whose foot-binding bandages
smelled like menstrual rags when he was forced to wash them ⟨*China Men*, 4⟩.
⟨. . .⟩ At night, these "bachelors" engage in more "woman's work": they cook
their own meals and hold eating races, with the loser washing the dishes. The
absence of wives is stressed, but this has to do as much with the difficulty of
taking on the menial tasks women would usually perform as with a sense of
emotional deprivation. Once Brave Orchid—Ed/BaBa's wife from China—
arrives in New York, the traditional roles resume: she cooks, cleans, and washes
for the men. Once again, the female narrator sympathizes with these fathers
but also critiques traditional gender roles.

Most criticism is leveled, however, at the dominant racist society. In what
appears a deliberate attempt to trap China Men in the stereotypical "feminine"
positions it had assigned them, American society perpetuated the myth of the
effeminate or androgynous "chinaman," while erasing the figure of the "masculine" plantation worker or railroad construction worker. We are all familiar
with the stereotype of the Chinese laundryman or waiter, but few know that
the railroads so essential to development in North America were built with
large numbers of Chinese laborers, who endured tremendous hardship and
isolation in the process, or that Hawaiian sugar plantations were carved out of
tropical forests with Chinese labor. ⟨. . .⟩

Hong Kingston seeks to redress this wrong of stereotyping and historical
erasure, not by a simple reversal ⟨of⟩ the figure of laundryman/cook and that

of railroad laborer/plantation worker, "feminine" and "masculine," respectively, but by a disruption of this gendered binary opposition—as we find in the Tang Ao and Tu Tzu-chun myths—which shows both roles and both job types to entail hardships and rewards. To this end she presents us with a variety of China Men from her family: Bak Goong, her "Great Grandfather of the Sandalwood Mountains," who endured the physical hardships of being a sugar plantation worker in Hawaii but who was also "a fanciful, fabulous man" (110); Ah Goong, her "Grandfather of the Sierra Nevada Mountains," a railway construction worker who risked his life from a suspended basket to set gunpowder charges in the mountains but whose intense loneliness at being a married "bachelor" finds expression in his nocturnal reveries on the myth of the Spinning Girl and her Cowboy (129); and BaBa, her father, the Chinese scholar who becomes an American laundryman. These generations of men are presented in all their pain and dignity.

—Donald C. Goellnicht, "Tang Ao in America: Male Subject Positions in *China Men*," *Reading the Literatures of Asian America*, ed. Shirley Geok-lin Lim and Amy Ling (Philadelphia: Temple University Press, 1992), 197–99

STEPHEN H. SUMIDA

As elsewhere in missionaries' campaigns to convert "heathen" people, in California the act of teaching English literacy to rescued women was aimed at enabling the converts not only to read the Bible but also to confess their sinful, pagan pasts and to make way for a new Christian life. Whatever the Chinese American convert's past, it was thus intertwined with a culture their "rescuers" considered not simply inferior, but sinful. Writing such an "autobiography" for the missionaries had to be quite different from the "confessing" to people of the same culture; for the Chinese woman autobiographer—to save her very life, if she had been a caged prostitute in San Francisco—had to deal with how she would, by her writing, be considered a representative of her culture for an audience that believed their own culture and notions of individual virtue to be superior to hers. In such an autobiography, a confession implied an apology to a higher authority.

Chinese American autobiography today inherits this history. By 1976 when Maxine Hong Kingston's *The Woman Warrior: Memoirs of a Girlhood Among Ghosts* was published, some Asian American writers and literary critics, notably Frank Chin and his fellow editors of *Aiiieeeee! An Anthology of Asian-American Writers* (1974), were raising questions about how Asian American first-person narratives affirmed, suggested ignorance of, or were indifferent to cultures and literary histories not only of racist depictions of Asians but also of coaching books and converts' autobiographies and the like. Kingston's book could be seen and judged as an attempt at two things, perhaps both at once: It could be

a critique of its narrator, a fictional first-person "I" meant to be questioned so
that her confusions about Chinese American identity and the causes and consequences of her American ignorance of China might be understood; or the
book could be entirely "transparent," not an interplay of hiding and revealing
but a clear revelation by means of explicit, descriptive statement of what it
means to grow up Chinese American and female. The selling of *Woman Warrior*
as nonfiction, a marketing practice that continues today, tended to throw
weight and judgment heavily on the side of the latter interpretation, so despite
Kingston's disclaimers that she was not "representing" but had made very significant changes in retelling them, certain stories are generally believed to be
nonfictional, transmitted as directly from Chinese tales as oral traditions allow.
Contrary to many reviews that took her versions for granted, Kingston implicitly questioned how a daughter would interpret her mother's Chinese culture,
given the American contexts, in which they both live, of idealism and racism,
sexism, and cultural, historical ignorance. So, for instance, in "White Tigers,"
the narrator's belief that a woman was proscribed from being a warrior is a
reflection on and critique of the prohibition in the American military, during
the time the narrator is growing up, against women entering combat. The
book's title, meanwhile, proclaims that unlike in America, in the mother's culture there *are* women warriors, exceedingly well-known military ones.
Kingston herself has made it explicit that she considers a critique of the book's
narrator and her constructs of American and Chinese cultures a key to its reading. *The Woman Warrior* in this way is a Chinese American woman's
Bildungsroman, a narrative not aiming to present how China, Chinese, and
Chinese Americans essentially are, but to plot the imaginative, psychological,
ethical, and bodily development of its main character, the narrator herself.
The work is, in short, an example of "growing up Asian American" in anything
but a simplistic sense.
    —Stephen H. Sumida, "Afterword," *Growing Up Asian American: An Anthology*, ed. Maria Hong
    (New York: William Morrow and Company, Inc., 1993), 402–3

BIBLIOGRAPHY

The Woman Warrior: Memoirs of a Girlhood among Ghosts. 1976.
China Men. 1980.
Hawaii One Summer. 1987.
Tripmaster Monkey: His Fake Book. 1988.